CONTEMPORARY Black Biography

ISSN-1058-1316

CONTEMPORARY

Black
Biography

Profiles from the International Black Community

Volume 62

THOMSON

GALE

Detroit • New York • San Francisco • New Haven, Conn. • Waterville, Maine • London

Contemporary Black Biography, Volume 62

Sara and Tom Pendergast

Project Editor
Pamela M. Kalte

Image Research and Acquisitions
Leitha Etheridge-Sims

Editorial Support Services
Nataliya Mikheyeva

Rights and Permissions
Beth Beaufore, Barb McNeil, Sara Teller

Manufacturing
Dorothy Maki, Cynde Bishop

Composition and Prepress
Mary Beth Trimper, Tracey L. Matthews

Imaging
Lezlie Light

ISBN 13: 978-0-7876-7934-7
ISBN 10: 0-7876-7934-8
ISSN 1058-1316

This title is also available as an e-book.
eISBN 13: 978-1-4144-2921-2
eISBN-10: 1-4144-2921-5
Please contact your Gale sales representative for ordering information.

Printed in the United States of America
10 9 8 7 6 5 4 3 2 1

Advisory Board

Contents

Introduction

Contemporary Black Biography provides informative biographical profiles of the important and influential persons of African heritage who form the international black community: men and women who have changed today's world and are shaping tomorrow's. *Contemporary Black Biography* covers persons of various nationalities in a wide variety of fields, including architecture, art, business, dance, education, fashion, film, industry, journalism, law, literature, medicine, music, politics and government, publishing, religion, science and technology, social issues, sports, television, theater, and others. In addition to in-depth coverage of names found in today's headlines, *Contemporary Black Biography* provides coverage of selected individuals from earlier in this century whose influence continues to impact on contemporary life. *Contemporary Black Biography* also provides coverage of important and influential persons who are not yet household names and are therefore likely to be ignored by other biographical reference series. Each volume also includes listee updates on names previously appearing in *CBB*.

Designed for Quick Research and Interesting Reading

- **Attractive page design** incorporates textual subheads, making it easy to find the information you're looking for.

- **Easy-to-locate data sections** provide quick access to vital personal statistics, career information, major awards, and mailing addresses, when available.

- **Informative biographical essays** trace the subject's personal and professional life with the kind of in-depth analysis you need.

- **To further enhance your appreciation** of the subject, most entries include photographic portraits.

- **Sources for additional information** direct the user to selected books, magazines, and newspapers where more information on the individuals can be obtained.

Helpful Indexes Make It Easy to Find the Information You Need

Contemporary Black Biography includes cumulative Nationality, Occupation, Subject, and Name indexes that make it easy to locate entries in a variety of useful ways.

Available in Electronic Formats

Diskette/Magnetic Tape. Contemporary Black Biography is available for licensing on magnetic tape or diskette in a fielded format. Either the complete database or a custom selection of entries may be ordered. The database is available for internal data processing and nonpublishing purposes only. For more information, call (800) 877-GALE.

On-line. Contemporary Black Biography is available on-line through Mead Data Central's NEXIS Service in the NEXIS, PEOPLE and SPORTS Libraries in the GALBIO file and Gale's Biography Resource Center.

Disclaimer

Contemporary Black Biography uses and lists websites as sources and these websites may become obsolete.

We Welcome Your Suggestions

The editors welcome your comments and suggestions for enhancing and improving *Contemporary Black Biography.* If you would like to suggest persons for inclusion in the series, please submit these names to the editors. Mail comments or suggestions to:

The Editor

Contemporary Black Biography

The Gale Group

27500 Drake Rd.

Farmington Hills, MI 48331-3535

Phone: (800) 347-4253

Tommy Amaker

1965—

Basketball coach

Amaker, Tommy, photograph. AP Images.

From the summer league games he played as a child, through his outstanding high school and college basketball careers, Tommy Amaker valued his coaches as mentors and friends. The men who trained and encouraged him on the court inspired him to choose coaching as his career and to devote his energy and talent to teaching young players. Amaker's dedication led him to become the youngest head coach in Big East conference basketball and the first African-American coach at Harvard University. Fiercely independent and generous with his energy, skills, and knowledge, Amaker has navigated the competitive world of college athletics with poise and integrity, earning the esteem of his colleagues and the trust and respect of his athletes.

Harold Tommy Amaker Jr. was born in the northern Virginia town of Falls Church on June 6, 1965, one of two children of Alma Deskins Amaker, a high school English teacher, and Harold T. Amaker, Sr., a career military serviceman. Tommy Amaker began playing basketball in local community centers and under a backyard hoop at his grandparents' house. He soon joined a summer league team, and, by the age of ten, he had already developed teamwork and a remarkable skill at ball handling that caught the eye of Red Jenkins, a basketball coach at the nearby W.T. Woodson High School.

Amaker's friendship with Jenkins prompted him to choose Woodson when he entered high school, and he joined the basketball team as a freshman. At first glance, the new recruit was unimpressive. At 15, Amaker was only five-feet, eight-inches tall and 108 pounds, and his mother had to hem his jersey at the shoulders so that his number did not disappear when he tucked the shirt into his shorts. However, the small freshman was a dynamo on the court, able to dribble and throw equally well with both hands, and willing to play cooperatively with his team. He was also a determined learner who practiced constantly to improve his skills.

Became a Strong Point Guard

Amaker found his strongest position on the team during his first season with the Woodson Cavaliers. The senior who played point guard was injured during a tournament game and Coach Jenkins sent Amaker in as a replacement. The point guard has a central role on a basketball team, controlling the ball and calling offensive plays. Amaker's speed, strength, and dexterity allowed him to step into that position of responsibility with confidence and flair. He would play starting point guard through his entire high school and college basketball careers. Jenkins gave Amaker the nickname "T-Bird" because he was low and fast like a Ford Thunderbird sports car. Even in the early 2000s, Jenkins still claimed that Amaker was the best point guard ever to play in Northern Virginia.

Amaker's skills on the court attracted the interest of several college athletic departments. He received an offer from North Carolina's Davidson College and hoped to get one from the University of Maryland, where his sister Tami attended college. However, while playing in a summer league Amaker met another coach who would influence both his basketball career and his life. Mike Krzyzewski, head coach of the Duke University Blue Devils men's basketball team, had come to

watch another player in the Washington, D.C., summer league tournament when his attention was drawn to the dynamic point guard from northern Virginia. According to Mirza Kurspahic in an on-line *Connection Newspapers* feature, when Krzyzewski was introduced to Amaker's mother, he greeted her with a confident promise: "Your son is going to look great in Duke blue."

As Krzyzewski predicted, Amaker did go to Duke. He was not only persuaded by the excellence of the North Carolina university's athletic department, but by the warmth and respect Coach Krzyzewski showed his players. Amaker played starting point guard for Duke for four years, leading his team to an NCAA championship in 1986 and becoming captain of the team and an All-American athlete in 1987. In 1986, he also won a gold medal in the World Championships as a member of the U.S. team.

Throughout his college career, Amaker maintained relationships of affection and respect with his teammates and his coach, becoming almost like a son to "Coach K." His constant support and instruction to other players caused them to call him the "coach on the floor," and his quiet, serious manner gave authority to his comments and suggestions.

Returned to Duke as Coach

After his graduation from Duke with a bachelor's degree in economics in 1987, Amaker was drafted by the Seattle Supersonics professional basketball team. He stayed with the Sonics only a short time, then joined the minor league Wyoming Wildcatters briefly, before deciding to return to Duke to work toward a graduate degree in business. While earning his MBA, he rejoined the Blue Devils, this time as assistant coach.

Amaker's strong court skills coupled with his quietly authoritative manner and his real affection for his players made him an effective coach. He remained at Duke for nine years, progressing from assistant to associate coach and guiding the team through two NCAA championships and five "Final Four" playoffs. During his career there, the Duke men's team achieved a record of 230 wins and 80 losses.

Colleges and universities constantly seek successful coaches, and Amaker received several job offers while working at Duke. In 1997, he decided to take a job as head coach of the men's basketball team at New Jersey's Seton Hall University. He had begun to feel that he needed to leave Duke to forge an independent career as head coach, and he decided that Seton Hall was the right place to launch that career. He remained at Seton Hall for almost four years, building and improving the team there through the aggressive recruitment of new players and his self-possessed, respectful teaching style. Under Amaker's leadership the Seton Hall Pirates achieved a record of 68 wins and 55 losses.

Amaker's first experience as head coach brought difficulties as well as successes. His job at Seton Hall had made him, at the age of 31, the youngest head coach of a basketball team in the Big East conference. As head coach, he bore most of the public responsibility for the team's successes and failures, and he became the focus of criticism if things went badly for the team. Amaker took on these additional responsibilities with his usual calm assurance, and, as he coached the Pirates through three National Invitation Tournaments and one NCAA tourney, he continued to attract the notice of college athletic departments around the country. In 2001, just after gaining Seton Hall one of the best recruiting classes in the nation, he left the university to take a job as head coach of men's basketball at the University of Michigan.

Rebuilt Respect for Basketball at Michigan

Working at Michigan in 2001 presented special challenges for a head coach. The university was still under the cloud of a recent financial scandal involving illegal gifts to players from wealthy team supporters. The athletic department suffered from league penalties, poor facilities, and weak recruiting practices, and the Michigan Wolverines had not made the NCAA Final Four playoffs since 1993. Amaker went to work to build the team into a national competitor once again. Within a few seasons, he had succeeded in bringing a renewed confidence and respect for basketball at Michigan, making the Wolverines once more the kind of team that could attract good high school recruits. By the 2006 season, the team was ranked 20th in the nation and had played three seasons with 20 wins. They played in three National Invitation Tournaments, winning the NIT in 2004, making Amaker the youngest black coach in the history of basketball to win a national tournament. However, the Wolverines had not earned the right to play in an NCAA tournament, the standard by which many fans and sports writers judge college basketball success. Since Amaker's team did not gain a place in the tournament after six seasons, he was fired as head coach at Michigan in April 2007.

However, other athletic departments sought Amaker's coaching skills, and within days of his firing by Michigan, Harvard University announced that Tommy Amaker would head up their men's basketball team. As coach of the Crimson, Amaker would become the first African-American head coach at the prestigious Massachusetts university since its founding in 1636.

Throughout his career, Amaker has studied the work of other coaches to improve his teaching skills. He has also worked to become a guide, mentor, and father figure to his players, just as his high school and college coaches were to him. He has built a reputation as a serious and devoted teacher who treats both players and referees with polite respect and retains his composure even during stressful moments. During games,

referees frequently call technical fouls on coaches who exhibit unsportsmanlike behavior, such as cursing, arguing, or threatening a referee. It says much about Amaker's self-control as a coach that in his nine years as head coach of a university basketball team, he has received only three technical fouls.

In 1992, Amaker married Dr. Stephanie Pinder, a clinical psychologist he met at Duke. Pinder-Amaker has accompanied her husband through his career changes and served on the faculties of both Seton Hall University and the University of Michigan.

Sources

Books

Weiss, Dick, *True Blue: Mike Krzyzewski's Career at Duke,* Sports Publishing, 2005.

Periodicals

Jet, April 7, 1997, p.47; April 16, 2001, p. 51.
Los Angeles Times, March 23, 2000, p.1; December 21, 2006, p. D1.
New York Times, March 12, 2006, p. 8.1; April 14, 2007, p. D5.
Sports Illustrated, February 16, 1998, pp.100-2.
Washingtonian, May 1983, p. 9.

On-line

"Amaker Dismissed After Six Seasons As Michigan Coach," *ESPN,* http://sports.espn.go.com/ncb/news/story?id=2802320i (July 4, 2007).
"Being Tommy Amaker," *Michigan Daily,* http://media.www.michigandaily.com/media/storage/paper851/news/2001/03/30/Sports/Being.Tommy.Amaker-1409277.shtml (July 4, 2007).
"#8, Tommy Amaker, Woodson Basketball, 1983," *The Connection Newspapers,* www.connection-newspapers.com/article.asp?article=69989&paper=73&cat=198 (July 4, 2007).
"H. Tommy Amaker," *Biography Resource Center,* http://galenet.galegroup.com/servlet/BioRC (July 4, 2007).
"Latest from the *Ann Arbor* News: 2006 profile: Who is Tommy Amaker?," *Mlive.com,* http://blog.mlive.com/annarbornews/2007/03/amaker_profile.html (July 4, 2007).
"Tommy Amaker Named Men's Basketball Coach at Harvard," *Harvard University,* www.gocrimson.com/ViewArticle.dbml?DB_OEM_ID=9000&ATCLID=860319 (July 4, 2007).

Other

Information for this profile was obtained through an email interview with Tommy Amaker on April 18, 2007.

—Tina Gianoulis

John Amos

1941—

Actor, producer, director

Amos, John, photograph. Fitzroy Barrett/Landov.

Actor John Amos will forever be associated with the miniseries *Roots*, in which he portrayed a proud African man sold into slavery and subjected to unspeakable cruelties. However, Amos is just as comfortable with comedy, and his powerful build and stern but wry expression suit him for a variety of character roles. Amos's break into stardom came with the *Mary Tyler Moore Show* in the early 1970s, and for most of that decade he worked in a string of situation comedies, including the highly popular *Good Times*. After nearly a decade focusing on film and theater work, Amos returned to the small screen in the 1990s, taking both starring and supporting roles in such series as *704 Hauser Street, The Fresh Prince of Bel-Air, The West Wing,* and *Men in Trees.*

Though Amos's fame comes from his work in television, he has also had a diverse career away from the small screen. Amos has played both dramatic and comedic roles in a string of feature films. Since 1990, Amos has been performing, producing, directing, and acting in his one-man show, *Halley's Comet.* He founded a film production studio, Colored Wind Productions, to give his son the opportunity to direct his first film, *The Watermelon Heist,* in 2003. Perhaps most meaningfully, in 1999 Amos founded the Halley's Comet Foundation, a charitable organization that "is committed to making a positive and long-lasting impact on today's youth by exposing them to learning the challenges and culture of the sea," according to its mission statement.

Avoided Youthful Troubles

Amos was born in 1941 and raised in Newark, New Jersey, the only son of an auto mechanic. He was a rebellious youngster, especially after his parents divorced. "I got in a lot of trouble as a kid and as a young man," he recalled in the *Washington Post.* "I never hurt another human being, but I took things that didn't belong to me. I was a candidate for prison, a very good candidate." More than once, Amos's mother—who had sole responsibility for him and his sister—was forced to bail her son out of jail. She finally informed Amos that she would no longer be humiliated by his behavior—he was on his own. "I straightened up," the actor said. "The idea of losing your last safety net, it scared the hell out of me more than any incarceration in any institution ever could."

At a Glance . . .

Born on December 27, 1941 (some sources say 1939), in Newark, NJ; son of John A. (a mechanic) and Annabelle P. Amos; married Noel J. Mickelson (divorced); married Lillian Lehman (divorced); married Elisabete De Sousa; children: Shannon Patrice (daughter), K. C. (son). *Education*: Attended Colorado State University and Long Beach City College.

Career: Professional football player, 1962-65; actor, producer, director, writer, c. 1965–.

Awards: Los Angeles Drama Critics Award nomination, 1971, for *Norman, Is That You?*; Emmy Award nomination for best actor, 1977, for *Roots*; National Association for the Advancement of Colored People (NAACP) Image Award nomination for best actor, 1985, for *Split Second*; Image Award for supporting actor in a comedy series, 1996, for *In the House*; TV Land Impact Award, 2006, for *Good Times*.

Addresses: *Office*—Step and One Half Productions, P.O. Box 587, Califon, NJ 07830. *Agent*— c/o Michael Mesnick and Assoc., 11300 Olympic Blvd., Suite 610, Los Angeles, CA 90064. *Web*—www.thehalleyscomet-foundation.org.

Scrapes with the law behind him, Amos plunged into sports. In high school, he worked on his skills as a football player and was good enough to earn an athletic scholarship to Colorado State University. There he studied social work in preparation for a career helping others in the black community. After leaving Colorado State he returned east to New York City, where he served briefly as a public defender trying to get bail reductions for people who were incarcerated while awaiting trial. That job proved terribly disillusioning; Amos became convinced that the criminal justice system in New York was biased against black males. A different sort of work beckoned him, and he decided to give it a try.

Though many young boys dream of playing professional football, few ever achieve that goal. Amos was invited to try out for the Kansas City Chiefs, who signed and then cut him. When the Denver Broncos did the same thing, Amos enrolled in a training program that would prepare him to manage a McDonald's franchise. He then heard from several semi-pro football teams as well as the Canadian Football League. He spent three

years in the American, Continental, and Canadian football leagues, including a brief stint with the British Columbia Lions. When the Lions also dropped him, Amos gave up on football. "I said to myself, 'John, you're getting a little long in the tooth to be going to [football] tryouts,'" the actor remarked in the *Washington Post*. "My daughter was then about a year and a half old, and I knew I was going to have to make a life's decision."

Turned to Show Business

Having performed as a stand-up comic in British Columbia, Amos decided to take a chance on a career in show business, figuring he could at least write for other people if he could not break in himself. Hollywood proved a tough arena for the former football player. "I'd go in when I first started in the business, trying to get a job as a writer, and they'd see a black guy with a 19-inch neck," Amos told *Newsday*. Once, he was informed that he could not possibly know anything about comedy. Amos refused to give up, though, and in the late 1960s he was hired as a writer-performer for the *Lohman and Barkley Show*, a cult classic in Los Angeles that also launched the career of director Barry Levinson.

The big break for Amos came in 1970, when he was cast as weatherman Gordy Howard on the *Mary Tyler Moore Show*. The role was small and intermittent, but it gave Amos the kind of exposure he needed to secure other, more meaningful parts elsewhere. He made his stage debut in 1971, in *Norman, Is That You?*, a drama that earned him a best actor nomination from the Los Angeles Drama Critics Circle. He also found better stand-up work as a regular on the Columbia Broadcasting System (CBS) series *The Funny Side*. The "black guy with a 19-inch neck" was well on his way to stardom.

In 1973 Amos took a small part on another CBS sitcom. On *Maude*, a spinoff from the highly popular *All in the Family*, Amos played Henry Evans, husband to Maude's maid, Florida. The Henry and Florida characters proved so popular that CBS created another show exclusively for them, *Good Times*, which debuted in 1974. The sometimes controversial show profiled a fictitious black family living in public housing and trying to make a better life for themselves. Originally conceived as a comedy that would explore the social concerns of poor families, *Good Times* gradually became a vehicle for comedian Jimmie Walker, whose ebullient personality and trademark quip "Dyn-o-MITE!" began dominating the show. Amos objected strenuously to the changes. "There was too much emphasis on wearing chicken hats and 'dyn-o-mite,' and no equal representation of the other side, which is the world of academia, the young black guy who's not grabbing his crotch or wearing his hat sideways, but who aspires to a good life through the old traditional values," Amos opined in *Newsday*. "While we shouldn't have been doing [educational and cultural programming that appears on] PBS every week we certainly should have been putting more emphasis on a more positive role model."

Amos eventually quarreled with Norman Lear, the producer of *Good Times*, and when their exchange grew heated, Lear terminated Amos's contract. The Henry Evans character was "killed off" by a heart attack, and *Good Times* continued for several more seasons without Amos. The abrupt end to his sitcom work was hardly devastating for Amos, however. He had accepted a major dramatic role in a miniseries that would ingrain itself in American culture.

Starred in Roots

The miniseries *Roots* was based on the story of writer Alex Haley, who had traced his ancestry back to an enslaved African man named Kunta Kinte. In several installments, the show follows Kunta Kinte's life from his youth on the African savannah to his old age as a brutalized but still proud plantation slave. Amos was cast as the adult Kunta Kinte—a man determined to preserve his African heritage for future generations. In one of *Roots*'s most memorable moments, Amos holds a child toward the night sky and says: "Behold! The only thing greater than yourself!" *Chicago Tribune* correspondent Allan Johnson referred to that scene as "surely one of the most significant moments in a drama filled with significant moments." Johnson further noted that Amos's work in *Roots* "sparked an awareness in African Americans of their heritage." The actor was nominated for an Emmy Award for his portrayal of Kunta Kinte.

At the time of its first broadcast in 1977, *Roots* drew the highest ratings of any television show in history. The miniseries has since been rerun many times, and Amos has become closely associated with his role in the drama. In the wake of *Roots*'s success the actor concentrated on theater and film work. He wrote his own one-man show called *Halley's Comet* and traveled across country performing it. He also took cameo roles—a villain here, a hero there—in such films as *Die Hard 2*, *Lock Up*, *Coming to America*, and *The Beastmaster*.

Middle age and the responsibility of caring for two growing children brought a gradual shift in Amos's political views. Once a "superliberal," as he described himself in the *Washington Post*, he has come to be more supportive of the conservative cause. This has not eroded Amos's social consciousness, however. Having moved back to New Jersey after years of living in California, he helped to open the first movie theater in downtown Newark since the 1960s and has worked with youngsters there who want to pursue theatrical careers. "I don't want to be blasé about it, but I go where the work is, and then I come home," Amos told *Newsday*, referring to his decision to live in New

Jersey. "Cause this is my home—because of the theater, and because of my involvement with various organizations in the state."

Steady Work in Supporting Roles

In an ironic twist, Amos's return to regular TV work came about through his work with Norman Lear—the man he had clashed with over race roles in the early 1970s. The 1994 television pilot *704 Hauser Street* teamed Amos with Norman once again in telling the story of Ernie Cumberbatch (played by Amos), a Vietnam War veteran and former civil rights activist who abhors Republican politics. The show effectively turns the old *All in the Family* formula upside down, featuring a liberal father and a conservative son living in the former home of the bumbling bigot and main character of *All in the Family*, Archie Bunker. While *704 Hauser Street* is filmed on the former set of *All in the Family*, the new comedy has taken care to present all of its characters as intelligent and well read, able to argue their points on an intellectual level as well as an emotional one. *Newsday* reporter Diane Werts pointed out that various episodes "get to the crux of contrasting views on discrimination, virginity, and other issues. Sometimes Amos seems right; sometimes his son seems right. All the time, they compel each other to ponder why they believe what they do."

Amos and Lear buried whatever differences they may have had in the past and worked together in harmony to create the new show. "We've both changed, obviously for the better," Amos observed in *USA Today*. "We have a great relationship now." Though the show was not on the air for long, it helped remind television producers what a fine actor Amos was, and other roles followed. Amos grabbed the role of Fred Wilkes for four episodes of *The Fresh Prince of Bel-Air* in 1994-95, then joined the cast of *In the House* for 11 episodes between 1995 and 1997. Amos's most notable role came in 1999 when he was cast in the recurring part of Admiral Percy Fitzwallace, a no-nonsense advisor to the president in the popular series *The West Wing*. In the autumn of 2006, Amos was cast in the role of Buzz in the Ann Heche comedy *Men in Trees*. In each of these series, Amos earned critical acclaim for his polished acting skills in supporting roles.

Led Active Life Offscreen

Supporting TV roles were probably best for Amos, who was quite busy pursuing other interesting projects beginning in the 1990s and 2000s. In 1990, Amos penned his own one-man play called *Halley's Comet*. The play tells the story of an 87-year-old man who relates his memories of life, beginning with his first sighting of the famous comet 76 years earlier. The play is "the love of my life, because I wrote the piece," Amos told Tavis Smiley. "Years ago, I realized that at any point as an actor, you're the extension of someone's ego. And unless your face is right on the top of that 8x10 pile, or whatever it is they select you from, you don't exist. So I said I'd better use the skills and the gifts that God has given me and write something for myself." Touring intermittently but consistently since 1990, the play has taken Amos to more than 400 cities.

Amos has also found real meaning through his work with the Halley's Comet Foundation. Amos started the foundation in 1999 when he purchased a 68-foot boat designed to look like a pirate ship. Amos hosts at-risk youth aboard the ship, where they master the techniques to keep the large boat on course while learning important lessons about success in life. Amos's passion for this work comes from the pleasure he takes in being a father and grandfather. Amos has two children: his daughter, Shannon, is a physical therapist, and his son, K.C., is a filmmaker. Amos takes great joy in his children's accomplishments and was able to work alongside K.C. in the early 2000s when he produced his son's first film, *The Watermelon Heist*. The pair plan another film based on Amos's early days as a football player. But Amos told *Blackfilm*: "Theatre is my first love, and whenever I am not involved in a TV or movie project and if I am not on an absolute vacation or doing some writing, I am probably involved in a theatrical production of some kind."

Selected works

Films

The World's Greatest Athlete, 1973.
Let's Do It Again, 1975.
The Beastmaster, 1983.
American Flyers, 1984.
Coming to America, 1988.
Lock Up, 1989.
Die Hard 2, 1990.
For Better or Worse, 1996.
Dr. Dolittle 3, 2006.
Ascension Day, 2007.

Television

Mary Tyler Moore Show, 1970-73, 1977.
Maude, 1973-74.
Good Times, 1974-76.
Roots (miniseries), 1977.
Future Cop, 1977-78.
Hunter, 1984.

704 Hauser Street, 1994.
The Fresh Prince of Bel-Air, 1994-95.
In the House, 1995-97.
The West Wing, 1999-04.
The District, 2000-01.
Men in Trees, 2006-07.

Plays

Actor, writer, director, and producer, *Halley's Comet*, toured 1990–.
Appeared in *Norman, Is That You?*; *The Emperor Jones*; *Master Harold...and the Boys*; *Split Second*; and *And Miss Reardon Drinks a Little*.

Sources

Books

Contemporary Theatre, Film, and Television, Vol. 4, Gale, 1987.

Periodicals

Back Stage West, July 17, 2003, p. 4.
Chicago Tribune, March 2, 1993, p. 14.
Huntsville (Alabama) *Times*, June 30, 2007.
Newsday, April 10, 1994, p. 20; April 11, 1994, p. B-25.
USA Today, April 27, 1994, p. D-3.
Washington Post, May 8, 1994, p. TV-6.

On-line

The Halley's Comet Foundation, www.thehalley-scometfoundation.org (July 23, 2007).
"John Amos: The First Dad of Black Life Telling It Like It Is," *Blackfilm*, http://blackfilm.com/0205/features/i-johnamos.shtml (July 23, 2007).
"John Amos' Unlikey, Oceanic Passion," *NPR*, http://216.35.221.77/templates/story/story.php?storyId=10821424 (July 23, 2007).

Other

Interviewed on *The Tavis Smiley Show*, May 4, 2006; transcript available at *Tavis Smiley*, www.pbs.org/kcet/tavissmiley/archive/200605/20060504_amos.html (July 23, 2007).

—Anne Janette Johnson and Tom Pendergast

Angela Bassett

1958—

Actress

"It's like Angela's not there anymore," actor Larry Fishburne told *Entertainment Weekly*, describing actress Angela Bassett's capacity to inhabit a character. "She becomes who she's playing." A Yale-trained actress, Bassett began her career on stage in the 1980s, performing on Broadway in such plays as *Ma Rainey's Black Bottom* and *Joe Turner's Come and Gone*. At a time when women and African Americans in Hollywood struggled to find interesting, well-written roles, Bassett emerged as a powerful, technically accomplished performer in such highly regarded films as *Boyz N the Hood*, *Malcolm X*, *Waiting to Exhale*, and *How Stella Got Her Groove Back*. With her portrayal of rock survivor Tina Turner in the biopic *What's Love Got to Do with It*, she became a star.

Inspired by Theatre

Born on August 16, 1958, Bassett grew up in public housing in St. Petersburg, Florida. She was first truly electrified by acting when, in 1974, she went on a field trip to Washington D.C. There she saw the illustrious black thespian James Earl Jones in a Kennedy Center production of the play *Of Mice and Men*. "I just sat there after the play, boo-hoo crying, weeping," Bassett recalled to Barbara Jones of *Premiere*. "I couldn't move, and I remember thinking, 'My gosh, if I could make somebody feel the way *I feel right now!*'" Upon her return home she immersed herself in plays and started "really concentrating." A very good student, she was admitted to Yale, thanks in large part to the encouragement of her mother, Betty, who raised Angela and her sister D'Nette without the help of a spouse: "After [high school] graduation I knew I wanted to act," the actress told *Upscale* magazine reporter Christie Smith. "I also wanted to play it safe, so I decided that I'd be a business woman. My mother suggested Yale. She even typed my application. Later, I changed my major to acting, and she supported me 100 percent."

It wasn't easy being a Floridian in the Ivy League. Bassett's southern drawl set her apart from most of her East Coast classmates. She told Smith, "I had a lot of regionalism and really needed…training." Fortunately, such training came from a supportive teacher. Lloyd Richards was head of the Yale School of Drama and had seen Bassett acting in some undergraduate productions. He later told *Premiere* he'd seen in the aspiring actress a "deep passion" and declared, "When she applied for admittance to the drama school, I was very pleased." Bassett spent a total of six years at Yale and earned a master's degree in drama in 1983.

Bassett began working in commercials in the early 1980s soon after graduation; she had a role for a time on the television soap opera *The Guiding Light* and took parts in some forgettable films, like *Critters 4*. Yet much of her work was, in the words of *Entertainment Weekly*'s Ty Burr, "high-minded indeed." She made her Broadway debut in the August Wilson play *Ma Rainey's Black Bottom*, was cast by Lloyd Richards in Wilson's *Joe Turner's Come and Gone* in 1988, and landed a role in director John Sayles's 1991 urban epic *City of Hope*.

Born on August 16, 1958; raised in St. Petersburg, FL, daughter of Betty; married Courtney B. Vance, 1997; children: son and daughter (twins). *Education*: Yale University, BA, Afro-American Studies, 1980; Yale University, MFA, drama, 1983.

Career: Stage, film, and television actress, 1982–.

Awards: Golden Globe Award for Best Actress in a Musical or Comedy, for *What's Love Got to Do With It*, 1994; NAACP Image Award for Outstanding Supporting Actress in a Motion Picture, 1993, 2002; NAACP Image Award for Outstanding Lead Actress in a Motion Picture, 1993, 1996; NAACP Image Award for Best Actress, 2001; NAACP Award for Outstation Performance by a Female Actor in a Television Movie or Miniseries, 2002; Soul Train Lady of Soul Award: Lena Horne Award for Outstanding Career Achievement, 2002; Chapman University, Dodge College of Film and Media Arts, Dream Maker Award, 2007.

Earned Successful Leading Roles

But it was her performance in John Singleton's highly successful 1991 film *Boyz N the Hood*—about a group of African American teens growing to manhood in the midst of urban violence—that brought Bassett some real attention. She played Reva, the sophisticated mother of the film's young protagonist, Tre. Bassett's recollections of her own mother's dedication became a key to approaching the role of Reva, a woman who sends her son to live with his estranged father so that the youth might benefit from a strong male presence in his life. "When the role came up, I knew I wanted it," the actress related to *Upscale*. "I mean, there's a finite number of one-hour TV dramas you can do. I had been in L.A. for a while, and things weren't up to speed. When I got it, I was appreciative and felt blessed. I identified with [characters like] Doughboy, Tre and the rest of them because when I grew up, the big thing was heroin; now it's crack, guns and everything in between."

Co-star Larry Fishburne, a friend of Bassett's, recommended her to the director, and she felt an immediate bond with the young filmmaker. "I remember looking at John Singleton, thinking how sincere he was," she recalled. "He was only 21, making this massive film. I just had so much enthusiasm and love for what he was trying to do. After the audition, we sat around and talked to each other about great poets, like Langston Hughes. It seemed like we'd known each other before.

I really just wanted to go over and hug him. He was just a baby."

Bassett had a supporting role in Sayles's well-regarded 1992 drama *Passion Fish*, but would garner much more attention that year for her portrayal of Betty Shabazz, the wife of Malcolm X, in Spike Lee's film about the renowned activist's life and tragic death at the hands of assassins. Her audition for the part astonished Lee, who told *Premiere*'s Jones that Bassett "*was* Betty. Betty Shabazz is the best work she's ever done on film. She makes you *feel* for this woman." In her interview with *Upscale*, Bassett noted: "Spike was surprisingly easy to work with. I mean we've all heard the rumors. He gave me a lot of room as an actress." She added that Lee "really respects actors, but he doesn't get credit for that. I found that I could really talk openly with him."

Lee's estimation of her work was confirmed by many viewers. "I watched as Angela Bassett reenacted Betty's reaction to Malcolm's assassination," Joe Wood of *Rolling Stone* recounted. "Take 1, take 2, take 3, and she wailed, screamed, really, and in that screaming I felt tears." Wood added that "Bassett's voice carried an essential portion of Malcolm, of his spirit." Reviewing the film for the same publication, critic Peter Travers referred to the actress as "the very fine but underused Angela Bassett." Co-star Denzel Washington, who played the film's title role, told Burr of *Entertainment Weekly* that Bassett is "one of the very few actresses, period, of *any* color, who are carrying movies of substance." The actress revealed in *Upscale* that she strove to "bring dignity to [the] performance." In a *Premiere* piece, she allowed some insight into this process of characterization: "Betty was just so calm, so I was calm. You just got to be about your plan. Be about your race and finish it. Because there're people who're going to applaud it and people who won't be impressed for one moment."

Bassett finally broke through to stardom in her first truly splashy screen role: playing Tina Turner in *What's Love Got to Do with It*. *Time*'s Richard Zoglin called it "the kind of star-making turn that every actress dreams of—and practically every black actress in Hollywood wanted." Bassett went into serious training for the role of the singer, whose tumultuous relationship with her husband, Ike—according to the film's source, Turner's autobiography *I, Tina*—included both emotional and physical abuse. "I had a dialect coach, a singing coach, a choreographer and a personal trainer for 30 days before the filming began," Bassett told Deborah Gregory of *Essence*. "I lifted weights for two hours a day, six days a week, and went on a high-protein, no-sweets diet—egg whites, tuna without mayo, vegetables—to get Tina's incredibly muscular physique. If I had had two months to prepare, I think I would've been able to enter a bodybuilding contest afterward."

Won Praise for Turner Portrayal

Larry Fishburne agreed to accept the role of Ike Turner only after he knew for sure that Bassett would play Tina. "She's a bad motherf—er," Fishburne exclaimed to *Premiere*. "Angie B. is all that *and* the Sunday papers. I sat down and thought, 'I could just go and do this movie just 'cause Angie's in it.'" He further commented to Burr of *Entertainment Weekly* that Bassett "is 100 percent committed" to the projects on which she works. The two actors managed to recreate the scenes of violence between Ike and Tina to a harrowing—and sometimes dangerously real—degree. Bassett suffered a broken hand during shooting and explained to Burr why she endured the physical strain of those scenes over repeated takes: "I'm the type of person who doesn't want to kid it. I have to really go there, or I feel like I'm cheating. It's painful to go there, but, hey, it's painful not to go there."

Best of all, Bassett had one other important figure for support during the making of the film: Turner herself. The singer flew in from Germany to see Bassett's audition. "When I walked into the room," Bassett recalled to Gregory of *Essence*, "she immediately hugged me and told her manager that she thought I was 'beautiful,' and then she started showing me some of the dance routines from her days with [musical group] the Ikettes." Bassett added: "When I walked out of that room, I was flying on cloud nine and I knew I would give the part *everything* I had!" The actress told Burr that Turner "did my makeup. She was my biggest fan. Can you imagine?"

Bassett noted in *Time* that she considered the role of Tina Turner "the biggest challenge of my career." She further described her hopes for the project in an *Ebony* interview: "I wanted to convey that [Tina] is a bright woman, a survivor and a fighter." Apparently Bassett succeeded in her aim. *Los Angeles* film critic Rod Lurie predicted that she "is going to be a bigger star than Lady Tina herself." *Rolling Stone*'s Travers, who had serious reservations about the film, nevertheless praised the actress's "fine, sexy strutting portrayal of Tina," calling her "a dazzler; she commendably resists playing Tina as a victim even when the script keeps pushing her down that familiar path." Owen Gleiberman of *Entertainment Weekly* insisted that Bassett "captures the erotic youthquake that was Tina Turner in the '60s and early '70s." Bassett's work in *What's Love Got to Do with It* earned her an Oscar nomination in 1993, and in 1994 a Golden Globe award for best actress in a musical or comedy.

Played Strong, Dramatic Women

Following her success in *What's Love Got to Do with It*, Bassett appeared again as Betty Shabazz in the 1995 film *Panther*, which detailed the history of the Black Panther Party. She also co-starred opposite Eddie Murphy in the film *Vampire in Brooklyn*. Bassett played the role of Rita, a police officer who is unaware that she is a vampire. Along with Ralph Fiennes, Bassett co-starred in the 1995 science fiction thriller *Strange Days*. In the film, she played the role of Lornette "Mace" Mason, a rugged, independent woman who teams with Fiennes's character to rescue his ex-girlfriend from a group of gangsters.

Perhaps Bassett's greatest triumph in 1995 was her work in the film *Waiting to Exhale*. Directed by Forest Whitaker and based on the novel by Terry McMillan, the film chronicles the lives of four African-American women as they search for lasting romance and love. In the film, Bassett plays the role of Bernadine, a woman whose husband is having an affair with his secretary and abandons her and her two children. *Waiting to Exhale*, which also co-starred Whitney Houston, Lela Rochon, and Loretta Devine, was a huge commercial success and earned accolades for Bassett. Stephen Holden, writing in the *New York Times*, remarked that "Bassett's fuming performance is the movie's riskiest and most compelling and gives the movie its dramatic backbone."

In 1997 Bassett played the role of Rachel Constantine, a deputy chief of staff to the president of the United States, in the highly acclaimed science fiction film *Contact*. The following year, she starred in the box office smash *How Stella Got Her Groove Back*. Bassett played the role of Stella, a successful stockbroker and single mother. Stella is singularly devoted to raising her son, and has little time for dating and romance. Encouraged by a friend to take a trip to Jamaica, she meets a handsome Jamaican man who is 20 years her junior. The film follows their relationship as it progresses from mere physical attraction to a deeper romantic love. *How Stella Got Her Groove Back* provided yet another example of Bassett's talents as an actress. Kevin Rodney Sullivan, who directed the film, told *Jet* magazine "Angela as an artist is all 88 keys. She's a virtuoso, and I'm astounded by her range, depth and ability to bring so many nuances to the role. When I ask her for chartreuse, she gives me chartreuse. When I ask her for lavender with peach highlights, she gives me exactly that." Like Stella, Bassett's life and career were in a wonderful groove. As she remarked to *Ebony*, "What's being in a groove? It's being self-assured, confident, growing, continually growing. My life is joyful! I think that's pretty groovy."

Adding to the joy she found in her acting career, Bassett wed longtime friend Courtney B. Vance in 1997. The couple had known each other for nearly 14 years before beginning to date seriously in 1996. They recorded their unique journey to finding themselves and each other in a sort of dual autobiography entitled *Friends: A Love Story*, published in 2007. Happily married, the couple added twins to their family via surrogate mother in 2006.

Meanwhile Bassett maintained a steady schedule of work, landing a wide variety of lead and supporting roles on stage and screen. She returned to the New York stage in 1999, appearing in *Macbeth* with Alec Baldwin, and appeared in Pasadena, California, in August Wilson's play, *Fences*, with Laurence Fishburne, in 2006. In the early 2000s, Bassett also tried her hand at producing made-for-television movies with *The Rosa Parks Story*, the story of the civil rights heroine, and *Ruby's Bucket of Blood*, a dramatic look at racial tension in the South when a black bar owner hires a white singer to entertain. For both she also gave award-winning performances as the lead character. She gained further critical acclaim for *Boesman and Lena*, in which she portrayed Lena, a South African woman who, with her husband, finds herself homeless and struggling to make sense of her desperate situation. Bassett offered audiences a fresh side of her strong character, playing a tough sports journalist in *Mr. 3000* opposite the comedic actor Bernie Mac. The role may have led to Tyler Perry casting her as his leading lady in *Meet the Browns*, a film scheduled for release in 2008; the movie is an adaptation of Perry's stage play in which a single mother living in the Midwest takes her children to the funeral of her father in the South, where she meets his family for the first time. No matter her role, Bassett exuded a rare strength of character that consistently appealed to viewers.

Selected works

Books

(With Courtney B. Vance) *Friends: A Love Story,* Harlequin, 2007.

Films

F/X, 1986.
Boyz N the Hood, 1991.
City of Hope, 1991.
Passion Fish, 1992.
Malcolm X, 1992.
What's Love Got to Do with It, 1993.
Panther, 1995.
Vampire in Brooklyn, 1995.
Strange Days, 1995.
Waiting to Exhale, 1995.
Contact, 1997.
How Stella Got Her Groove Back, 1998.
Music of the Heart, 1999.
Supernova, 2000.
Boesman and Lena, 2001.
The Score, 2001.

Mr. 3000, 2004.
The Lazarus Child, 2004.
Akeelah and the Bee, 2006.
Meet the Robinsons (animated film), 2007.

Plays

Ma Rainey's Black Bottom, Broadway, 1985.
Joe Turner's Come and Gone, Broadway, 1988.
Macbeth, Joseph Papp Theater, 1999.
Fences, Pasadena Playhouse, 2006.

Television

Doubletake (made-for television movie), 1985.
The Cosby Show, 1985.
The Jacksons: An American Dream (miniseries), 1992.
Ruby's Bucket of Blood, (made-for-television), 2001.
The Rosa Parks Story (made-for-television), 2002.
Alias, 2004–.

Sources

Periodicals

Daily Variety, February 16, 2007, p. 12.
Detroit Free Press, March 29, 2007, p.
Ebony, July 1993, pp. 110-12; September 1998, pp. 68-72.
Entertainment Weekly, November 13, 1992, pp. 66-68; June 25, 1993, pp. 37-38.
Essence, December 1992; July 1993, p. 52.
Jet, August 17, 1998, p. 28-32.
Los Angeles magazine, June 1993, p. 123.
New York Times, December 22, 1995.
Parade, February 14, 1993, p. 2.
Premiere, December 1992, pp. 39-40; July 1993, pp. 50-51.
Rolling Stone, November 26, 1992, pp. 34-40, 80; June 24, 1993, p. 89.
Time, February 8, 1993, p. 71; June 21, 1993, p. 65.
Upscale, February 1993, pp. 76-77.
Woman's Day, March 6, 2007, p. 60.

On-line

"Angela Bassett Interview: *Mr. 3000*," About.com, http://movies.about.com/od/mr3000/a/ mr3000ab090204.htm (July 26, 2007).

—David G. Oblender, Shirelle Phelps, Simon Glickman, and Sara Pendergast

Sanford Biggers

1970—

Artist

Sanford Biggers creates mixed-media art installations that explore the many ways in which different cultures are interconnected. The relationships between Asian traditions and African-American popular culture particularly interest him, and he employs sculpture, found objects, movement, and video to address this theme. As he explained to *Cincinnati Enquirer* writer Marilyn Bauer, "The spirituality of Shinto in Japan, Buddhism in India and the spirituality of the African Diaspora – Yoruba and Santeria…I think these traditions are still inside us, latent. We don't get to express them until we tap into them with film, art, dance."

Influenced by Eclectic Artistic Sources

Born on September 22, 1970, in Los Angeles, California, Biggers grew up in the city's middle-class Baldwin Hills neighborhood, where he absorbed influences from both mainstream popular and hip-hop cultures. The family took trips to Disneyland, for example, but Biggers also grew up break dancing, deejaying, and doing graffiti. In fact, he told Bauer, "Graffiti is how I started doing art."

Biggers gained a wider appreciation for and knowledge of art and culture in college. He attended Syracuse University's international program in Florence, Italy, in 1991, and earned a bachelor's degree from Morehouse College in 1992. After graduation he lived in Japan for two years, teaching English and art in the city of Nagoya. While in Japan, Biggers began to study Zen

Buddhism, a spiritual practice that has remained a major influence in his work. He did further training at the Maryland Institute College of Art and at the Skowhegan (Maine) School of Painting and Sculpture before earning an M.F.A. at the School of the Art Institute of Chicago in 1999. Since then he has been based in New York City.

Though he began as a painter, Biggers soon discovered that he was more interested in objects themselves than in how he was able to represent them on a canvas. As he observed to Lauren Wilcox in an interview in *Tout-Fait*, he realized that objects he picked up on the street held inherent power. "It isn't about depicting— it's about seeing authenticity right in front of you," he explained. The way in which the object displayed wear and tear, for example, conveyed much about how and by whom the object had been used and what it had meant. Such objects became the focal points of Biggers's art installations. In 1993 he had his first solo exhibition, "In the Mind's Eye," in Los Angeles, and in 1996 his "Gomi no Tendankai" was shown in Nagoya, Japan. His works were also included in several group exhibitions in the 1990s and early 2000s, including "Magical, Mythical, Monumental" at Baltimore's Green Street Space and "Freestyle" at the Studio Museum in Harlem.

"I begin with found and mass-produced materials that bespeak a pre-existing history and a point of reference," Biggers explained in comments quoted in *Contemporary Artists*. "However seemingly abstract or distant, I transform them." This transformation sometimes communicates the object's spiritual importance;

At a Glance . . .

Born on September 22, 1970, in Los Angeles, CA. *Education:* Syracuse University, Department of International Programs Abroad, Florence, Italy, 1990-1991; Morehouse College, Atlanta, GA, BA, 1992; Maryland Institute College of Art, Baltimore, MD, 1996-1997; Skowhegan School of Painting and Sculpture, Showhegan, ME, 1998; School of the Art Institute of Chicago, IL, MFA, 1999.

Career: English and art instructor, Nagoya, Japan, 1992-94; California Afro-American Museum, painting and drawing instructor, 1995; Youth Opportunities Unlimited, painting and drawing instructor, 1996; Chelsea Vocational High School (Eyebeam/New York City Annenberg Challenge for Arts Education), New York, NY, teacher-in-residence, 2000; Cooper Union Saturday Program, New York, NY, codirector, 2000–; Studio Museum in Harlem, New York NY, artist-in-residence, 2000; P.S. 1 Studio Residency, 2000, Socrates Sculpture Park, World Trade Center, artist-in-residence, 2001; ARCUS Project, Japan, artist-in-residence, 2003.

Awards: School of the Art Institute of Chicago, James Nelson Raymond Fellowship, and Graduate Incentive Scholarship, 1999; Pennies From Heaven/New York Community Trust Grant, 2004.

Addresses: *Web*—www.sanfordbiggers.com.

it can also offer a critique of the ways in which these objects are commercialized. "Mandala of Co-option," for example, consists of five clear plastic Buddha statues inside of which float various objects, many of which are associated with hip-hop culture, such as thick gold chains, fat shoelaces, and microphones. The Buddhas are manufactured in Mexico, and the souvenirs are made in Hong Kong, Taiwan, and Korea. According to the artist's Web site, the piece shows how easily we accept cultural co-option—the process by which one culture incorporates elements of another as its own. Taking a less ironic approach, "Mandala of the B-Bodhisattva II" explores the confluence of breakdancing and Asian spirituality. The piece, a linoleum floor installation fashioned like a Buddhist mandala (a circular pictogram used as an aid in meditation), was used for the Bronx Community College's Battle of the Boroughs break dance competition in 2001.

Explored Various Cultures

While several of his works refer to Asian culture, Biggers focuses on middle-class America for his project entitled "a small world." The project juxtaposes home-movie footage from his childhood and that of a friend, showing both children playing piano, eating dinner with family, and playing with toys. In comments on *The Charlie Rose Show*, included on the artist's Web site, Biggers said that the piece "basically compares the life of a middle-class Jewish family from the east coast and a middle-class black family from the west coast." The footage shows that each family engages in rituals that are basically identical, yet neither family is at all aware of the other. What Biggers found especially interesting about this project, he told Rose, was that it shows that the country's diverse cultures are united by economic status, which dissolves ethnic differences; at the same time, however, this dynamic makes ethnicity all the more important, since it is the only thing by which a culture can maintain a distinct identity.

Among Biggers's other cultural explorations is "Both/And Not Either/Or," an installation of 12 pieces displayed at the Cincinnati Contemporary Arts Center in 2004. The largest piece, a painting entitled "Kalenda," consists of footprints suggesting dance notation. Biggers told *Cincinnati Post* writer Jerry Stein that the piece refers to dances that slaves did to communicate secretly among themselves. In "Kalenda," however, the steps are from pop dances of the 1970s. According to Stein, "Biggers sees the original slave dances plotting freedom as having descended into frivolous disco use." Another piece, "Hip Hop Ni Sasagu (In Memory of Hip Hop)" features a Buddhist prayer bell made from melted-down hip-hop jewelry. Biggers explained that his intent was to return hip-hop to its more spiritual origins. "Sticky Fingers," a mixed-media installation, features a giant leather pick-comb with a clenched fist above a bed with shiny red sheets and faux-fur covering. The work suggests the co-option of symbols popular during the Black Power movement of the early 1970s. A highlight of "Both/And Not Either/Or" is the video work "Danpatsu." In this piece Biggers, wearing traditional Japanese robes, sits in a forest while a Japanese woman in a kimono cuts his dreadlocks. This action suggests the ritual haircutting of a sumo wrestler's topknot when he retires. The piece, wrote Bret McCabe in *Baltimore City Paper*, indicates "Biggers' earnest respect for both the artistry of hip-hop and Buddhism's and Shinto's symbolic reverence."

In an interview in *Buddha Mind in Contemporary Art*, featured on Biggers's Web site, the artist observed that work, for him, is akin to a meditative state: "Your hands, mind, and eyes are not necessarily relaying coherent thoughts and signals to each other," he explained. "It is no longer being 'inside' your mind, but having a visceral, preconscious notion of how to work." At the same time, he added, it is crucial to invite audience participation in his art: "To me experience is so magical that it becomes what my work is about," he said. "I think there is a 'universal vibe' that connects us even if we never have the chance to meet...I think some of my projects are basically experiments around this idea."

Biggers returned to Japan in 2003 as an artist-in-residence with the ARCUS project. He has also been artist-in-residence at Socrates Sculpture Park, the World Trade Center, and the Studio Museum in Harlem. His works are in several collections, including the Studio Museum in Harlem, the Doron Sebbay Art Collection in Israel, and the Altoid Curiously Strong Collection in New York.

Selected works

Group exhibitions

Magical, Mythical, Monumental, Green Street Space (MICA), Baltimore, MD, 1997.
Doing Our Own Thing, Christopher Art Gallery, Prairie State College, Chicago, IL, 1998.
Freestyle, Studio Museum in Harlem, NY, 2001.
Whitney Biennial, Whitney Museum of American Art, New York, NY, 2002.
Black Belt, Studio Museum in Harlem, NY, 2003.
Somewhere Better Than This Place, Contemporary Art Center, Cincinnati, OH, 2003.
Reverse Negatives, The Gershman Y, Philadelphia, PA, 2004.
Double Consciousness: Black Conceptual Art Since 1970, Contemporary Arts Museum, Houston, TX, 2005.
The Dalai Lama Portrait Project: The Missing Peace, the 100 for Tibet, traveling, 2005.

Solo exhibitions

In the Mind's Eye, Wight Gallery, Los Angeles, CA, 1993.
Gomi no Tendankai, Cabaret Mago, Nagoya, Japan, 1996.

Psychic Windows, Matrix Gallery, Berkeley Art Museum, Berkeley, CA, 2002.
Afro Temple, Contemporary Arts Museum, Houston, TX, 2002.
Creation/Dissipation, Trafo Gallery, Budapest, Hungary, 2002.
Both/And No Either/Or, Contemporary Arts Center, Cincinnati, OH, 2004.
Sanford Biggers, Mary Goldman Gallery, Los Angeles, CA, 2004.
Sanford Biggers, Triple Candie, New York, NY, 2005.
Notions, Kenny Schachter Gallery, London, UK, 2005.

Sources

Books

Pendergast, Sara, and Tom Pendergast, eds., *Contemporary Artists,* 5th ed., Vol. 1, Gale, 2002.

Periodicals

Art in America, January, 2005, p. 132.
Cincinnati Enquirer, May 23, 2004.
Cincinnati Post, June 8, 2004.
New York Arts, March-April, 2007.

On-line

"In Review: Urbanite #7, January 05," *Urbanite,* www.urbanitemagazine.com (June 29, 2007).
"Ninja, Please," *Baltimore City Paper,* www.citypaper.com/news/story.asp?id=9342 (June 28, 2007).
Sanford Biggers, www.sanfordbiggers.com/ (April 9, 2007).
"Transformation and Tradition: Interview with Sanford Biggers," *Tout-Fait,* www.toutfait.com/issues/volume2/issue_4/ArtandLiterature/bigger/bigger.htm (April 9, 2007).

—E. M. Shostak

Golden Brooks

1970—

Actress

As one of the lead characters on the hit television show *Girlfriends,* which debuted in 2000, Golden Brooks has become one of the most recognized faces in the country. After eight seasons playing the character of Maya Wilkes, she has also begun to find fame on the big screen, garnering a steady stream of film roles including the 2008 release, *A Good Man is Hard to Find,* which she described to *AOL's Black Voices* as "one of those things that you wait your whole life as an actress." Her success is a testament to not only her talent, but her tenacity. Just out of high school, she auditioned for a play at Fresno City College. The director, not impressed, told her that she was no actress. Instead of giving up, Brooks, known for her positive personality, persevered. "I am glad he said that to me," she told the *Fresno Bee* in 2002. "To this day, I have not forgotten that. It pushes me."

Golden Ameda Brooks was born in Fresno, California, on December 1, 1970, a month premature and weighing only three pounds. Her earliest days were a struggle just to survive. "She has always been a fighter," her father Walter Brooks told the *Fresno Bee.* "No matter what she has done, she has always been very, very determined. I sure wouldn't want to go to war with her." When she was two, her father moved the family to Lagos, Nigeria, where he worked briefly as a teacher. Upon returning to California, her parents divorced and Brooks and her brother went to live with their mother Barbara in San Francisco. They later moved to Los Angeles during Brooks' high school years.

Independence and personal growth were a constant in their household. "My mother gave my brother and me so much independence to discover and explore and I think because of that, it kept me open," Brooks told *Jet.* "I could go in any room and talk to anyone. Whether it is the president of the United States or a room of angry right-wing conservatives or Southern White people, I have that ability to blend in and assimilate." Her mother also encouraged Brooks to express herself through sports and the arts. She excelled in gymnastics, figure skating, and theater, but it was dance that was her true love. "I was a dancer in high school. I did ballet, modern, jazz," she told the *Fresno Bee.* "After high school, all I wanted to do was dance." However, after a disappointing stint with a dance company, she decided to pursue college instead.

Brooks attended the University of California, Berkeley, where she majored in sociology and did research on media representations of minorities. She also spent more and more time in the theater, appearing in university productions of Ntozake Shange's *For Colored Girls,* Anton Chekov's *The Brute,* and William Shakespeare's *Romeo and Juliet.* After graduating in 1994, Brooks moved to New York where she earned a master's degree in creative writing from Sarah Lawrence College. She also further immersed herself in theater both on stage and in theoretical classes. "Theatre is the core where acting comes from, just like blues and jazz is the core where all music stems from," she told *Back Stage West.* "For me theatre has been the foundation of my training."

Returning to California in the late 1990s, Brooks continued to work on stage, becoming an active mem-

At a Glance . . .

Born on December 1, 1970, in Fresno, CA. *Education:* University of California Berkeley, BA, sociology, 1994; Sarah Lawrence College, MA, creative writing.

Career: actress, 1990s–; Robey Theater Company, CA, member, 1990s–.

Awards: Multi-Cultural Prism Award, for Best Actress in a Comedy, 2003; BET Comedy Award, for Outstanding Supporting Actress in a Comedy Series, 2006.

Addresses: *Agent*—Nine Yards Entertainment, 8530 Wilshire Blvd., 5th fl, Beverly Hills, CA, 90211.

ber of the Robey Theater Company, a non-profit theater that promotes black performances, both experimental and established. There, she shared the stage with Danny Glover. In 1998, Brooks made the leap to television when she landed a co-starring role alongside Pam Grier on the Showtime cable sitcom, *Linc's*. Based in a Washington D.C. bar owned by a black Republican, the show dealt with issues of politics, race, and sex all under the guise of comedy. Though it garnered several awards nominations and a fair amount of critical acclaim, the show was cancelled after just two seasons. Brooks told *Men's Magazine Online*, "My character was the only one people related to—the hard-working girl, single mother, living check to check. It caught people off guard. Middle America wasn't ready for those ramifications. It scared people."

Brooks didn't stay unemployed long. In 2000, she landed the role of Maya Wilkes on the UPN (now The New CW) show *Girlfriends*. Based on the lives of four female friends as they navigate life and love in Los Angeles, the show became a smash hit, running for an impressive eight seasons—the network's longest-running sitcom. Brooks attributed the show's success to keeping it real. "We keep the information accessible and the characters honest," she told *Men's Magazine Online*. "All are flawed and humbled. They make mistakes that don't get cleared up in 24 minutes." Brooks plays a sassy, brassy girl from the ghetto made good. Brooks told *The Fresno Bee*, "I'm a lot like Maya in the sense of Maya is very comfortable in her skin. She is very outspoken, very family-oriented, very grounded and a very strong person," Brooks says. The role earned Brooks a Multi-Cultural Prism Award for Best Actress in a Comedy and a BET Comedy Award for Outstanding Supporting Actress in a Comedy Series. Her high profile also landed her several guest appearances on shows such as *Moesha*, *The Jamie Foxx Show*, *The Parkers*, and *Star Trek: Enterprise*.

As her small screen stature grew, Brooks slowly made ascended in stature on the silver screen. After appearing in bit parts in several forgettable films in the early 2000s, Brooks landed a major role in the 2005 Queen Latifah film *Beauty Shop*. Alongside Alicia Silverstone, Andie MacDowell, and Alfre Woodard, Brooks held her own as the saucy stylist named Chanel. She followed that film a year later with a part in *Something New*, a sophisticated comedy about a professional black woman dating a sexy white landscaper. Next, she landed a role as one of three leads in the film *A Good Man Is Hard to Find*, based on the gospel play of the same name. However, even as these films raised her celebrity, Brooks still found it hard to find what she called the "right roles." "It's very competitive to land those few roles that come along," she told the *Oakland Tribune*. "I thought that after Halle Berry won the Oscar for *Monster's Ball* that things were changing. The roles are getting better, but there's just a lack of them." She then added with characteristic optimism, "But I'm still encouraged." Her growing legion of fans are as well.

Selected works

Films

Hell's Kitchen, 1998.
Timecode, 2000.
Impostor, 2002.
Motives, 2004.
Beauty Shop, 2005.
Something New, 2006.
A Good Man Is Hard to Find, 2008.

Television

Linc's, 1998.
Girlfriends, 2000-07.

Sources

Periodicals

Back Stage West, September 12, 2002, p. 1.
Fresno Bee (Fresno, CA), August 4, 2002, p. H1.
Jet, February 13, 2006, p. 40.
Oakland Tribune (Oakland, CA), April 1, 2005.

On-line

"Golden Brooks: Over 'Girlfriends'?," *AOL Black Voices,* http://blackvoices.aol.com/blogs/2007/05/07/golden-brooks-the-future-of-girlfriends/ (May 25, 2007).
"Golden Brooks: Simply Golden," *Men's Magazine Online,* www.mensmagazineonline.com/golden_brooks.asp (May 25, 2007).

—Candace LaBalle

Mehcad Brooks

1980—

Actor

Mehcad Brooks won a highly coveted role for any young, relatively unknown actor when he was cast in the hit ABC series *Desperate Housewives* at the end of its first season in 2005. Since then, the former high school basketball star from Texas has gone on to a slew of other choice roles in such films as *Glory Road,* the story of the dramatic tournament victory of a college basketball team, and *In the Valley of Elah,* an Iraqwar thriller from Academy Award-winning director Paul Haggis.

Brooks, Mehcad, photograph. AP Images.

Brooks began modeling at the age of 15. Yet his work did not keep him from becoming engaged in high school. He was a talented basketball player at L.C. Anderson High School, starting on its varsity team and serving as captain for three years. He was twice elected class president, and after graduation in 1999 Brooks entered the University of Southern California (USC) on an academic scholarship. The bulk of his coursework was concentrated in USC's renowned School of Cinema-Television, but he suffered a personal tragedy not long after leaving home when a cousin who was raised with him and his brother was shot to death at age 17. "He was a good kid, just the wrong place, wrong time," Brooks said of his cousin Ian in an interview with *USA Today* writer William Keck. "He was the strongest person I knew. He played the cello and football and was on his way to college. He was an inspiration to me every day."

Determined to Be an Actor

Brooks was born on October 25, 1980, in Austin, Texas, to Alberta Phillips, a journalist who later became a columnist and editorial writer for the *Austin American-Statesman,* and Billy Brooks, a professional football player who spent much of his career as a wide receiver for the Indianapolis Colts. His parents divorced, and his mother later remarried an attorney and settled Brooks—whose given name is pronounced "muh-COD" and means "wise one" in Ethiopian—and his brother in a predominantly white neighborhood of Austin.

Brooks worked a variety of jobs during his time at USC to pay for his living expenses. He also found time to audition for acting roles on the side. "I was working three jobs to go to college and making nothing," he explained to *Boston Herald* writer Stephen Schaefer

At a Glance . . .

Born Mehcad Jason McKinley Brooks, on October 25, 1980, in Austin, TX; son of Billy Brooks (a former professional athlete) and Alberta Phillips (a journalist). *Education:* Attended University of Southern California School of Cinema-Television, 1999-2002(?).

Career: Teen model, mid-1990s; Los Angeles, CA, odd jobs including window-washer, 1999-2004; actor, 2002–.

Addresses: *Home*—Los Angeles, CA. *Agent*—Mosaic Media Group, 9200 Sunset Blvd, 10th Fl, Los Angeles, CA 90069.

about his decision to leave USC. "I kept getting fired from my clothing store jobs because I'd be leaving for auditions and getting back three hours late." He decided to drop out of college when he was cast in a planned football movie from Austin filmmaker Richard Linklater that never went into production.

Brooks's first on-screen role came alongside his brother Billy in a 2002 short film by Katina Parker shown at various film festivals called *Radimi: Who Stole the Dream.* Later in 2002 he won a guest role in a sitcom, *Do Over,* and then another on an episode of *Malcolm in the Middle.* His breakout performance came in four episodes of the hit drama *Boston Public* in 2003 when he played Russell Clark, who romances the principal's daughter. After that, he appeared in a made-for-television movie, *Tiger Cruise,* and an episode of *Cold Case.*

Desperate Housewives Role Brought Fame

Winning a role on *Desperate Housewives,* ABC's top-rated drama at the time, was not easy, and by this point Brooks's brother was also living in the Los Angeles area and trying out for roles, including the *Desperate Housewives* part of Matthew Applewhite. Part of a new storyline on *Desperate Housewives,* Matthew moves onto Wisteria Lane at the end of the first season with his mother Betty, played by Alfre Woodard. Brooks described the series of seven tryouts for the series, including a standard ABC network audition, as "nerve-racking" in an interview with Diane Holloway in the *Austin American-Statesman.* "You walk into a room with a bunch of people who make 20 grand an hour and say, 'Hey, here I am…please like me.'"

Brooks noted in another interview that the fictional suburban street of *Desperate Housewives* was not that different from where he was raised, telling Keck in *USA Today,* "it's freaky how much my neighborhood was like Wisteria Lane." But it seems unlikely that anyone in his Austin neighborhood kept a close family relative locked up in the basement, as the Applewhite storyline revealed. Over the course of second season, the bizarre situation was exposed as the family's decision to keep Matthew's brother—who murdered Matthew's girlfriend—incarcerated at home rather than turn him over to the authorities. When the storyline began with the first-season cliffhanger, both Brooks and Woodard hinted that romances would develop between his character and some of the other teenagers who populated Wisteria Lane, but that never happened. In the end, Brooks was unhappy with his 18-episode run. "There was seniority and priority," he told *USA Today*'s Keck, "and we were marginalized and completely segregated from every family except the Van De Kamps."

Continued Film Career

Brooks proved a natural casting choice for his next role, the basketball movie *Glory Road.* He was cast as Harry Flournoy in the 2006 feature film, a real-life player for the Miners at the school that later became the University of Texas at El Paso. Based on a true story, the film recounts the Miners's journey in 1966—when the school was called Texas Western College—to a stunning upset in the finals of the National Collegiate Athletic Association (NCAA) tournament. The Miners beat a heavily favored University of Kentucky team with the first all-black starting line-up ever to play in the tournament, a controversial decision by the coach that ushered in a new era for college hoops. "The film does a good job of showing just how momentous that game was, immersing the audience in a world pervaded by racism, both casual and intense," wrote *New York Times* film critic A.O. Scott. A review from *Variety*'s Brian Lowry asserted that Brooks, along with castmates Josh Lucas as the white coach and Derek Luke as the Miners's star player, "[lead] a solid cadre of youthful players who manage to both look convincing on the court and convey the mix of anger and enthusiasm that the youths felt."

Brooks followed *Glory Road* with another sports drama, *Fly Like Mercury,* and *In the Valley of Elah,* another film set for 2007 release that traces a father's search for his missing son, who has recently returned from a tour of duty in the Iraq war. Brooks was cast in the Tommy Lee Jones–Jonathan Tucker movie as Army Specialist Ennis Long in the *Elah* project, written and directed by Paul Haggis, who won the Academy Award for the racial-tension drama *Crash.*

Brooks shares a house in the San Fernando Valley with his brother Billy and claims he has had to learn some hard lessons about managing his personal finances. At one point before his *Desperate Housewives* stardom, he was forced to take a job washing windows on Rodeo Drive, the world-famous pricey retail strip in Beverly

Hills. Admitting he loves the menswear designs of both Gucci and Hugo Boss, he told *People* that he fails to receive any ego boost from shopping in such stores now, because "I know I'm the same guy who was their window washer." However, it seems unlikely that Brooks may ever have to wash windows again.

Selected works

Films

Glory Road, 2006.
Fly Like Mercury, 2007.
In the Valley of Elah, 2007.

Television

Boston Public, 2003.
Tiger Cruise (movie), 2004.
Desperate Housewives, 2005-06.

Sources

Periodicals

Austin American-Statesman, May 22, 2005, p. K1.
Boston Herald, January 12, 2006, p. 43.
Film Journal International, February 2006, p. 27.
New York Times, January 13, 2006, p. E1.
People, October 26, 2005, p. 58; November 28, 2005, p. 184.
USA Today, May 20, 2005, p. 2E; May 19, 2006, p. 2E.
Variety, January 16, 2006, p. 33.

On-line

"An Interview with Mehcad Brooks," *Blackfilm.com,* www.blackfilm.com/20060106/features/mehcad-brooks.shtml (June 28, 2007).

—Carol Brennan

George Leslie Brown

1926-2006

Politician, journalist, business executive

George Leslie Brown's election as Colorado's lieutenant governor in 1974 made him the first black lieutenant governor in the 20th century, yet that pioneering achievement was only one among many in his esteemed career. Brown was appointed to a vacant seat in the Colorado House of Representatives in 1955 and then elected to five consecutive terms in the state Senate starting in 1956—he was the first black to serve as a senator in the state. He was also the first African American to work as an editor at a major daily newspaper in the Rocky Mountain region. And when he joined the Grumman Aerospace Corporation in 1979 he became the first black corporate officer in a major U.S. aerospace firm.

Started in Journalism

Brown was born in Lawrence, Kansas, on July 1, 1926. When he was one year old, his family moved to Kansas City, where his two sisters, Harriet and Laura, were born. The family moved back to Kansas—to his grandparents' farm in North Lawrence—when he turned five, and he lived there until his graduation from high school. A star athlete at Liberty Memorial High School, he excelled in football, baseball, and track. Immediately after graduation in 1944, he enlisted as a flight cadet in the Tuskegee Airmen, a black, Alabama-based unit of the Army Air Force. After the war he entered the University of Kansas, intending to study engineering. When he learned that it was nearly impossible for blacks to get jobs as engineers, he switched

to journalism, and in 1950 he earned a Bachelor of Science degree in that field.

Brown was to become prominent in journalism, politics, and business, but he made his mark first as a journalist. He had chosen journalism as his major because black reporters were in demand at the time to cover black-related issues. Upon graduation he received 17 job offers, and he accepted a position as a reporter with the *Denver Post*. He subsequently rose to the position of night city editor at the paper, becoming the first black editor at a major Rocky Mountain daily. During the same period he was also hosting a local radio talk show and teaching at the University of Colorado and the University of Denver. In 1959 he was named a King Fellow at the Colorado School of Journalism. In 1962 the U.S. State Department selected him as one of a group of journalists that was sent on a tour of Europe and 14 African countries to conduct seminars on journalism and communications. In an oral history recorded in 1973 by Juanita Gray and James Davis, held in the *Collaborative Digitization Program*, Brown recalled, "We spent most of the [tour] in Africa working with journalists, trying to establish a freer press in countries that up to that point had government-controlled press," He left the newspaper business in 1965. The University of Kansas's School of Journalism and Mass Communications formally recognized his achievements in 1976 with the inauguration of the George Brown Urban Journalism Scholarship. In 2003 the University awarded him its Distinguished Service Citation.

At a Glance . . .

Born on July 1, 1926, in Lawrence KS; died on March 31, 2006, in Boca Raton, FL; married Modeen Broughton, 1978; children: Gail, Cindy, Kim, Laura. *Education:* University of Kansas, BS, journalism, 1950; Harvard Business School, University of Colorado, and University of Denver, graduate studies.

Career: *Denver Post,* Denver, Colorado, writer and editor, 1950-65; Colorado House of Representatives, representative, 1955-56; Colorado State Senate, senator, 1956-75; State of Colorado, lieutenant governor, 1975-79; Grumman Ecosystems, vice president of marketing, 1979; Grumman Energy Systems, senior vice president of business development; Grumman Aerospace, chief Washington lobbyist, 1981-90; various positions with Prudential Securities, Greenwich Partners, L. Robert Kimball Associates, and Whitten & Diamond.

Memberships: 4H Board of Trustees; Board of Trustees of Davis and Elkins College; Board of Trustees of the World Trade Center, Washington; Democratic National Committee; Denver Citizen's Committee on Juvenile Delinquency; Executive Committee of the SW Regional Council of the National Association of Housing and redevelopment Officials; Governor's Coordinating Committee on Implementation of Mental Health and Mental Retardation Planning; Harlem Boys and Girls Choir Board of Trustees; the National Panel of the National Academy of Public Administration Foundation Neighborhood-Oriented Metro-Government Study; National Policy Council of the U.S. Department of HEW; National Task Force for Secondary Education Reform; Nutrition Advisory Board for the Colorado Social Services Department.

Awards: Colorado Black Caucus, Achievement Award, 1972; Colorado School of Journalism, King Fellow, 1959; Congressional Black Caucus, Adam Clayton Powell Award for Political Achievement, 1975; Kappa Alpha Psi, Achievement Award, 1974; NAACP (Denver Metro branch), Exceptional Man Award, 1972.

Long Career in Public Office

Brown also distinguished himself in politics and public service, beginning in 1955 when Colorado's Democratic Party appointed him to the state's House of Representatives to fill the seat vacated by Elvin Caldwell after his election to the Denver City Council. Brown, who had worked on Caldwell's campaign as a speech-writer, served in the House for a year and a half. In 1956 he made a successful bid for the state Senate, becoming Colorado's first African-American senator. He served in the Senate for five consecutive terms, during which he co-sponsored far-reaching civil rights laws on issues including fair housing, open records, fair employment, and prison work release. A particular source of pride for him was the central role he played in repealing the state's miscegenation laws, which forbade blacks and Chicanos from marrying whites. Of his time in the Senate, Brown said in his oral history, "I wouldn't trade [it] for anything in the world. It's been an education. It's been frustrating. I had to learn to compromise, which is one of the hardest things for me. It became easier when I realized that I didn't have to compromise past my line of conviction, and I don't think I ever have."

A significant portion of Brown's life in public service saw him as the leader or a member of a number of committees, boards, and government agencies. From 1965 to 1969, he was the assistant director of Denver's Housing Authority. During his tenure he helped to craft programs for senior-citizen health and youth recreation and supervised the creation of family housing developments and community centers. In 1969 he served as executive director of the Metro Denver Urban Coalition, in which capacity he brought members of the minority community together with representatives from business, education, religion, and the media to devise new approaches to social problems. Much of Brown's public-service work was directed at young people. He told Juanita Gray and James Davis, "It's been said many times that the future of the world is in our young. But that future doesn't necessarily have to be good unless you've worked with young people and helped them see the need for constructive change, the need for active participation. And I don't think you can do that except by demonstration." To support these convictions, Brown served in the Denver Citizens' Committee on Juvenile Delinquency and the White House Conference on Youth, and he also sat on the boards of trustees for such groups such as 4H and the Boys and Girls Choir of Harlem.

Brown ran for Lieutenant Governor in 1974 as the running mate of Richard Lamm. He had been approached in the two previous elections about the possibility of running for lieutenant governor, but on those occasions he didn't think that Colorado was ready for a black gubernatorial candidate. Lamm's campaign was successful, and in 1975 Brown was sworn in as the first black lieutenant governor of the 20th century. His term was marked by controversies that may have undermined his long-term political prospects. While Lamm was on vacation, for instance,

Brown pardoned a convicted murderer named Sylvester Lee Garrison, who had been a friend of Brown's. When Lamm returned to work, he rescinded the pardon. Lamm later withheld some of Brown's pay because Brown had overspent his budget. One episode in particular spurred a flurry of negative publicity. At a speech before the 1975 National Lieutenant Governors Conference in Alabama, Brown claimed that during his Tuskegee Airmen days, he had crash landed in an Alabama field. He said that a farmer found him and branded a letter "K" onto his chest, possibly a reference to the Ku Klux Klan. It was soon revealed, however, that the brand was actually from Brown's Kappa Alpha Psi fraternity. The story got plenty of play in the local press, and there were calls for his ouster. Lamm dropped Brown from the ticket in his 1978 re-election campaign. In 1980, Brown sued for $500,000 in back pay and was awarded $10,000.

Left Elected Office for Industry

Brown spent the remainder of his life primarily in the business arena. In 1979 was hired by the Grumman Corporation, making him the first black executive in a major aerospace firm. He served in a number of roles in various Grumman divisions: In 1979 he was named vice president of marketing at Grumman Ecosystems, and from 1979 to 1981 he served as senior vice president of business development at Grumman Energy Systems. In 1981, following his completion of Harvard Business School's Advanced Management Program, he was appointed Grumman's chief lobbyist in Washington, D.C., a position he held until 1990. He left Grumman in 1990, and went to work for a variety of firms, including the law firm Whitten & Diamond, Prudential Securities' public finance office, the architectural/engineering outfit L. Robert Kimball Associates, and the public finance firm Greenwich Partners. Even while immersed in the business world, Brown remained active in civil rights, a commitment that led *Ebony* magazine in the late 1990s to name him one of America's 100 most influential African Americans. Just weeks before his death he co-chaired the National Black People's Unity Convention in Gary, Indiana. He had also co-chaired a similar meeting in Gary in 1972 that was credited with increasing the role of blacks in the Democratic Party.

In his 1973 oral history, Brown reflected on his time in the Senate, and he summarized those years in a way that could stand as a declaration of his life's mission. "I want to find ways to work…for my people," he said. "When I say that, I want everybody to understand that, yes, I have a priority on black people, but I include all people when I say, 'I want to work for my people.'" Brown died of cancer in Boca Raton, Florida, on March 31, 2006.

Sources

Books

Who's Who Among African Americans, 19th ed., Gale, 2006

Periodicals

Denver Westword, April 1, 1999.
Indianapolis Recorder, August 16, 2005.
Jet, April 24, 2006, p. 17.
Los Angeles Times, April 5, 2006, p. B9.
New York Times, April 6, 2006, p. 23.
State News, May 2006, p. 23.
Washington Post, April 7, 2006, p. B6.

On-line

"Brown, George L.," *Black Past.org: Remembered and Reclaimed,* www.blackpast.org/?q=aaw/brown-george-l-1926-2005 (July 31, 2007).
"Colorado Lieutenant Governors," *Colorado State Archives,* www.colorado.gov/dpa/doit/archives/offic/ltgov.html (July 31, 2007).
"Death of George Brown, KU Distinguished Service Citation Recipient," *Monday Memo: William Allen White School of Journalism and Mass Communications,* www.journalism.ku.edu/faculty/monday-memos/spring06/4-3-06%20Monday%20Memo.pdf (July 31, 2007).
"Eight Elected to National 4-H Council Board of Trustees," *Clover Corner News,* http://4hblogs.org/ccn/archives/2004/04/index.html (July 31, 2007).
"Former Lieutenant Governor George Brown Dies," *CoGen Blog* www.cogenblog.com/index.php?s=george+l.+brown (July 31, 2007).
"George L. Brown Biography," *HistoryMakers,* www.thehistorymakers.com/biography/biography.asp?bioindex=389&category=PoliticalMakers&occupation=Political%20Leader&name=George%20L.%20Brown (July 31, 2007).
"George L. Brown 1926-2006 Boca Raton," *LJWorld.Com,* www2.ljworld.com/obits/2006/apr/11/george_brown/ (July 31, 2007).
"George L. Brown: Oral History," *Collaborative Digitization Program,* www.cdpheritage.org/streaming/index.cfm?filename=DPL-OH47.tape1.sideA (July 31, 2007).
"George L. Brown: Oral History," *Collaborative Digitization Program,* www.cdpheritage.org/streaming/index.cfm?filename=DPL-OH47.tape1.sideB (July 31, 2007).
"George L. Brown: Oral History," *Collaborative Digitization Program,* www.cdpheritage.org/streaming/index.cfm?filename=DPL-OH47.tape2.sideA (July 31, 2007).
"Isaac E. Moore, Jr. Papers," *Blair-Caldwell African American Research Library: Denver Public Library,* http://aarl.denverlibrary.org/archives/imoore.html (July 31, 2007).
"Leaders in Service to Receive Honors on Commencement Weekend," *Kansas University Connection,* www.kuconnection.org/2003apr/people_1.asp (July 31, 2007).

—Bob Genovesi

Rosemary Brown

1930-2003

Legislator, social activist, feminist

Rosemary Brown, a pioneer of 20th century Canadian politics, devoted her life to the cause of justice and equality for women and minorities. When she was elected in 1972 as a Member of the Legislative Assembly (MLA) in the British Columbia provincial legislature, she became the first black woman to serve in a Canadian parliamentary body. She was also the first black female candidate for leadership of the New Democratic Party. In addition to her work in elected office, Brown served as the Chief Commissioner of the Ontario Human Rights Commission and as a member of the Judicial Council of British Columbia. She was a founding member of the Vancouver Status of Women Council and the Canadian Women's Foundation. Lt. Governor Iona Campagnolo summed up Brown's life mission as "lighting her way through the thickets of residual discrimination, whether racist, sexist, or classist, using her fine mind and elegant manners to set old ideas on fire with their inherent inconsistencies and working to replace them with values for a world in which the common good was served first in a society dedicated to inclusion, justice, and active support for human rights," at the 2005 inauguration of British Columbia's Rosemary Brown Award for Women. Brown died of an apparent heart attack on April 26, 2003.

Brown was born in Jamaica on June 17, 1930. Her father died when she was young, and she grew up with her mother and grandmother in her grandmother's middle-class neighborhood. In her autobiography, *Being Brown: A Very Public Life,* she described her upbringing as safe and supportive, in a house ruled by women: "It was [a] large place that was filled with the noise of women and children, with their laughter, their joy, their anger...The men who came and went, uncles, brother, cousins—did so quietly and with respect."

Such an upbringing left her unprepared, however, for the trauma of confronting racism and sexism when she moved to Canada in 1950. Arriving at age 20 to study at McGill University in Montreal, she encountered hostile immigration authorities and rejections from potential landlords and employers. She ended up with a private dorm room at McGill because white students refused to be her roommate. Despite the obstacles, Brown earned a Bachelor of Arts degree from McGill in 1955, and at the University of British Columbia she earned a Bachelors degree in social work in 1962 and a Master's degree in that field in 1967. Her college experiences laid the foundation for her subsequent commitment to social activism as well her achievements in political office. In a 1973 speech she recalled the experiences and the attitude they engendered in her: "To be black and female in a society which is both racist and sexist is to be in the unique position of having nowhere to go but up."

Her activities in public service began around 1955, when she moved to Vancouver, British Columbia, to marry William Brown. She and her husband became founding members of the British Columbia Association for the Advancement of Coloured People. In the early 1960s, she joined the Voice of Women, an anti-nuclear group that lobbied for arms control and the elimination of nuclear weapons. She also hosted a weekly television program called *People in Conflict.* In her private

At a Glance . . .

Born on June 17, 1930, in Jamaica; died on April 26, 2003 in Vancouver, British Columbia; married Dr. William Brown; children: Gary, Cleta, Jonathan. *Education:* McGill University, BA, 1955; University of British Columbia, BSW, 1962; University of British Columbia, MSW, social work, 1967.

Career: Government of British Columbia, Member of Legislative Assembly, 1972-86; MATCH International, chief executive officer, 1989; Victoria University, professor at the School of Social Work, 1986-87; Simon Frazer University, Ruth Wynn Woodford Professor of the Endowed Chair in Women's Studies, 1987-88; University of British Columbia, professor at the School of Social Work,1988; Ontario Human Rights Commission, chief commissioner, 1993-96.

Memberships: Advisory Council of the Global Fund for Women, board member; British Columbia Association for the Advancement of Coloured People, founding member; Canadian Centre for Policy Alternatives; Canadian Women's Foundation, founding member; Queen's University, board member; South African Educational Trust Fund, board member; Vancouver Status of Women Council, founding member.

Awards: National Black Coalition Award, 1972; United Nations, Human Rights Fellowship, 1973; YWCA, Woman of Distinction Award, 1989; University of British Columbia Alma Mater Society, Great Trekker Award, 1991; Government of British Columbia, Order of British Columbia, 1995; Government of Jamaica, Commander of the Order of Distinction, 2001; Canadian Labour Congress, Award for Outstanding Service to Humanity, 2002; Harry Jerome Award, 2002; Government of Canada, Order of Canada.

life during the 1960s, she worked as a social worker with such institutions as the Children's Aid Society of Vancouver, the Riverview Mental Hospital, and the Montreal Children's Hospital.

Her plunge into electoral politics came in 1972. Brown was working as the coordinator of the Vancouver Status of Women Council's Ombudsoffice for Women. The council was involved in a project to get feminist women elected to positions of power, and they backed Brown in a bid for the British Columbia legislature. When she won her seat on the legislature, representing Vancouver-Burrard, she became the first black woman to serve in a Canadian parliament. She was re-elected to the seat in 1975. Because of redistricting she subsequently represented Barnaby-Edmonds from 1979 to 1986. During her tenure in parliament she helped found the Berger Commission on the Family, introduced bills to curb discrimination based on sex or marital status, led an effort to remove sexism from educational curricula and textbooks, and got a law passed making seatbelts mandatory for children. In 1975 she campaigned for leadership of the Federal New Democratic Party, running on the slogan, "Brown is Beautiful." She came in second after four ballots, but nevertheless won the distinction of being the first black woman to run for leadership of a national party in Canada.

Brown retired from the legislature in 1986 but remained as active as ever. She taught at Simon Fraser University as the Ruth Wynn Woodford Professor of the Endowed Chair in Women's Studies from 1987 to 1988 as well as at Victoria University's School of Social Work from 1986 to 1987 and at the School of Social Work at the University of British Columbia in 1988. Her autobiography, *Being Brown: A Very Public Life,* was published by Random House in 1989. The same year she became the chief executive officer of MATCH International in Ottawa, a nongovernmental development agency that helps fund projects run by feminist groups in Africa, Asia, the Caribbean, and South America to empower women. She served as the organization's CEO for three years, followed by stints as special ambassador and then president. She also served as the Chief Commissioner of the Ontario Human Rights Commission from 1993 to 1996.

Brown died of an apparent heart attack on April 26, 2003. More than one thousand people attended a memorial service held on May 5. Speaking at the memorial, British Columbia NDP opposition leader Joy MacPhail summed up Brown's achievements: "Her legacy will live on amongst the thousands of women and people of color who were inspired and have become involved in politics through her role as an activist, educator, and role model," as quoted on the New Democratic Party of British Columbia Web site.

Sources

Books

Being Brown: A Very Public Life, Random House, 1989.

Periodicals

Canadian Review of Sociology & Anthropology, August 1999, p. 355-369.
Herizons, Summer 2003, p. 5.

Maclean's, July, 8, 1996, p.2.
Share News, May 1, 2003.
Toronto Star, June 15, 2003.

On-line

"Black Feminist Leader Receives Great Trekker Award," *University of British Columbia Library,* www.library.ubc.ca/archives/pdfs/ubyssey/UBYSSEY_1991_09_27.pdf (June 24, 2007).

"In Memoriam," *McGill University Alumni Quarterly,* www.mcgill.ca/news/2003/fall/memoriam/ (June 24, 2007).

"In Memoriam Rosemary Brown," *University of British Columbia; The School of Social Work and Family Studies Two-Year Annual Report, 2002-2004,* www.swfs.ubc.ca/fileadmin/template/main/images/departments/social_work/annrep0204.pdf (June 26, 2007).

"Obit—Rosemary Brown," *CBC Radio: As It Happens,* www.radio.cbc.ca/programs/asithappens/national/2003/obit_brown_280403.html (June 24, 2007).

"Rosemary Brown," *Canadian Heritage,* www.canadianheritage.gc.ca/progs/multi/black-noir/commemoration/brown-rosemary_e.cfm (June 24, 2007).

"Rosemary Brown (1930-2003)," *Heroines.ca,* www.heroines.ca/people/brown.html (June 26, 2007).

"Rosemary Brown, A Canadian Political Fixture," *African American Registry,* www.aaregistry.com/african_american_history/2204/Rosemary_Brown_a_Canadian_political_fixture (June 24, 2007).

"Rosemary Brown—Activist," *Cool Women,* www.coolwomen.org/coolwomen/cwsite.nsf/vwWeek/D2F3F31CA37DA0885256CF40076F6A1?OpenDocument (June 26, 2007).

"Rosemary Brown Award for Women Presentation and Tea," *Office of the Lieutenant Governor, British Columbia,* www.ltgov.bc.ca/whatsnew/sp/sp_mar08_2_2005.htm (June 24, 2007).

"Rosemary Brown Fonds," *University of British Columbia Library,* www.library.ubc.ca/spcoll/AZ/PDF/B/Brown_Rosemary.pdf (June 26, 2007).

"Rosemary Brown, She Will Be Missed, " *Canadian Labour Congress,* http://canadianlabour.ca/index.php/april_03/192. (June 24, 2007).

"The Title and Degree of Doctor of Laws, (honoris causa) Conferred at Congregation, June 2, 1995" *University of British Columbia Library,* www.library.ubc.ca/archives/hdcites/hdcites11.html (June 26, 2007).

"2002 Harry Jerome Award Recipient—Lifetime Achievement," *Black Business and Professionals Organization,* www.bbpa.or/Harry/rosemaryb.html (June 26, 2007).

Other

For Jackson: A Time Capsule from His Two Grandmothers (documentary film), LRS Productions, 2003.

—Bob Genovesi

Rae Dawn Chong

1961—

Actress

Actress Rae Dawn Chong became famous in the 1980s for a string of film roles that maximized her exotic, multiracial looks for the big screen. Of mixed African-American, Native American, Asian, and Anglo ancestry, Chong gained fame in Hollywood at the start of her career as the daughter of popular comedian Tommy Chong. In the 1990s and beyond, her career seemed to falter, though she was occasionally seen as a guest star on such television series as *That's So Raven.* Chong, however, seemed troubled little by her intermittent time in the limelight, admitting to Paul E. Pratt of *Asianweek* that "I've never been one to think of my body of work as anything more than 90 minutes of popcorn."

Chong, Rae Dawn, photograph. Kevin Winter/ImageDirect/Getty Images.

Chong was born in February 28, 1961, in Edmonton, Alberta, Canada; some sources cite her year of birth as 1962 and the city in which she was born as Vancouver, British Columbia. Her father was of mixed Scottish-Irish and Chinese-Canadian ancestry, and her mother, Maxine, was African-American and Native American and just 17 years old at the time of Rae Dawn's birth. Chong was raised primarily by her father, first in Vancouver and later in Los Angeles, where his career as a nightclub comic eventually segued into a popular comedy duo with Cheech Marin known as Cheech & Chong. The pair's drug-addled comedy routine and stoner characters were a hit with young audiences in the 1970s, and they began appearing in a string of hit movies beginning in 1978 with *Up in Smoke.*

Child of Hollywood

Chong's family came to include several half-siblings, and her mixed ancestry sometimes caused problems for her in her teens. She was sent to a boarding school in Ojai, California, for a time, and began venturing into the entertainment business herself. She made her television debut in 1974 Disney movie *The Whiz Kid and the Mystery at Riverton,* and was almost cast in a popular sitcom a few years later, *Diff'rent Strokes,* as the girlfriend of Willis, one of the two African-American kids being raised by a wealthy white bachelor. Producers of the hit NBC series reconsidered, however, and hired the less-exotic Janet Jackson for the role instead.

Chong made her feature-film debut in *Stony Island,* a 1978 urban drama set on Chicago's South Side that featured an R&B music-industry storyline and compel-

At a Glance . . .

Born February 28, 1961, in Edmonton, Alberta, Canada; daughter of Tommy Chong (an actor) and Maxine Sneed; married Owen Baylis (a stockbroker), 1982 (divorced); married C. Thomas Howell (an actor), 1989 (divorced, 1990); children: (with Baylis) son Morgan.

Career: Actor, 1974–.

Addresses: *Agent*—Metropolitan Talent Agency, 4526 Wilshire Blvd, Los Angeles, CA 90010.

ling soundtrack. Her breakout role, however, came in 1981 with *Quest for Fire,* a saga of prehistoric man from French director Jean-Jacques Annaud. Its story centered around the Ulam, a community of hunters who do not know how to make fire, but recognize its importance when nature provides the spark for them. The Ulam send out a search party to find a flame and bring it back, and along the way rescue a young girl named Ika (Chong) from death at the hands of cannibals. Ika leads them to her own people, who know the secret of making fire, and along the journey a romance develops between her and one of the Ulam.

Quest for Fire was a large-scale, joint French/ Canadian production that was shot in Scotland, Kenya, and Alberta, Canada, and attracted a great deal of media attention when it was released in early 1982. The cast, which included future *Beauty and the Beast* star Ron Perlman, studied animal behavior for weeks before shooting began, and for their dialogue memorized a script made up entirely of a primitive language created by British novelist Anthony Burgess. The movie's premise that early human civilization was driven by conflicts between Neanderthals and more advanced Homo sapiens was criticized by anthropologists, as was the main point of the plot: that 80,000 years ago primitive man did not yet know how to make fire. Scientists believe that this knowledge dated back some 500,000 years instead. But there was also a great deal of press focused on Chong, who was essentially naked save for some mud stripes throughout the film, and said that she spent nearly 17 weeks like that on location. "It was horrible, cold, dirty work, but the exposure was worth it," she told Deirdre Donahue in *People.*

A Few Busy Years

Quest for Fire won two César Awards, the French equivalent of the Academy Award, both for best director, and best film. Few of Chong's subsequent projects would fare as well, however. She appeared in the breakdancing drama *Beat Street* in 1984, put in a well-reviewed performance in another film that same year, *Choose Me* from Alan Rudolph, and followed it with a role as a lesbian stripper in *Fear City* and then a pictorial in Playboy. In 1985 she became the center of another minor controversy when Mick Jagger chose her to appear in a 90-minute video for his first solo album, *She's the Boss,* that featured some graphic love scenes. Publicity of a different type followed that when Chong narrated 20-minute educational film produced for the New York City public schools, *The Subject Is AIDS,* which was lauded by a long list of prominent public-health officials but mired in legal battles for years because it failed to explicitly endorse abstinence as a way to prevent AIDS. The film, which was shown outside of New York as well, has an alternate title, *Sex, Drugs and AIDS.*

Fame brought some pitfalls for Chong, she admitted in the 1985 *People* interview. She married a stockbroker in 1982 and had a son, but the union was short-lived, and she said that substance abuse had marred her first years of success in Hollywood. "I think if it had not been for the birth of my son I'd have gone right over the edge," she told Donahue in *People.* "It's an old problem in this town." She went on to appear that same year in *The Color Purple,* Steven Spielberg's adaptation of Alice Walker's acclaimed novel, and won a plum role as the sidekick to Arnold Schwarzenegger in another 1985 film, *Commando,* an action movie that followed on the heels of Schwarzenegger's success as *The Terminator.* "I knew Arnold would make the film a hit, and I wanted to be part of that," she told *People.* "I want studio executives and producers to start to say to themselves, 'Rae Dawn is bankable.' I am here to make money, but I am also here to make every part I get special."

That box-office clout never happened for Chong, however, perhaps because she was a bit too outspoken about the Hollywood system. "I have to work 20 times harder for a part because I have brown skin, black curly hair and big lips," she asserted in that same interview and added, "I know there are certain actors who won't work with me romantically because I am ethnic." In 1986, she appeared in *Running Out of Luck* and *Soul Man,* and later married her co-star from the second movie, C. Thomas Howell. Films that followed included *Chaindance* and *Rude Awakening,* both from 1990, *Amazon* in 1992, and *Boca* in 1994. Later in the decade she appeared in *Goodbye America, Highball, Small Time,* and *Dangerous Attraction,* along other largely ignored films.

Scored Well with The Visit

Chong received some long-overdue good reviews with *The Visit* in 2000, which co-starred her alongside Hill Harper as a young man dying of AIDS in prison after being wrongly convicted of rape. Chong was cast as childhood friend who still visits Alex after surviving her own traumas, including murder and drug addiction. "The initial conversation between Alex and Felicia is one of the funniest and most surprising in the movie," wrote A.O. Scott in a *New York Times* review. "Her glow of spiritual satisfaction seems downright obnoxious, and he responds by mocking her and questioning her good faith." She followed the film with roles on two short-lived television series, *Mysterious Ways* and *Wild Card.*

In 2005, Chong appeared in *Constellation* with Billy Dee Williams, the story of mixed-race Southern family. She continued to make guest appearances on television, and had a roster of credits that ranged from *Melrose Place* to *Judging Amy*, but her best-known role remained *Quest for Fire*, which was released on DVD in 2003. Chong and Perlman added commentary to the disc version of the movie, which a *Washington Times* journalist called "a funny, rousing and poignant adventure that hasn't aged a whit since its initial release."

In addition to her acting, Chong also wrote and directed films. Her first was the 1994 *Boulevard*. In 2001 she directed the horror movie *Cursed, Part 3*, and in 2002 she wrote and filmed the short film *Mary Stigmata*, about a woman struggling to make a decision in an abortion clinic. Her screenplay *Blunt*, described as a "modern day Cheech and Chong movie," won the 2007 WildSound Screenplay Challenge in Toronto, Canada. With her own material to fuel her, Chong seemed poised for many more years in the entertainment industry.

Selected works

Films

Stony Island, 1978.
Quest for Fire, 1981.
Beat Street, 1984.
Choose Me, 1984.
Fear City, 1984.
The Color Purple, 1985.
Commando, 1985.

Running Out of Luck, 1986.
Soul Man, 1986.
Chaindance, 1990.
Rude Awakening, 1990.
Amazon, 1992.
Boca, 1994.
Small Time, 1996.
Goodbye America, 1997.
Highball, 1997.
Dangerous Attraction, 2000.
The Visit, 2000.
Constellation, 2005.

Television

The Whiz Kid and the Mystery at Riverton (made-for-television movie), 1974.
Deadly Skies (made-for-television movie), 2005.

Other

She's the Boss (Mick Jagger solo LP video), 1985.
(As narrator) *The Subject Is AIDS* (documentary; also known as *Sex, Drugs and AIDS*), 1986.

Sources

Periodicals

Asianweek, November 17-23, 2005, p. 14.
New York Times, February 7, 1982; January 13, 1985; October 4, 1985; November 1, 1986; December 15, 2000.
People, November 18, 1985, p. 75.
Times (London, England), April 7, 1982; p. 9.
Washington Post, February 2, 2007, p. T33.
Washington Times, April 3, 2003, p. M22.

On-line

"Rae Dawn Chong," *Wildsound*, www.wildsound-film-making-feedback-events.com/rae_dawn_chong.html (July 23, 2007).

—Carol Brennan

Mayme Agnew Clayton

1923-2006

Collector, librarian

Dr. Mayme Agnew Clayton gathered one of the largest and most significant collections of black Americana in existence. She kept much of it in the garage behind her modest home in the West Adams district of Los Angeles, California. When Clayton died in 2006 her garage was spilling over with an estimated two million artifacts of African-American history. Her collection included rare books, letters, posters, photographs, newspaper clippings, and films. Its most valuable item was the only known signed copy of the first book published by a black American—*Poems on Various Subjects, Religious and Moral*—written by Phillis Wheatley in 1773. Although astoundingly eclectic, Clayton's collection was particularly strong in books and documents of the Civil-War era and the Harlem Renaissance.

In an interview for *The History Makers* Web site Clayton explained: "I always had a desire to want to know more about my people.... It just snowballed, it just kept going. I have invested every dime that I have, everything that I have, in books for future generations. It may change somebody's life—you can never tell." According to the Web site of the Western States Black Research and Education Center (WSBREC), Clayton collected so that "children would know that black people have done great things."

Inspired by Mary McLeod Bethune

Mayme Agnew was born on August 14, 1923, in Van Buren, Arkansas. Her father, Jerry Monique Agnew, Sr., owned a general store and was the town's only black merchant. Mayme's mother, Mary Dorothy

(Knight) Agnew, was a homemaker and renowned cook. The Agnews were determined to expose Mayme and her siblings to the many accomplishments of black Americans. In 1936 Jerry Agnew took his family to Little Rock, Arkansas, to hear Dr. Mary McLeod Bethune, the famous educator, speak. Mayme developed a strong interest in black literature and history and later collected Bethune artifacts.

Mayme Agnew graduated from high school at the age of 16. She briefly attended Lincoln University in Missouri. In 1944, at the age of 21, she moved to New York City where she worked as a model and photographer's assistant. Andrew Lee Clayton was a handsome soldier and a barber, 16 years older than Mayme, who returned to the studio repeatedly on the pretext of being photographed. After a ten-month courtship Agnew married Clayton in New York on January 22, 1946. The couple returned to Van Buren for a reception and then moved to California, to the West Adams bungalow. There the Claytons raised their three sons in a tradition of social responsibility and pride in black accomplishments. Mayme Clayton began collecting.

In 1952 Clayton became a librarian's assistant at the University of Southern California. In 1959 she moved to the University of California at Los Angeles (UCLA) law library. When UCLA established its Afro-American Studies Center Library in 1969, Clayton, already known for her collection of African-American literature, was loaned out as a consultant and she began building the library's collection. However UCLA was interested in contemporary black studies and Clayton was frustrated by their refusal to purchase out-of-print

At a Glance . . .

Born Mayme Agnew on August 4, 1923, in Van Buren, AK; died on October 13, 2006, in Inglewood, CA; married Andrew Lee Clayton, 1946 (died 1987); children: Avery, Renai, Lloyd. *Education:* AR Baptist College, 1940-41; Lincoln University, 1944-46; University of Southern California, 1958-59; University of California, Berkeley, BA, history, 1974; Goddard College, MLS, 1975; Sierra University, PhD, humanities, 1983.

Career: Collector of black Americana, 1940s-2006; Doheny Library, University of Southern California, Los Angeles, assistant, 1952-57, engineering library assistant, 1956-59; University of California, Los Angeles, assistant law librarian, 1959-72, Afro-American Studies Center, 1970-71; Universal Books, Hollywood, CA, co-owner, 1971-72; Third World Ethnic Books, Los Angeles, owner, 1972; WSBREC, Los Angeles, founder, executive director, president, 1972-2006; Black History Department, Claremont College, 1973-74; Black American Cinema Society, Los Angeles, founder, executive director, 1976; BTOP Film Festival, Los Angeles, executive producer, 1977-91; *Black American Odyssey* video series, consultant, 1987.

Selected memberships: Afro-American Studies Center Library, UCLA, founding member; Black Cultural Entertainment Network, founder; International Black Book Dealers, organizer; Sierra University, director; Urban League.

Selected awards: Iota Phi Lambda, Woman of the Year Award, 1973, Lola M. Parker National Businesswoman Woman of the Year Award, 2005; Southern Christian Leadership Conference, Rosa Parks Award, 1990; Los Angeles Mayor's Award, 1992; Black Business Association, Pioneer Award, 2006; California State Legislature, Woman of the Year, 2006.

books. She had become acquainted with collectors and experts in black history and she began to buy the out-of-print books herself, specializing in the authors of the Harlem Renaissance.

Her Hobby Became Her Avocation

In 1972 Clayton left UCLA and went to work at Universal Books, a used bookstore in Hollywood with a huge selection of black literature. Eventually she became co-owner. When her partner lost their profits at the horse races, Clayton agreed to take possession of his collection rather than suing him. She ran Third World Ethnic Books out of her home. Clayton also went back to school, earning her bachelor's degree in history from the University of California at Berkeley in 1974, her master's in library science from Goddard College in Vermont in 1975, and her doctorate in humanities from the now-defunct Sierra University in Santa Monica in 1983.

Every weekend for more than 40 years, Clayton combed bookstores, antique shops, garage and estate sales, flea markets, attics, and even dumps, adding to her collection. Whenever a black newspaper closed, she bought their photos. She was also a competitive golfer and the organizer and sponsor of Mayme A. Clayton Celebrity Golf Tournaments. She traveled the country and as far as Africa playing in golf tournaments and collecting.

Clayton was an aggressive and competitive collector and was famous for getting the best of any bargain. She bought the Wheatley book from a New York dealer for $600 in 1973. In 2003 it was appraised at $30,000. She bought the first issue of *Ebony* for a dime and refused to lend it back to the magazine's publisher. Over the years, by living modestly and selling books, Clayton spent hundreds of thousands of dollars on building her collection.

Clayton's collection grew to include some 30,000 rare, first-edition, and out-of-print books by and about blacks. She had first editions and correspondence by Langston Hughes, Richard Wright, George Washington Carver, and Zora Neale Hurston. She had plantation inventories and slave bills-of-sale. She had the complete set, 1830-1845, of the first American abolitionist journal *The African Repository*. She had personal letters of black leaders and entertainers. She had 75,000 photographs and 9,500 sound recordings, as well as music scores and sheet music. Her son Avery Clayton told William Booth of the *Washington Post* in December of 2006: "She was a hoarder, she was. But she was a hoarder with a vision."

Clayton founded the WSBREC in 1972 as the world's largest privately held collection of African-American historical materials. She served as its executive director for many years, eventually becoming its president when her son Avery took over as executive director. Alex Haley, author of *Roots*, served as national board chairman. For four decades Clayton ran programs through the WSBREC.

Founded the Black American Cinema Society

In 1975 Clayton founded the Black American Cinema Society (BACS) as the home of the Clayton Library Film Archives. It was the world's largest collection of pre-1959 black films, with more than 1,700 titles and more than 350 movie posters. Clayton had original prints of many of the films of Oscar Micheaux, the most prolific director and producer of race movies, including *Body and Soul,* the silent film that first brought Paul Robeson to the screen.

Clayton taught African-American Cinema at California State University. She also worked on black programming for network and cable television. In 1977 with films from her collection, Clayton launched the Black Talkies on Parade (BTOP) Film Festival at the Los Angeles Museum of Science and Industry. It was the country's first public black film festival. In conjunction with BTOP Clayton initiated the annual Black Student and Independent Filmmakers Competition. In 1993 she contributed over $50,000 in cash grants for the BACS Awards. The Mayme A. Clayton Library revived the BTOP film festivals in 2005. In 2006 it collaborated on the first annual Black and Yiddish Film Festival.

In 1999 Clayton co-founded the annual Reel Black Cowboy Film and Western Festival at the Gene Autry Museum. Clayton wanted the public to know that one out of every three cowboys of the American West was black. Avery Clayton told the *Washington Post* in 2006: "She bought a poster for a thousand dollars a few months before her transition and I still don't know where she got the money." It was for *The Bronze Buckeroo,* a black cowboy movie.

Clayton's efforts on behalf of black film made her much more than an expert on the films' subjects; she developed a deep understanding of how to preserve film. Clayton appeared in a 1999 video, *Keepers of the Frame,* on attempts to preserve film heritage as a record of the twentieth century. In 1995 her own collection had been moved to a climate-controlled vault in a film warehouse owned by Eastman Kodak.

Worried About the Future

Clayton had been unable to find a permanent home for her collection, where it would be available to scholars and the public alike. Portions were scattered in storage rooms around Los Angeles and her dilapidated shed was filled to the brim. There was mold. The roof could leak. Her dog provided the only security and she had no insurance. Los Angeles County Supervisor Yvonne B. Burke recalled how years before she had expressed concern about the security of Clayton's collection, as reported in the *Los Angeles Sentinel.* Clayton replied, "In my neighborhood they do not steal books."

Avery Clayton left his job as an art teacher to lead the effort to move the collection. On October 12, 2006, the day before Clayton's death from pancreatic cancer, Culver City agreed to lease a 22,000-square-foot former courthouse to the WSBREC for $1 per year. Purportedly the deal enabled Mayme Clayton to die at peace.

Clayton's life was celebrated at the Agape International Spiritual Center in Culver City by more than 800 attendees. The *Los Angeles Sentinel* quoted actor Glen Turman remembering that she had "such a zest for life and a profound interest in many things and knew so much. Talking with her was like listening to a sage who really knew everything. She had the heartbeat of the community and it was never about her. It was always about the other person." Others recalled how in her later years Clayton became known as the "Queen of E-mail," sending out spiritual messages and bawdy jokes alike to her numerous correspondents.

Clayton Collection Moved to Temporary Home

In February of 2007 movers specialized in handling documents began transporting materials from the Clayton shed to the temporary home of the Mayme A. Clayton Library and Cultural Center in Culver City. Avery Clayton had raised $40,000 to fund the move. Universities had agreed to supply the technical staff for organizing and curating the Mayme A. Clayton Collection of African American History and Culture, composed of seven separate collections. Mayme Clayton's sons Lloyd and Renai Sr. were in charge of music and sports, respectively.

Some experts believed that Clayton's collection might rival that of the Schomburg Center for Research in Black Culture in Harlem. Sara Hodson, curator of literary manuscripts at the Huntington Library, who planned to include Clayton materials in a 2009 exhibition, told the *Los Angeles Times* in 2007: "A lot of it is material that might not have been preserved if Mayme Clayton had not gone after it, as single-minded and devoted as she was."

Although Avery Clayton hoped to open the collection to the public by 2008, as of 2007 more than $500,000 were still needed to organize and display it for a year. There were hopes that the State of California would take it over as a museum. Representatives from the Library of Congress were examining the collection. The Public Broadcasting System's *History Detectives* was producing a one-hour special on it. In its March 2007 issue *Arts & Antiques* magazine posthumously named Dr. Clayton one of the "Top 100 Collectors Who Are Making a Difference."

Avery Clayton told the *Los Angeles Times* in 2007: "Most African American history is hidden. Information just sort of died on the vine. What's exciting about this is that we're going to bring it back and show that black culture is rich and varied." Thanks to Mayme Clayton, the depth of African-American cultural contributions can be better appreciated, and thanks to Clayton's sons, the work she started continues.

Sources

Periodicals

Diverse Issues in Higher Education, January 25, 2007, p. 13.

Library Journal, November 15, 2006, p. 19.

Los Angeles Sentinel, October 26-November 2, 2006, pp. A7, A12.

Los Angeles Times, June 16, 2002, p. E1; October 21, 2006, p. A1; February 13, 2007, p. B2.

New York Times, December 14, 2006, p. A1.

Washington Post, August 1, 2000, p. 2; December 13, 2006, p. C1.

On-line

"Dr. Mayme Clayton: 40 Years of Collecting African American Works," *Education Update,* www.educa-tionupdate.com/archives/2006/Feb/html/cov-drmayme.htm (June 18, 2007).

"Large Collection of Black Memorabilia Goes Public," *News & Notes,* www.npr.org/templates/story/story.php?storyId=6461161 (June 18, 2007).

Mayme A. Clayton Library & Museum, www.wsbrec.org (June 18, 2007).

"Mayme Clayton Biography," *The History Makers,* www.thehistorymakers.com/biography/biography.asp?bioindex=879&category=educationMakers (June 18, 2007).

—Margaret Alic

Donald Coleman

1952—

Advertising executive

Donald Coleman, the chief executive officer of Global-Hue, the largest minority-owned full-service multicultural communications agency in the United States, has overseen key campaigns for several major companies, including Chrysler Corporation, Kmart, and Domino's Pizza. His company's ads, described in *Black Enterprise* as "intelligent and delightfully entertaining," target a demographic group that has until recently received little attention: hip, urban people of color who have money to spend. This multicultural focus has helped make GlobalHue one of the fastest-growing ad agencies in the country.

GlobalHue's roots go back to 1988, when Coleman founded his first company, Don Coleman & Associates (renamed Don Coleman Advertising in 1997). Coleman had started his agency to tailor advertising specifically for minorities. In one DCA print ad, the caption under a photo of a cup of coffee read, "How do you take your advertising? Well, if you want it to be successful, you take it rich and full-bodied. And if you want it to be strong, you take it Black." Coleman built DCA into the third largest African American-owned advertising agency in the United States. He remained at the helm as CEO when it was restructured as GlobalHue in 2002, after a series of mergers. Despite exceptionally difficult conditions for the advertising sector in the early 2000s, the company quickly became one of the top-earning agencies in the country, with sales of approximately $350 million in 2002.

Athletic Career Was Cut Short

Donald Alvin Coleman did not originally set out to pursue a business career. Born on January 11, 1952, he grew up in Toledo, Ohio. He majored in journalism at the University of Michigan, where he was a star athlete. After graduating in 1974 he was drafted by the New Orleans Saints. He played four seasons as a linebacker in the National Football League, having been traded to the New York Jets early on, but knee injuries put him on the bench for long periods. During this injury time he began to study marketing at Hofstra University, where he earned an M.B.A. By the time his knee problems forced him to retire from professional football in 1977, Coleman had the training to make a new career start in the business sector.

Coleman joined Campbell-Ewald Advertising in Warren, Michigan, and by 1982 had been promoted to a vice president and management supervisor. Increasingly interested in the growing African American and Hispanic markets, which he felt Campbell-Ewald was ignoring, he joined the country's preeminent black-oriented advertising agency, Burrell Communications Group in Chicago, in 1985. Eager to go out on his own as soon as possible, Coleman launched Don Coleman & Associates on January 11, 1988, in Southfield, Michigan, with himself as the sole employee. The company planned events and promotions for local businesses, including the Detroit Receiving Hospital, Grace Hospital, and Schlitz Malt Liquor. In 1991 DCA signed its first major client, Domino's Pizza.

DCA grew quickly, attracting talented professionals who appreciated Coleman's vision of building a leading firm that marketed in a fresh, savvy way to African Americans. As DCA senior vice president W. Juan Roberts explained to *Black Enterprise* writers Cassandra Hayes and Jules Allen, "We stay away from the 'ghetto,'" his term for the stereotyped images so often used in ads targeted to blacks. "If our work is to be effective, it must have energy and insight and be relevant to the marketplace. We try to present an intelligent African American image and mindset in everything we do." By 1998 DCA (which now stood for Don Coleman Advertising) was the third largest African American-owned ad agency in the United States.

Attracted Major Clients

In 1994 DCA began its relationship with one of its most important clients, Chrysler Corporation (now DaimlerChrysler), landing the firm's substantial minority account. The campaigns it created for the Neon, Cirrus, Intrepid and Jeep vehicles were a huge success. "We had to show African Americans that these cars fit

their lifestyle," Coleman told Hayes and Allen in *Black Enterprise*. "Previously, Jeep was positioned as a wilderness buster, but most African Americans live in cities of concrete and asphalt, so we had to make the car luxurious and fit those environments." To create this sophisticated image for Jeep, DCA used voice-overs by soul crooner Barry White, while the agency put the Parliament song "Flashlight" behind its commercial for the Dodge Neon. DCA's campaigns for Chrysler were so successful that the agency increased its share of black automotive marketing from 13.8 percent in 1994 to 17.9 percent in 1996.

In quick succession DCA picked up other major clients, including General Mills, Kmart, and Shell Oil Company. "What works with the general market may not work as well with the African American market," commented General Mills director of ethnic marketing, Autumn Boos, to Hayes and Allen in *Black Enterprise*. "By using DCA, we wanted to get unique insights and tap the right emotional levels in order to connect with the African American consumer."

In 2000 American Airlines, citing Coleman's impressive record in marketing to black Americans, chose DCA to increase its business among this demographic group. Other major clients that signed with DCA included Ameritech, Western Union, and the Michigan State Lottery.

Mergers Created Multicultural Powerhouse

DCA also grew through mergers and acquisitions. In 1999 it became part of the New American Strategies Group of True North Diversified Companies, with Coleman named as head of NASG. This move gave DCA the resources to broaden its reach beyond just the African American market. "This network represents a new and compelling model with the potential to create a strong link between the mainstream advertisers and America's growing multicultural communities," Coleman observed in a *Black Enterprise* interview. "The credibility and experience we are providing now will make corporate America more comfortable in addressing multiculturalism. It's going to be a lot easier for companies to get involved in these markets through us because we are all working together."

In another step to strengthen DCA's position as a multicultural marketer, Coleman approached Montemayor y Asociados, a leading Hispanic ad agency, with a buyout offer in 2000. The merger was completed in 2002, the same year that Chrysler reshaped its multicultural marketing approach. Abandoning its earlier strategy of creating separate campaigns for separate groups, the company decided to "speak to the multicultural market through a unified urban voice," as Richard Linnett reported in *Advertising Age*. To do so, it chose to hire a single advertising agency to handle its

$40 million multicultural marketing budget. DCA was now in a position to offer full-service representation, and it competed successfully against approximately 60 other agencies for the lucrative account. What made DCA stand out in the field was its ability to handle marketing that was comprehensively multicultural and not targeted only to a particular subgroup.

In 2002 DCA acquired Innovasia, a full-service Asian American agency with clients that included Qwest, Samsung, UPS, and Wells Fargo. This merger created GlobalHue, the largest minority-owned full-service multicultural communications agency, with offices as of 2006 in New York City, Los Angeles, San Antonio, Miami, and Detroit. The company targets the entire multicultural market, including not only racial groups but also the gay, lesbian, and transgendered market. "We are the market. We are the most diverse ad agency in the country," Coleman told *DaimlerChrysler.com*. "My people always have a foot in their original culture and that's the key to communication. You've got to understand the culture, the lifestyle."

Coleman's broad strategy has proved remarkably successful. By 2003 GlobalHue's client list included Verizon Wireless, Miller Brewing Company, and Johnson & Johnson, the U.S. Internal Revenue Service, the U.S. Navy, and State Farm. In addition, its account with Chrysler grew from $40 million to a whopping $140 million. In 2003 GlobalHue competed successfully for Microsoft's African American advertising campaigns. According to a Microsoft press release, GlobalHue was chosen because of its "demonstrated understanding of the ethnic audiences [it] serve[s] and [its] ability to translate that understanding into strategic, creative advertising."

Positioned to Capitalize on Minority Growth

Commenting on the success of Coleman's company, *Target Market News* president Ken Smikle told Hays and Allen in *Black Enterprise* that "they have the ability to blend sophistication and hipness in their creative approach. What really accounts for the agency's success is the excellence they bring not only to the creative side, but also to their strategic planning." His business philosophy, Coleman told Hays and Allen, is a simple one. "It's to learn everything about the client, strategically attack the competition, establish product identity and grow the client's business." Having an insider's knowledge of the market is key. As he explained to *Automotive News* writer Laura Clark Geist about his campaigns for Chrysler, "These multicultural markets are not like the general market where you can throw in a lot of incentives and it will get what you're looking for." Ads for cars, he added, "have to say something to consumers other than 'I got a great price on it.'"

GlobalHue continues to be on the vanguard of multicultural marketing, a segment expected to play an increasingly prominent role in the U.S. economy through the 2000s. As *Black Enterprise* writer Alan Hughes noted, the 2000 U.S. census data show that African Americans, Hispanics, and Asian Americans are expected to represent 40 percent of the U.S. population by 2020. And not only are minority populations growing; their incomes are growing as well. The combined spending power of U.S. minority groups in 2007 is expected to be more than $2 trillion, with the greatest share among Hispanics, who will control about $926.1 billion. African Americans and Asian Americans will likely control $852.8 billion and $454.9 billion, respectively. These numbers, according to Coleman, prove the importance of multicultural marketing. "Marketers are seeing this is not fad," he emphasized to Hughes. "This is for real."

Acknowledging Coleman's role as a pioneer in the field of multicultural advertising, *Black Enterprise* named Don Coleman Advertising its Advertising Agency of the Year in 1998. This honor was repeated in 2003, when the award went to GlobalHue. *Overtime* Magazine singled out Coleman in 2005 for its MVP Award, honoring him for proving "that the end of a pro-sports career can be the beginning of something far greater, including helping others to achieve their own dreams of success," according to *Overtime* publisher and Editor-in-Chief Ryan McNeil in *Screen Magazine*. Coleman told *Screen* that advertising was his "passion." *Target Market News* reported in 2007 that GlobalHue grew 17 percent in 2006 and had 220 employees in offices in major urban centers across the country. Among some 400 companies surveyed by *Advertising Age* that year, GlobalHue ranked 29th overall; it also nabbed first and second place, respectively, among African American and Hispanic multicultural agencies. His company's outstanding performance, Coleman said in *Target Market News*, "is the result of our talent, organic and new client opportunities and an increased recognition by companies to better appreciate the buying power of the multicultural market."

Sources

Periodicals

Advertising Age, April 1, 2002, p. 1.
Automotive News, October 13, 2003, p. 4M.
Black Enterprise, June 1, 1998, pp. 164-169; September 1, 2001, p. 21; December 1, 2002, p. 30; June 1, 2003, pp. 186-189.
Jet, May 1, 2000, p. 12.

On-line

"A Chance to Shine," *DaimlerChrysler.com*, www.daimlerchrysler.com/dccom/0-5-886353-1-890 33-0-1-0-0-0-0-0-36-876574-0-0-0-0-0-0-0.html (July 23, 2007).
"Don Coleman Biography," *History Makers*, www.thehistorymakers.com/ (July 23, 2007).

GlobalHue, www.globalhue.com (July 23, 2007).

"Global Hue Ranks 29th in Advertising Age's 2006 Agency Special Report," *Target Market News*, www.targetmarketnews.com/ (July 23, 2007).

"Microsoft Selects GlobalHue and López Negrete To Lead Ethnic Advertising Initiatives," *Microsoft*, www.microsoft.com/presspass/press/2003/jul03/07-02lopezglobalhuepr.mspx (July 23, 2007).

"Working Overtime: Donald A. Coleman Wins the OT MVP Award," *Screen Magazine*, www.screenmag.tv/feature.aspx?fid=677 (July 23, 2007).

—Brenna Sanchez and E. M. Shostak

Tony Corley

1949—

Founder of the Black Surfing Association

Tony Corley's love of the beach and the ocean led him to try surfing. His stubborn determination kept him at it until he mastered the challenging sport, and his sense of playfulness and joy turned his accomplishment into a lifelong passion. After many years of being one of very few black faces in a sea of blond surfers, Corley set out to create a black surfing community. Beginning with a letter to a surfing magazine in 1973, Corley set up first an informal network, then an organization for black surfers to find each other and share their love of riding the waves. The Black Surfing Association continues to unite surfers of African descent into the 2000s, and Corley remains at the heart of the loosely organized group. Still an avid surfer, both on his home shores in central California and in the warmer waters of Baja, Mexico, Corley dreams of visiting the coast of Africa, where his ancestors may have been among the first to discover the freedom and fun of surfing.

Discovered Love of Surf

Anthony Leroy Corley was born on August 11, 1949, in the small town of Paso Robles, a hot springs resort and winemaking area in central California. His father, James F. Corley, worked as a maintenance engineer for the state of California, and his mother, Esmon Turner Corley, was a nurse. Though the vast majority of Paso Robles' population was white, the Corleys lived in a largely black and Latino neighborhood. Growing up in the rural community, young Tony Corley enjoyed playing street games and little league baseball with his neighborhood friends and fishing with his grand-

mother, an accomplished fisherwoman who took him to nearby lakes and taught him to catch catfish and bluegill with a cane pole.

The Pacific Ocean lay only 30 miles away from Paso Robles, and the Corley family made trips to the beach at least once or twice a month. From early childhood Tony Corley loved playing in the ocean and riding the waves on an inflatable air mattress. He also loved watching the surfers ride the powerful breakers, and when he was 12, he and a friend rented surfboards to try the exciting sport.

The first time Corley surfed, he learned that it was not an easy skill to master. In the 1960s, surfboards were heavy, cumbersome, and slippery, and trying to control one in the pounding surf was difficult. However, he was determined to keep at it until he could ride a wave while standing on his board. He taught himself to surf, progressing slowly from lying on his stomach to kneeling, until he finally succeeded at riding on his feet. By the time he was 13, he was ready to buy his own board. He had saved money from gardening and selling newspapers in hopes of buying a go-kart, but his parents, concerned about his safety, refused to allow him to buy the small, motorized vehicle. However, they did allow him to spend his savings on his own surfboard. They drove him to a nearby town to a sporting goods store that sold Dewey Weber surfboards, designed by one of the great surfers of the 1950s and 1960s, and Corley's surfing career began in earnest.

The more Corley played in the waves, the more he fell in love with the sea and the beach, and the more he

At a Glance . . .

Born Anthony Leroy Corley on August 11, 1949, in Paso Robles, CA; married Rosemarie Garza, 1979; children: Vyctor, Cleo Moraia, Aquila Rose, and Anthony Silas. *Education:* California Polytechnic State University, BS, social sciences, 1975; California Polytechnic State University, MA, education with an emphasis on psychology, 1978.

Career: California Youth Authority, teaching assistant, group supervisor, youth counselor, 1968-2003; Black Surfing Association, founder and member, 1974–.

Memberships: Black Surfing Association, founder.

Addresses: *Home*—Paso Robles, CA. *Web*—www.blacksurfing.com.

identified himself as a surfer. He did not, however, identify with the blond beach bum surfer image made famous in films like *Beach Party* and *Gidget Goes Hawaiian*. Some of the white surfers he met and his black friends made their opinions clear: blacks did not surf.

Cultivated Community of Black Surfers

However, Corley's love of surfing was not dampened by these attitudes, and he continued to provide living proof that some black people did indeed enjoy surfing. In 1964, he was happy to meet another African-American surfer, James Norman, an army captain at Camp Roberts, a military base close to Paso Robles. Norman became a friend and mentor to the 15-year-old Corley and the two surfed together regularly until 1966 when Norman was sent to take part in the growing conflict in Viet Nam. Corley and Norman would remain lifelong friends. Corley found another role model in 1965 when *Ebony* magazine profiled a black surfer named Frank Edwards, who had taken up the sport after moving from Alabama to California during the 1960s.

During his non-surfing hours, Corley attended Paso Robles Joint Union High School, where he ran track and played football. After his graduation in 1967, he entered Cuesta College near his home. While attending classes at Cuesta, he worked as a teaching assistant for the California Youth Authority, teaching remedial reading to young people who had been locked up for

committing crimes. He worked at various jobs at the CYA, taking leaves to attend California Polytechnic State University, where he earned his bachelor's degree in social sciences in 1975 and his master's degree in education and counseling in 1978. He had hoped to become a community college counselor, but government cuts in social service funding meant fewer jobs in the community college system. Corley returned to the CYA for the remainder of his career, becoming a group supervisor and youth counselor. In 1979, he married Rosemarie Garza, a sixth generation California Mexican from Santa Barbara County whom he had met while attending Cuesta College, and the two started a family.

As he continued to surf and enjoy the central California beaches, Corley missed his old surfing buddy Jim Norman and looked for a way to find other African Americans who loved playing in the waves the way he did. In 1973 he wrote a letter to the editor of *Surfer*, one of the few magazines devoted to the sport, hoping that there might be a few black readers who would see his letter and contact him. *Surfer* published his letter in January 1974, and Corley was soon excited to begin receiving letters and phone calls from African Americans who were also anxious to connect with other black surfers. Though he received some racist hate mail as well, he was undaunted as he began to compile a file of contacts, to arrange surfing gatherings, and to publish a series of newsletters.

In 1975, Corley officially started the Black Surfing Association. The file in his home continued to grow with increasing membership, and the organization sponsored many informal gatherings, particularly in southern California. In 1983, *Surfer* magazine featured a story titled "The Black Surfers of the Golden State," highlighting the accomplishments of Corley and others. By the 2000s, the growth of the Internet allowed word to spread even further, creating more opportunities for black surfers to meet and play together. Young African Americans interested in surfing no longer had to feel alone and isolated, but could find role models on the Internet and at BSA gatherings, such as the annual May surfing contest and beach day, introduced by the group during the early 2000s. Corley attends such events proudly, feeling, as he told *Contemporary Black Biography,* "like a grandfather at a family reunion."

Tony Corley retired from CYA in August 2003. He continues to surf and enjoy the beach, passing on his love of the sea to his children and grandchildren, who enjoy fishing, skateboarding, and riding the waves on short boogie boards near Paso Robles or at the family vacation home in Baja, Mexico. At the southern California surf mecca of Venice Beach, a pair of 40-foot murals honors the history of black surfing. Titled "Old Wave" and "New Wave," one giant painting depicts

Tony Corley, crediting him as "Black Surfing Association founder and soul surfer since the 1960's." Facing Corley is another huge mural of a young African-American woman riding a wave, titled, "Andrea Kabwasa—competing in uncharted waters in 2005." Besides his own children and grandchildren, the new generation of black surfers represented by Kabwasa is perhaps Tony Corley's proudest legacy.

Sources

Periodicals

Ebony, April 1965, pp. 109-13.
Essence, October 2005, pp. 86.

On-line

"The Barbershop Club," *Wet Sand: World Wide Waves,* www.wetsand.com/article.asp?locationid=5-&resourceid=3743&ProdId=0&CatId=848&Tab-ID=0&SubTabID=0 (June 28, 2007).
"Black Surfing Association," *Blacksurfing.com,* www.blacksurfing.com/meet.htm (June 28, 2007).

Other

Information for this profile was obtained through an interview with Tony Corley on April 23, 2007.

—Tina Gianoulis

Merrin Dungey

1971—

Actress

Actress Merrin Dungey is best known for her television portrayals of characters she has referred to as "sassy black sidekicks," according to *Back Stage West.* Most well-known for her best-friend roles in the spy show *Alias* and the soap opera-style *Summerland,* Dungey also gained attention for comedic turns on *Malcolm in the Middle* and *The King of Queens.* She also landed a starring role in the pilot episode of the *Grey's Anatomy* spin-off *Private Practice,* in which she portrayed Dr. Naomi Bennett, the best friend of central character Addison Montegomery-Shepherd, played by Kate Walsh. Despite being replaced by Audra Mc-Donald in *Private Practice,* Dungey remained a sought-after actress.

Dungey was born on August 6, 1971, in Sacramento, California. She has been performing since she was a child, including ballet at age four and piano recitals and figure skating competitions through her teen years. She began appearing on television while she was still a student at Sacramento's Rio Americano High School, hosting a local talk show for teens and appearing in commercials. She graduated from high school in 1989, and despite her performance background, she entered UCLA intent on majoring in English. She appeared in plays at the school, however, and after winning the university's prestigious American Theater Award as a sophomore—the youngest person ever to win the award—she switched her major to theater. Dungey's father later told Mike McLaren of the *Fair Oaks Guardian* the on-line newspaper for Fair Oaks, California, that the best part of the award ceremony for his daughter was that Denzel Washington presented the prize.

After graduation in 1993 Dungey studied with acting coach Milton Katselas at the legendary Beverly Hills Playhouse acting school. As an assignment for the class, she developed a comic monologue about her experiences growing up in a white suburb, which she eventually expanded into a one-woman show called *Black Like Who?* In an interview with *PopGurls.com* she said, "Believe me, the journey of a black girl who had to hide her Valley Girl accent and love of Duran Duran, and learn to be 'black' to make it in Hollywood, had some yuks in it, if not for the slide show of my prom pictures alone." The show was broadcast on HBO's *Comedy Workspace.* She even adapted a portion of the show into a stand-up comedy routine. The success of *Black Like Who?* enabled Dungey to land representation by the influential William Morris Agency.

Dungey quickly built an impressive resume of recurring and guest roles on a variety of television shows. Comedy provided her entrée to her first series, the 1996 FOX situation comedy *Party Girl,* on which she played a librarian's assistant. A recurring role on the CBS sitcom *The King of Queens* as the wife of series star Kevin James's best friend proved a saving grace. She landed the part in 1998, at a time when "I was working three day jobs," Dungey told Bruce Fretts of *Entertainment Weekly.* "I was delivering Zone food to people like Hank Azaria, I was a personal assistant to an executive at Warner Bros., and I was working at a bar. After the first season, I was able to quit them all."

At a Glance . . .

Born Merrin Dungey on August 6, 1971, in Sacramento, CA. *Education:* UCLA, BA, theater, 1993.

Career: Actor in numerous television series, including *Alias, Summerland, The King of Queens,* and the forthcoming *Private Practice.*

Awards: UCLA School of Theater, American Theater Award, 1990.

Addresses: *Agent*—William Morris Agency, One William Morris Place, Beverly Hills, CA, 90212.

Dungey continued to win dozens of smaller roles in television series and films. She won a recurring role on *Malcolm in the Middle* in 2000, as Kitty Kenarban, the overprotective mother of Stevie. She also guest starred on series such as *The West Wing, Friends, Seinfeld, Babylon 5, Boston Legal,* and *Curb Your Enthusiasm.* She branched out to appear in such films as *Ed TV, Deep Impact,* and *Scream at the Sound of the Beep.*

The role that she considered her big break came in 2001 when Dungey was cast as Francie Calfo, the best friend of CIA double agent Sydney Bristow on ABC's *Alias.* The part enabled her to display the range of her acting talent, especially in the show's second season when her character was killed and replaced by an evil double. She considered that role her best to date, telling *PopGurls.com,* "An evil twin! Is that, or is that not, the dream part?" Dungey was so enamored of the part that when she later put together an amateur rock band she called it Bad Francie. However, she knew that the evil character's days on the series were numbered. "If you start out bad on *Alias,* you can set up some real estate," she told Jennifer Armstrong of *Entertainment Weekly.* "But if you turn bad...You better start looking for a new home." Dungey moved on in 2004 to play the part of the best friend and business partner of a fashion designer played by Lori Loughlin on the WB's beachside drama, *Summerland.* Discussing her "sidekick" roles with *Back Stage West,* Dungey said, "With the parts I've been given, I've just tried to make the most of what I have on the page.... Sometimes it's very specific, and you have to just play what's on the page, but the more you get to make it your own, the better."

She appeared in the pilot episode of the keenly anticipated show *Private Practice,* a spinoff of the popular ABC series *Grey's Anatomy.* The pilot of *Private Practice* served as the season finale of *Grey's Anatomy. Grey's Anatomy* fans were introduced to the medical practitioners and support staff at a Los Angeles, California, wellness center when Addison Montgomery-Shepherd, played by Kate Walsh, traveled there to meet up with Dungey's character, her friend from medical school and renowned fertility expert, Naomi Bennett. The anticipation that *Private Practice* would enjoy the high ratings of *Grey's Anatomy* would have made this Dungey's biggest role, yet she was cut from the cast in July 2007 for creative reasons. Speculators suggested that the onscreen chemistry between Dungey and other characters on the show lacked spark. Nevertheless, Dungey would likely find another more suitable vehicle for her rising star.

Selected works

Television

Party Girl, Wanda, 1996.
The King of Queens, Kelly Palmer 1998-2007.
Grosse Pointe, Joan, 2000-01.
Malcolm in the Middle, 2000-04.
Summerland, 2004-05.
Alias, 2001-03, 2006.
Private Practice, 2007.

Films

Deep Impact, 1998.
EdTV, 1999.
The Sky Is Falling, 2000.
Scream at the Sound of the Beep, 2002.

Sources

Books

Who's Who Among African Americans, 20th ed. Gale, 2007.

Periodicals

Back Stage West, May 12, 2005, p. 7.
Ebony, October 2001, p. 114.
Entertainment Weekly, November 23, 2001, p. 63; June 25, 2004, p. 153.
Sacramento Observer, May 10-16, 2007, p. E2.
Seattle Times, May 10, 2007, p. F2.
Self, December 2002, p. 78.

On-line

"Alias," *TV.com,* www.tv,com/alias/show/3451/summary.html?q=Alias&tag=search_results;more;0 (June 26, 2007).
"The King of Queens," *TV.com,* www.tv.com/the-king-of-queens/show/239/summary.html?q=the%-20king%20of%20queens&tag=search_results;more;0 (June 26, 2007).
"Malcolm in the Middle," *TV.com,* www.tv.com/malcolm-in-the-middle/show/248/summary.html?

q=malcolm%20in%20the%20middle&tag=search_results;more;0 (June 26, 2007).

"Merrin Dungey," *Internet Movie Database,* www.imdb.com/name/nm0242257 (June 26, 2007).

"Merrin Dungey," *Starpulse,* www.starpulse.com/Actresses/Dungey,_Merrin/index.html (June 26, 2007).

"Merrin Dungey," *TV.com,* www.tv.com/merrin-dungey/person/6179/summary.html (June 26, 2007).

"Party Girl," *TV.com,* www.tv.com/party0girl/show/2287/summary.html?q=party%20girl&tag=search_results;more;0# (June 26, 2007).

"Pride of the Lions President Shines for his Daughters," *Fair Oaks Guardian,* http://cwww.com/FOG/text/story10.htm (June 26, 2007).

"Summerland," *TV.com,* www.tv.com/summerland/show/20542/summary.html?=summerland&tag=search_results;more;0 (June 26, 2007).

"20 Questions with *Summerland*'s Merrin Dungey," *Popgurls,* www.popgurls.com/article_show.php3?id=469 (June 26, 2007).

"UCLA Alumni Cross Paths in 'Alias,'" *The Daily Bruin,* www.dailybruin.ucla.edu/archives/id/16774 (June 26, 2007).

—Bob Genovesi

Paris Michele Finner-Williams

1951—

Psychologist, lawyer, author

Trained as a clinical psychologist and as a lawyer, Paris Michele Finner-Williams has enjoyed a distinguished career as a mental health administrator, holding positions in local, county, and state mental health departments in and around her native Detroit, Michigan. In addition she is a Christian counselor, specializing in marriage counseling and male-female relationship issues. With her husband, Robert D. Williams, a clinical psychiatric social worker, she maintains a private practice that offers counseling to families and individuals.

Finner-Williams began her career as a clinical psychologist before deciding to earn a law degree. She joined the Michigan Department of Mental Health right out of college in 1972, taking a position as a rehabilitation counselor with the state's Office of Rehabilitation Services. In 1978 she became a department administrator for the Detroit-Wayne County Community Health Board's office of developmental disabilities. Among her responsibilities were development and management of the Job Seeking Skills Training Program for the State of Michigan, which provides services to help individuals with emotional, mental, and physical disabilities obtain employment.

Finner-Williams also developed the Wayne County Family Support Subsidiary Program, which provides financial support to help families that have children with developmental disabilities care for their children at home. In addition, Finner-Williams served as administrator of the Wayne County Community Mental Health Service programs for persons with developmental disabilities. In this position she developed and oversaw the Wayne County Probate Court Pre-Screening Program

as well as the Wayne County Jail Mental Health Department.

In 1979 Finner-Williams, who had earned a master's degree in educational psychology in 1974 and a doctorate in psychological counseling in 1977, established a private clinical practice, Finner-Williams and Associates Psychological Services. The practice focuses on family and relationship issues, as well as addiction counseling. Realizing that she could enhance her ability to serve her patients if she had the benefit of legal training, Finner-Williams took on the additional challenge of law school while balancing the demands of two busy jobs. She completed her J.D. in 1989, and two years later she established the legal professional association, Paris M. Finner-Williams, Esquire, P.C.

As both a certified trauma services specialist and a forensic examiner diplomat, Finner-Williams is well-equipped to deal with some of the more troubling elements that patients reveal in family counseling, such as spousal abuse or child molestation. Her training in forensic psychology, in which the scientific and professional elements of psychology are applied to questions and issues relating to law and the legal system, especially enables her to help patients whose needs require the intervention of the courts. These circumstances can include physical abuse, divorce cases, child custody cases, restraining orders, and other matters.

In 1992 Finner-Williams left her job with Wayne County to focus fulltime on her private practice, which she runs with her husband. "After Rob and I got married the emphasis became in creating a private

At a Glance . . .

Born on March 19, 1951, in Detroit, MI; married Robert Dee Williams, 1988. *Education:* University of Detroit, BA, 1972; Wayne State University, MEd, 1974; University of Michigan, PhD, 1977; Detroit College of Law, JD, 1989. *Religion:* Baptist.

Career: State of Michigan Rehabilitation Services, Detroit, counselor, 1972-78; Detroit-Wayne County Community Health Board, Detroit, MI, department administrator, developmental disabilities, 1978-92; Finner-Williams and Associates, founder and chief executive officer, 1979–; Paris M. Finner-Williams, Esq., P.C., 1991–; Black African-American Christian Counselors Division of the American Association of Christian Counselors, founder; Finner-Williams Christian Counseling Ministry, cofounder and chief executive officer.

Memberships: Association of Black Psychologists; Michigan Association of Black Psychologists; Association of Rehabilitation Counselors; National Rehabilitation Association; National Council of Community Mental Health Centers; Association for Retarded Citizens of Michigan; National Association for the Retarded; Westside Citizens Association for the Retarded; Phi Delta Kappa; Pi Lambda Theta.

Awards: Office of the Wayne County Executive, Distinguished Service Award; Spirit of Detroit Award, 1986; Board of Commissioners, Certificate of Appreciation, 1986; Association of Black Psychologists, Distinguished Psychologist of the Year Award, 1986; Professor Harold Norris Brass Turtle Award, 1987.

Addresses: *Office*—Finner-Williams and Associates, 17620 West McNichols Road, Detroit, MI 48235.

practice...where we could be more independent in our choices on how to serve people," Finner-Williams explained to *Black News* writer Shekini Jennings. "God has been faithful since. Now I have more control over who we serve, how we serve, and am able to serve those who can't afford to pay for services." One of their primary interests is marriage counseling and counseling for couples. With her husband, Finner-Williams has authored numerous articles for popular magazines, such as *Ebony* and *Jet,* and has appeared on radio and television talk shows. She is often asked to provide advice on such issues as child rearing, dating, and intimacy.

Of particular importance in Finner-Williams's work is her Christian faith. She is a fervent believer in church-based Christian counseling, and founded the Black African-American Christian Counselors Division of the American Association of Christian Counselors, serving as its first chairperson. In addition she offers free monthly training services to Christian Counselors in the Detroit area through her nonprofit corporation, Finner-Williams Christian Counseling Ministry.

With decades of experience in couples counseling, Finner-Williams and her husband have written two books about building and maintaining positive loving relationships: *Marital Secrets: Dating, Lies, Communication and Sex* and *Single Wisdom.* They have also written *How to Develop a Church Based Ministry.* Their books on marriage and relationships emphasize the importance of making wise and "Godly" choices and of following the example of those in stable, committed relationships. In *Single Wisdom,* Finner-Williams and her husband encourage those who are unmarried to embrace their lives as single individuals, and to prepare themselves to be faithful and "Godly" spouses if they do marry. The book includes a chapter that draws moral and behavioral lessons from the 1939 film *The Wizard of Oz.* Finner-Williams told Jennings in *Black News* that this chapter is probably the most empowering one in the book for African-American singles because it is "focused on...changing the way you perceive your encounters in life and knowing the power you have through Jesus Christ to be in control of self to make the most purposeful choices in life. We really wanted to put the emphasis on self empowerment in this book." Robin Caldwell, reviewing the book in *Gospel City,* praised its positive message for singles and noted that "its greatest strength is in promoting singleness as a holy, righteous and honorable lifestyle filled with positive (and doable) choices."

Though oriented toward those who are and will likely remain unmarried, *Single Wisdom* also includes the Finner-Williams Pre-Marital Screening Questionnaire, comprised of 157 questions designed to help those in love move beyond initial infatuation to discover who their beloved really is as an individual. The authors encourage readers to learn as much a possible about their loved one, including not only personal tastes and interests but also such practical concerns as job history and financial status. Too often, Finner-Williams notes, women and men jump into marriage without sufficient knowledge about each other, which is a major reason for the high rate of divorce. *Single Wisdom* emphasizes the wisdom in couples' taking time to know each other well before they take steps toward a permanent relationship.

Finner-Williams earned the attention and praise of those in her profession and community. She has received several public service awards. In 2006 the Association of Black Psychologists named her one of its distinguished psychologists of the year.

Selected works

Books

(With Robert D. Williams) *Marital Secrets: Dating, Lies, Communication and Sex*, RP Publishing, 2001.
(With Robert D. Williams) *Single Wisdom*, RP Publishing, 2005.
(With Robert D. Williams) *How to Develop a Church Based Ministry,* RP Publishing 2005.

Sources

Periodicals

Ebony, April 1, 2002, p. 84; May 1, 2003, p. 80; January 1, 2004, p. 140; March 1, 2004, p. 120;

June 1, 2004, p. 16; December 1, 2005, p. 84.
Jet, October 14, 2002, p. 16; April 3, 2006, p. 14.

On-line

"Congratulations to the ABPsi 2006 Distinguished Psychologists; Dr. Attorney Paris Michele Finner-Williams & Dr. James R. Lanier," *Association of Black Psychologists,* www.abpsi.org/distinguished. htm (July 16, 2007).
"Dr. Attorney Paris M. Finner-Williams Empowers Singles, Divorcees, Widows, and Widowers through *Single Wisdom*," *Black News,* www.blacknews. com/pr/singlewisdom101.html (July 16, 2007).
Finner-Willliams and Associates, www.finner-williams.com (July 17, 2007).
"*Single Wisdom*: Entertain Your Belief," *Gospel City,* www.gospelcity.com/dynamic/articles/books_theater/106/ (July 18, 2007).

—E. M. Shostak

Morgan Freeman

1937—

Actor

Morgan Freeman is a versatile actor who has performed in numerous roles from children's television to Shakespearean drama. He is best known for his appearances in a string of well-regarded motion pictures, including *Driving Miss Daisy, Lean on Me, Glory,* and *Million Dollar Baby.* The latter won him an Academy Award in 2005 for best supporting actor. Freeman has won several other awards and award nominations. *Time* correspondent Janice C. Simpson said Freeman's performances "are so finely calibrated that [the] characters emerge as men of true heft and substance." Freeman, a private man who says acting "comes easy" for him, does not care for the movie star label and all that it implies. The actor observed in *Ebony* that "once you become a movie star, people come to see you. You don't have to act anymore. And, to me, that's a danger." Now in his eighth decade, the actor brings a gravity and sense of wisdom to every role he plays, whether it be a superhero's quiet aide in the ongoing *Batman* series, the South African hero Nelson Mandela, or God himself.

The big screen has brought Freeman to a wider audience, but he has long been a figure in New York theater, appearing only in Broadway and off-Broadway plays that suit his very particular tastes. As early as 1967 he held a part in the Broadway cast of *Hello, Dolly,* that starred Pearl Bailey, but the bulk of his work has come in nonmusical, intensely serious dramas that relate various aspects of the African-American experience. "I have a special affinity for seeing to it that our history is told," Freeman said in *Ebony.* "The black legacy is as noble, is as heroic, is as filled with adventure and conquest and discovery as anybody else's. It's just that nobody knows it."

Endured Tumultuous Childhood

Freeman endured a tumultuous childhood, and he prefers not to reveal much in interviews about his early years. The fourth child in the family, he was born on June 1, 1937, in Clarksdale, Mississippi. While still an infant, he was sent to live with his maternal grandmother. She died when Freeman was six years old, and he spent the next several years traveling with his mother from Chicago to Nashville, Tennessee, and finally to Greenwood, Mississippi, where they settled down.

Like most youngsters of his generation, Freeman loved the movies. "When I was a kid, it cost 12 cents to go to the movies," he related in a *People* interview with Susan Toepfer. "If you could find a milk bottle, you could sell it for a nickel. Soda and beer bottles were worth 2 cents. If you were diligent, you could come up with movie money every day." The World War II-era films Freeman saw inspired him to be a fighter pilot. At first, drama served mainly as a pastime until he could enter the armed services.

Freeman's acting hobby began in junior high school. He was trying to gain the attention of a girl named Barbara by pulling her chair out from beneath her. His teacher grabbed him and took him to a room where they were preparing for a drama tournament. Freeman recalled to *New York,* "Well, we do this play 'bout a

At a Glance . . .

Born on June 1, 1937, in Clarksdale, MS; son of Grafton Curtis and Mayme Edna (Revere) Freeman; married Jeanette Adair Bradshaw, October 22, 1967 (divorced, 1979); married Myrna Colley-Lee (a costume designer), June 16, 1984; children: Alphonse, Saifoulaye, Deena, Morgana; ten grandchildren. *Education*: Attended Los Angeles City College. *Military*: U.S. Air Force, 1955-59.

Career: Actor, 1959–. Ground Zero Blues Club, Clarksdale, MS, co-owner; Madidi Restaurant, Clarksdale, MS, co-owner.

Selected awards: Clarence Derwent Award, Drama Desk Award, and Antoinette Perry Award nomination, 1978, *The Mighty Gents*; Obie Award, 1987, for stage version of *Driving Miss Daisy*; NYC Film Critics Circle Award, Los Angeles Film Critics Award, Golden Globe nomination, and Academy Award nomination, 1987, *Street Smart*; Golden Globe Award and Academy Award nomination, 1989, *Driving Miss Daisy*; Academy Award nomination for *The Shawshank Redemption*, 1994; Academy Award winner for best supporting actor for *Million Dollar Baby*, 2005; Image Award, NAACP, for *Million Dollar Baby*, 2005; Guest of Honor, Cairo Film Festival, 2006; University of California-Los Angeles Spencer Tracy Award, 2006.

Addresses: *Home*—Clarksdale, Mississippi. *Agent*—c/o WMA, 146 West 57th St., New York, NY 10019.

family with a wounded son just home from the war—I play his kid brother. We win the district championship, we win the state championship, and dadgummit, I'm chosen as best actor. All 'cause I pull this chair out from under Barbara."

Freeman's tale shows that he exhibited talent early but did not take acting seriously, even when others recognized his skill. After graduating from high school in Greenwood he entered the U.S. Air Force, hoping to become a pilot. Aptitude tests showed that he had the ability, but he was instead assigned duties as a mechanic and a radar technician. "I was aced out," he explained in *Esquire*. "Racism, the southern old-boy network. I had a sergeant who interposed himself between me and the casual barracks [stockade]—I was insolent. I called a horse's ass a horse's ass, even if it

was wearin' brass. The whole thing in the service, you're supposed to look down. Never could do that."

First Hollywood, Then Broadway

Freeman spent his spare time while in the Air Force contemplating other careers, and he ultimately decided to become an actor. He left the service in 1959 and headed straight for Hollywood. Once there, he looked up the address of Paramount Studios in the telephone book and went over to apply for a job. Only when he noticed that the questions on the application concerned familiarity with office machinery and typing did it dawn upon him that he would not be hired as an actor on the spot. He opted to follow a more conventional route, taking acting classes at Los Angeles City College while supporting himself as a clerk. He also took dancing lessons, becoming good enough to land a part-time job performing at the 1964 World's Fair in New York.

By his own admission, Freeman did not gain much insight from his acting classes. "I'm not much for talking about acting," he noted in *New York*. "I've been called an intuitive actor, and I guess that's right. I go with what I feel. It doesn't do me any good to intellectualize about it." Freeman moved to New York in the early 1960s and supported himself with a series of day jobs while auditioning for theatrical roles. At one point he even served as a counter man in a Penn Station doughnut stand. His first important part came in an off-Broadway play called *The Nigger-Lovers*, which opened and closed quickly in 1967.

Freeman's brief experience in *The Nigger-Lovers* was valuable, however, because it helped him land a role in the all-black cast of *Hello, Dolly*, that opened on Broadway in 1967. When the show closed, he moved on to a series of off-Broadway and repertory plays in New York and elsewhere. In 1971 he was cast in *The Electric Company*, a television series produced by the Public Broadcasting System. On the air for five years, the educational show was aimed at school-aged children, and Freeman played a hip character called Easy Reader. The actor commented in *People* that he is still remembered for his role. "It's like being known as Captain Kangaroo," he said. "It irks me when I meet people who are parents now who talk about how they grew up with me."

Freeman drew his first major awards for his role in the play *The Mighty Gents*, produced at New York's Ambassador Theatre in 1978. Even though he won the Clarence Derwent Award, Drama Desk Award, and earned a Tony Award nomination, the play closed in nine days and Freeman was out of work. For a while he found himself scuffling for jobs. This experience taught him that awards do not guarantee success, and he has been decidedly indifferent about them ever since. Even when he won his Oscar in 2005 for *Million Dollar Baby*, his acceptance speech was brief.

Excelled on the Stage

The New York Shakespeare Festival ultimately proved fertile ground for Freeman. There he appeared as the lead in *Coriolanus* in 1979 and had principal roles in *Julius Caesar* and *Mother Courage and Her Children*. His work in *Coriolanus* and *Mother Courage* earned him yet more awards, this time Obies. The breakthrough play for Freeman was *The Gospel at Colonus*, first performed in 1983. The musical, based on the ancient Greek drama about Oedipus—a mythical character who kills his father and marries his mother—is set in a modern Pentecostal church. *The Gospel at Colonus* featured Freeman as the preacher, a charismatic Oedipus figure around which the frenzied action revolved. Freeman won yet another Obie Award as best actor in a drama, and the play eventually moved to Broadway in 1988 with Freeman still in the lead.

Freeman's success with the New York Shakespeare Festival helped him to land a starring role in the stage play *Driving Miss Daisy*, for which he won an additional Obie Award. The drama examines the close friendship that develops between a wealthy Jewish widow and her black chauffeur, Hoke, in the post-Civil War South. By the time he appeared in *Driving Miss Daisy*, on stage, Freeman had also earned several film roles, most notably in the Robert Redford vehicle *Brubaker* and *Harry and Son*, starring Paul Newman. And because of *Driving Miss Daisy*'s success in the theater, Freeman was eager to portray Hoke in a film version.

The actor almost missed his chance. In 1987 he took the part of a near-psychotic pimp in the movie *Street Smart*. Although the film was a box-office flop, Freeman's powerful performance earned him an Academy Award nomination. "*Street Smart* essentially serves as a backdrop for Freeman's tour de force performance," Anthony DeCurtis wrote in *Rolling Stone*. "As the Yoo-Hoo-swilling Fast Black, he alternates fierceness with irresistible charm, engaging intelligence with a bone-chilling capacity for evil. He is the epitome of knowingness." The stage director of *Driving Miss Daisy* admitted that he never would have hired Freeman to play Hoke had he seen the actor as the menacing Fast Black first.

Drove "Miss Daisy" to a Film Career

Freeman's portrayal in the violent *Street Smart*, however, did not deter the makers of the critically acclaimed 1989 film version of *Driving Miss Daisy* from casting him in his original role of the kind-hearted Hoke. Once again Freeman was nominated for an Academy Award for best actor. That year he took another important role, this time as a grave digger-turned-soldier in the Civil War epic *Glory*. The film, a poignant drama about an all-black regiment that was chosen to lead an assault on a Southern fort, received much praise and provided

Freeman just the sort of work he relished. "I've been offered Black quasi-heroes who get hanged at the end," he said in *Essence*. "I won't do a part like that. If I do a hero, he's going to live to the end of the movie." Freeman's character in *Glory*—eventually promoted and decorated—is indeed one of the last fighters to die as his battalion storms the fort.

Noted for his subtle but scathing critiques of negative representations of African Americans on stage and in films, Freeman chooses his roles carefully. After ending the 1980s with a hectic spate of film and stage work, he took a brief breather before accepting work on a new project. Cast as Petruchio in the New York Shakespeare Festival's production of *The Taming of the Shrew* in 1990, Freeman generated lavish reviews, and he subsequently appeared as Azeem, a Moor, in the 1991 *Robin Hood: Prince of Thieves*. *Robin Hood* opened to mixed reviews. It was labeled a politically correct film.

Freeman received another Academy award nomination for his portrayal of a prisoner in *The Shawshank Redemption*. He also made his debut as a director in *Bopha!* with Danny Glover and Alfre Woodard, but told Jerry Roberts of *Variety*, "For directing, you've got to really enjoy it. It's time-consuming and it's not lucrative. Call me an actor who has directed."

Freeman also turned in standout performances in such films as *Outbreak*, *Unforgiven*, and *Deep Impact*. He had an important role in *Amistad*, a historically based film about slavery-bound Africans who revolted and fought for their freedom all the way to the Supreme Court. Freeman was given his first starring vehicle, *Kiss The Girls*, and another film, *Seven*, was his first top-grossing film. Known for playing good guys and everyday Joes, he portrayed the villain in *Chain Reaction* and *Hard Rain*. Freeman told Morgan Dean of WRIC-TV that he was "looking for characters to play and looking to have fun playing. I'm not drawn to any certain characters at all. I like playing what's eclectic."

A Veteran Supporting Actor

In 2004, Freeman starred in *The Big Bounce*, an adaptation of a book by Elmore Leonard. His best year came in 2005, when he won his Oscar for *Million Dollar Baby*. Freeman played Eddie "Scrap-Iron" Dupris, an ex-fighter who helps trainer Frankie Dunn (Eastwood) develop waitress Maggie Fitzgerald (Swank) thrive in the ring. Swank won best actress, Eastwood best director, and the film itself took best picture. Freeman also earned an Image Award from the National Association of the Advancement of Colored People (NAACP). In 2006, Freeman starred in *Lucky Number Slevin*, a slick crime thriller, in which he plays a crime boss. In *Hollywood Reporter*, Kirk Honeycutt wrote that the film is "stylish as hell with sharp dialogue, a tongue-in-cheek plot and visual and editing razzle-dazzle." In that same year, he received the

Spencer Tracy Award from the University of California-Los Angeles. The award ceremony included a video retrospective of Freeman's career, including his performance in *Lucky Number Slevin*.

As he passed his 70th birthday, Freeman continued to find a variety of roles that took advantage of his wry smile and his calm yet playful disposition. In 2007 Freeman played the role of God in 2007's *Evan Almighty,* a comedy that co-stars Steve Carrell, and was also cast as Jack Doyle in *Gone Baby Gone,* a crime thriller that marked the directorial debut of Ben Affleck. He was scheduled to appear in the next installment in the Batman franchise, *The Dark Knight,* in 2008, but Freeman's fans were most excited about his scheduled appearance as South African president Nelson Mandela in *The Human Factor,* scheduled for 2009. Freeman said: "I have known Nelson Mandela personally for quite some time, and am continually in awe of his enormous presence in the world. The opportunity to portray him in this film is a great honor."

Success has allowed Freeman to indulge himself at length in his favorite hobby—sailing. One of his acquisitions is a 38-foot sailboat that he has piloted through the Caribbean and the North Atlantic. "When you live in the world of make-believe, you need something real," he remarked in *Time.* "I go sailing, I'm in the real world." Freeman is often accompanied on his trips by his second wife, costume designer Myrna Colley-Lee, and one of his seven grandchildren, E'Dena Hines.

When not working, Freeman can also be found on his 44-acre farm near Clarksdale, Mississippi. There, Freeman has opened a blues bar, the Ground Zero Blues Club, and a fine-dining restaurant, Madidi. Freeman loves being far away from the glamour and pressures of Hollywood, he explained to the *Washington Post.* "The big question was, 'My Lord, you *can* live anywhere in the world you want, why did you choose Mississippi?' My glib answer was, because I can live anywhere. But the true answer is that of any place I've ever been, this feels most like home. When I come here, when I hit Mississippi, everything is right." Freeman does not see himself as a star. "As you work, you realize that stardom is really not what you want. You want steadiness," he told the Associated Press in *Jet.* "Steady work is better than stardom. And for a character actor, stardom is anathema because once you become a star, it becomes you." Being one of the best character actors in show business, Morgan Freeman no longer needs to worry about steady work.

Selected works

Films

Brubaker, 1980.
Eyewitness, 1980.
Harry and Son, 1983.
Teachers, 1984.
Street Smart, 1987.
Clean and Sober, 1988.
Johnny Handsome, 1988.
Lean on Me, 1989.
Driving Miss Daisy, 1989.
Glory, 1989.
The Bonfire of the Vanities, 1990.
Robin Hood: Prince of Thieves, 1991.
Unforgiven, 1992.
(Director) *Bopha!,* 1993.
The Shawshank Redemption, 1994.
Outbreak, 1995.
Seven, 1995.
Moll Flanders, 1996.
Chain Reaction, 1996.
Kiss the Girls, 1997.
Amistad, 1997.
Deep Impact, 1998.
Hard Rain, 1998.
(And executive producer) *Under Suspicion,* 2000.
Nurse Betty, 2000.
(And producer) *Along Came a Spider,* 2001.
High Crimes, 2002.
The Sum of All Fears, 2002.
(And executive producer) *Levity,* 2003.
Dreamcatcher, 2003.
Bruce Almighty, 2003.
Guilt by Association, 2004.
The Big Bounce, 2004.
Million Dollar Baby, 2004.
Danny the Dog, 2005.
Batman Begins, 2005.
War of the Worlds, 2005.
Edison, 2005.
An Unfinished Life, 2005.
Lucky Number Slevin, 2006.
The Contract, 2006.
Evan Almighty, 2007.
Gone Baby Gone, 2007.
The Dark Knight, scheduled 2008.
(And producer) *The Human Factor,* scheduled 2009.

Plays

The Nigger-Lovers, 1967.
Hello, Dolly, 1967.
Jungle of Cities, 1969.
Sisyphus and the Blue-Eyed Cyclops, 1975.
Cockfight, 1977.
The Mighty Gents, 1978.
White Pelicans, 1978.
Coriolanus, 1979.
Julius Caesar, 1979.
Mother Courage and Her Children, 1980.
Buck, 1982.
The Gospel at Colonus, 1983.

Medea and the Doll, 1984.
Driving Miss Daisy, 1987.
The Taming of the Shrew, 1990.

Television

The Electric Company, 1971-75.
Hollow Image, 1979.
Attica, 1980.
Another World, 1982-84.
The Atlanta Child Murders, 1985.
Resting Place, 1986.
Flight for Life, 1987.
Clinton and Nadine, 1988.
The Civil War, 1990.
The Promised Land, 1995.
(Producer) *Mutiny,* 1999.
Slavery and the Making of America, 2005.

Sources

International Dictionary of Films and Filmmakers, Vol. 3: *Actors and Actresses,* 4th ed., St. James Press, 2000.
Tracy, Kathleen, *Morgan Freeman: A Biography,* Barricade Books, 2006.

Periodicals

Chicago Defender, June 22-24, 2007, p. 22.
Ebony, April 1990.
Entertainment Weekly, October 22, 1993; December 1, 2006, p. 31.
Esquire, June 1988.
Essence, December 1988.
Hollywood Reporter, January 23, 2006.
Jet, March 6, 1989; October 16, 1995; March 27, 2006, p. 32.
New York, March 14, 1988.
New York Times, June 22, 2007, p. E10.
People, April 4, 1988.
Rolling Stone, May 5, 1988.
Time, January 8, 1990.
Variety, September 1, 1997; February 6, 2006, p. 101; June 25, 2007.
Village Voice, July 24, 1990.
Washington Post, November 13, 2005, p. P01.

On-line

Ground Zero Blues Club, www.groundzerobluesclub.com/home.php (July 24, 2007).
"Morgan Freeman," *IMDb,* www.imdb.com/name/nm0000151/ (July 23, 2007).

—Mark Kram, Ashyia N. Henderson, and Tom Pendergast

Tyrese Gibson

1978—

Singer, actor, fashion model, business executive

Tyrese Gibson, best known simply as Tyrese, first caught public attention for his smiling face in a Coca-Cola commercial when he was just 16. From that ad, Tyrese steadily built himself into a multimedia giant, amassing multimillion dollar modeling contracts, selling multi-platinum albums, nabbing principal roles in films, and creating a multimedia company called Headquarter Entertainment. Tyrese developed into a brand unto himself. His striking physique, mature-beyond-his-years vocal style, keen acting sense, and positive public message and attitude enabled him to appeal to a broad swath of the entertainment market.

Gibson, Tyrese, photograph. AP Images.

Possessed Stunning Good Looks, Smooth Singing Style

Tyrese Gibson was born on December 30, 1978, and grew up in the tough south-central Los Angeles neighborhood of Watts. He was the youngest of four children raised by his single mother, Priscilla Murray. The scene of civil unrest both in the 1960s and after the Rodney King verdict in the 1990s, Watts was a neighborhood beset by drugs and gang warfare, but Tyrese was determined to avoid falling into the way of life they represented. He threw himself into one school activity after another, playing football and basketball and joining the track team. "Everything I could do to stay out of harm's way, I did," he told *People*.

A popular and naturally outgoing student, Tyrese was voted most talented in his class and also class clown. "I've always been the in-your-face, nothing-to-hide kind of guy," he recalled in *People*. But one school activity above all others kept him centered: music. Tyrese found encouragement and guidance from Locke High School music teacher Reggie Andrews, who commented to *People* that his young student "turned a negative energy around to a positive." When Tyrese was 14, he began to enter, and to win, local talent contests around Los Angeles.

Two years later, Coca-Cola advertising directors looking for fresh talent came to Locke High School. Tyrese's career got off to an unpromising start when he almost missed his audition, but he turned the situation around with his rendition of Stevie Wonder's "Ribbon in the Sky." It didn't take Coke's executives long to sign him for an upcoming television commercial. That

At a Glance . . .

Born Tyrese Darnell Gibson on December 30, 1978; grew up in Los Angeles, CA, in Watts neighborhood; youngest of four children; mother's name: Priscilla Murray Gibson. *Education*: Locke High School, Los Angeles, 1996.

Career: Coca-Cola television commercial, actor and singer, 1995; RCA label, recording artist, 1998-2001; Guess brand, model, 1999; actor, 2001–; Headquarter Entertainment, founder, 2001–; J Records, recording artist, 2002–.

Awards: Grammy award nomination, Best R&B Male Vocal Performance, for "Sweet Lady," 2000; American Music Award, for Favorite New Artist, 2000;

Addresses: *Office*—Headquarter Entertainment, 1635 N. Cahuenga Blvd., 2nd Floor, Los Angeles, CA 90028. *Web*—www.headquarterentertainment.com.

advertisement went on to become one of the most distinctive and memorable in the company's long history of media campaigns. It featured Tyrese boarding a city bus with an earphone radio over his head, singing quietly to himself. Though the song merely extolled the virtues of Coke as a soft drink, viewers reacted positively to the smooth stylings and natural good looks of the spot's young lead actor.

The commercial did not escape the notice of talent watchers in the Los Angeles music industry, just then in the early stages of planning a massive effort to appeal to teenage consumers by signing artists of that same age group. Pop artists such as Britney Spears, country singers such as LeAnn Rimes, and urban contemporary artists such as Brandy and Monica had demonstrated the potential appeal of teenage vocalists, and a bidding war erupted among several labels vying for the services of the hot new phenomenon. Tyrese finally signed with the RCA/BMG conglomerate in 1998. He kept a hand in the modeling arena as well, appearing in advertisements for the Tommy Hilfiger clothing firm and others.

Asserted Own Ideas Early in Career

Far from being simply a pretty face that served as the vehicle for the musical and marketing ideas of others, Tyrese had considerable creative input into his debut album release, entitled simply *Tyrese*, which appeared in the fall of 1998. He co-wrote the album's first single, "Nobody Else," and, despite the common practice of incorporating guest appearances by big-name rappers into the releases of new artists, performed the song's rap himself. The album won critical praise, and "Nobody Else" cracked the top 15 on *Billboard* magazine's R&B singles chart and even crossed over to the Pop Top 40.

Various top creative talents in the R&B field were brought in to work on *Tyrese*, but Tyrese himself proved to have the versatility to succeed in several different musical styles. The follow-up to "Nobody Else," the harmony-laden "Sweet Lady," became the album's biggest hit, reaching the top spot on the R&B chart in 1999. The song earned Tyrese a Grammy Award nomination for Best R&B Male Vocal Performance at the awards ceremony held the following year. Tyrese also gained strong airplay for a third single from the album, "Lately." His efforts were rewarded with platinum level sales and an American Music Award for Favorite New Artist in 2000.

Tyrese immediately set about building upon the success of the album. He contributed a song, "Criminal Mind," to the soundtrack of the hit Martin Lawrence film *Blue Streak*, and landed a host slot on the hip-hop oriented *MTV Jams* program on cable television. Guest slots on television series flowed his way: he appeared on *Martin*, *Sister Sister*, *Moesha*, and *Hangin' with Mr. Cooper*. He appealed to audiences of many different backgrounds; though firmly rooted in the R&B and hip-hop genres, he expressed a desire to collaborate musically with country superstar Garth Brooks. The pursuit of sheer exposure was the smartest move Tyrese could have made, for his physical appearance was remarkable.

Sporting a bald head shaved since age 16, a pierced lower lip (the ring he wore was dropped in the year 2000), and nine tattoos, Tyrese was best known for his bodybuilder physique. MTV veejay Ananda Lewis, quoted in *People*, spoke admiringly of his "12-pack abs." But few knew of the concentrated stretch of weightlifting that the entertainer had put into forging his new physical image, which had not come naturally to him at all. "I had to get in shape for my first video," he told *Ebony*. "I wasn't in shape at all. My trainer, Sandy Alexander Cochran, got me in shape in three months. What you see in that video is just three months of work." The work paid off: in *Ebony*'s words, "[H]e has one of those bodies that might as well be made of neon for all the attention it attracts." In late 1999, Tyrese became the first male model under exclusive contract to the successful Guess jeans line, signing a multi-million dollar deal.

The success of his debut album enabled Tyrese to attract the talents of such producers as Babyface, Jermaine Dupri, Rodney Jenkins, and Diane Warren, for his sophomore CD release, *2000 Watts*. Tyrese co-wrote many of the songs on the album and hoped that the sound would tap into the quality works of R&B classics, explaining to *Jet* that "there's something about R&B oldies that you can play 'em today and they still sound good and make you feel good. That's what I'm trying to get back in touch with on this album, and I just hope people are going to enjoy it not just for the moment, but for many years from now." The album ultimately went platinum. He followed it with another R&B album in 2002, *I Wanna Go There*.

Scored Silver Screen Roles

More than a toned physique and smooth voice, Tyrese had other talents to offer. Director John Singleton picked Tyrese to play a principal role in his first movie to revisit social dilemmas in South Central Los Angeles since *Boyz N the Hood*. In *Baby Boy*, Tyrese played Jody, a young man drifting through his life without a strong sense of responsibility for his future path. *Chicago Defender* movie critic Earl Calloway found the movie "seriously compelling" and Tyrese's performance "truly profound." Singleton picked Tyrese again for subsequent projects, including *2 Fast 2 Furious* in 2003 and *Four Brothers* in 2005.

Tyrese did not have to rely on Singleton to build his acting career, however. Tyrese filmed on location in Africa for *Flight of the Phoenix*, a 2004 remake of a 1965 film about surviving a plane crash in the desert, and followed that with a turn as a strict Naval officer in *Annapolis*. By his sixth film, *Waist Deep*, Tyrese secured his first starring role. He played O2, a recently released convict who struggles to retrieve his kidnapped son without landing himself back in prison. Evidence of Tyrese's time in the limelight came when he landed a role in the Steven Spielberg blockbuster *Transformers*. The live-action film was released in 2007 at a time when 1980s style had once again become fashionable. Adults who remembered the action figure toys, animated television series, and popular film about the characters from their childhood in the 1980s were as enthralled with the live-action film as legions of young adults being introduced to the characters by Spielberg. Tyrese spoke about the popularity of the film with Sandy Cohen of the *Seattle Times*, saying "You feel good talking about the Transformers as a grown man. It doesn't make you feel like you're talking about the Care Bears or something."

Introduced Alter Ego

As Tyrese worked on films, he did not abandon his music. In Africa, he came up with the notion for an original concept for an R&B crooner. He decided to make a double album, *Alter Ego*, with two distinct parts: one hip-hop raps and another R&B songs. After multi-platinum sales of his earlier R&B albums, Tyrese's experimentation with his "alter ego," Black-Ty the rapper, seemed fresh. No other singer had recorded such a project. Rapping was not new to Tyrese; during his teenage years he had rapped as a part of a group called Triple Impact, as he told Allison Kugel of

PR.com. While Tyrese thrilled to the idea of introducing another facet of his personality to his fans, he acknowledged that his two identities might not appeal to the same crowd. He planned to keep his musical styles separate and identifiable to his fans by continuing to use the moniker Black-Ty for his emcee work. "Because Tyrese is an R&B singer and Black-Ty is an emcee. I didn't want my fans to show up to buy a Tyrese CD and hear me rapping on it. It's two different experiences, two different worlds," he told Kugel. Tyrese described his hip-hop music as a "man's man album" to Audrey J. Bernard of the *New York Beacon* and added that "The R&B side is for the ladies." The album quickly went multi-platinum.

Tyrese had plans to cultivate his female fan base in the fall of 2007. Joining with Ginuwine and Tank as a musical super group, Tyrese scheduled "The Shirts Off Tour," which promised to highlight the attractive, chiseled physiques of the men, as well as their smooth, soulful voices. "It's going to be the ultimate female experience," Tyrese told August Brown of the *Los Angeles Times*.

Laid Foundations of Media Empire

As Tyrese's fame grew, he did not cut off one portion of his career to pursue another. Instead he maintained a well-rounded approach that enabled him to lay the foundations of what would become a multimedia empire. Tyrese explained his business approach to Bernard: "My mom taught me when I was young, you're blessed with so many talents, so many capabilities that you have to expose things one at a time. You don't want to overwhelm people."

His empire rested firmly on his roots. At the onset of his commercial success, Tyrese did something quite unusual: he generously acknowledged and thanked those who had helped him when he had nothing. With his first flush of success, he purchased a plush suburban home for his mother. As his star rose, he maintained an interest in helping others. He returned frequently to his Watts neighborhood, appearing at community festivals, working with inner-city young people, visiting schools, and consistently speaking out against the scourge of drugs. Through his 2000 Watts Foundation, he raised and donated millions of dollars to give back to his community. "I don't want the children's dreams," he explained to *People*, "to be as small as the houses they live in." As his star has continued to rise, Tyrese's reputation as a kind and generous community member remained intact, only adding to his commercial appeal.

Cultivating so many facets of his career required more than Tyrese's personal drive. He needed an organization. After returning from filming in Africa, Tyrese set up Headquarter Entertainment in 2001 as a multimedia company, with film, graphic arts, management, recording, publishing, and travel among its many divisions. Tyrese developed the company to grow whether or not his star continued to rise. "At the end of the day, I love fame and popularity, but the day that it all stops I will still be able to run something that's successful," Tyrese told Kugel.

Selected discography

Albums

Tyrese, RCA, 1998.
2000 Watts, RCA, 2001.
I Wanna Go There, J Records, 2002.
Alter Ego, J Records, 2006.

Films

Baby Boy, 2001.
2 Fast 2 Furious, 2003.
Four Brothers, 2005.
Flight of Phoenix, 2004.
Annapolis, 2006.
Waist Deep, 2006.
Transformers, 2007.

Sources

Periodicals

Chicago Defender, June 27, 2001, p. 19; June 23-25, 2006, p. 5.
Ebony, October 1999, p. 62.
Jet, June 5, 2000, p. 41; June 25, 2001, p. 60.
Los Angeles Times, June 3, 2007, p. F14.
New York Beacon, January 4-10, 2007, p. 18.
People, November 13, 2000, p. 111; July 30, 2001, p. 83.
PR Newswire, May 30, 2000, p. 0233.
Seattle Times, July 11, 2007, p. F6.
Star Interviews, July 9, 2001, p. 1.
WWD, November 11, 1999, p. 13.

On-line

"Tyrese Gibson, R&B Singer and Actor, Opens Up About His New Double CD "Alter Ego," then Talks Shop with Film Director John Singleton," *PR.com,* www.pr.com/article/1057 (July 24, 2007).
Tyrese/Black-Ty, www.tyrese.com (July 24, 2007).

—James M. Manheim and Sara Pendergast

Adele Givens

19(??)—

Comedian, actor

Growing up in a poor, inner-city neighborhood on the west side of Chicago, Illinois, Adele Givens listened to comedians telling jokes on television and the radio and dreamed that someday she would be one of them. Though her life was not always easy, her sharp intelligence and quick wit enabled her to turn her pain into humor and to use that humor to comment on everyday events and social issues. When friends encouraged her to enter a local comedy competition, Givens won the contest and introduced her raunchy, street-smart comedy to a young African-American audience that was eager to see urban hip-hop culture reflected in their entertainment.

Swept up in an explosion of confrontational urban black comedy that gained tremendous popularity during the 1990s, Givens began a successful career performing in comedy clubs and comedy shows on cable television, which soon led to appearances in television series and films. Though enjoying her success, Givens has maintained a strong commitment to her own integrity, carefully choosing material and roles that promote respect and positive social change. As her career has progressed, she has begun to combine her comedy writing with her love of poetry to step beyond standup comedy into the art of spoken word performance.

Givens was born and raised in a largely black working-class neighborhood in the urban center of Chicago. She learned to face life's difficulties with laughter from her mother, Nellie Bell, who she described in an interview by Darryl Littleton in his 2006 book, *Black Comedians on Black Comedy: How African Ameri-*cans *Taught Us to Laugh,* as the "funniest lady you ever heard."

Her parents had moved to Chicago from Kentucky, and occasional visits to her grandmother in Kentucky became an escape from the poverty and violence of an inner-city childhood. Television and radio were also escapes, and young Adele often tuned in to comedy acts, watching and listening carefully, learning which jokes worked and which did not, trying to imagine how she might perform her own act. She especially longed to be on the radio because she was insecure about her looks; there she could be both public and hidden.

For many years Givens only performed her humorous commentary for family and friends, but in 1990, friends persuaded her to enter a comedy competition sponsored by Crown Royal. Givens not only wowed the audience in Chicago's Regal Theater on February 3, 1990, but won the contest and became immediately addicted to performing. She quickly left her job as a Social Security clerk and launched headlong into a career as a standup comic.

She was soon performing regularly at comedy nightclubs and standup venues around town, meeting other young African-American comedians, such as fellow Chicagoan Bernie Mac. In 1992, she was invited to appear on a new kind of comedy show, HBO's *Def Comedy Jam. Def Comedy Jam* was produced by Russell Simmons. Simmons was an African-American businessman who had founded the hip-hop record label Def Jam in the mid-1980s, and had pioneered other hip-hop-influenced businesses, including Phat Farm, a trendy clothing line.

At a Glance . . .

Born Adele Givens in 19(??) in Chicago, Illinois; married, children: two (adopted).

Career: Royal Crown Comedy Competition, Chicago, winner, 1990; comedian, 1990–; actor, 1998–; WGCI Chicago, *The New Howard "Crazy" McGee and Adele Givens Morning Show,* 1999-2000; Queens of Comedy Tour, 2000; Crown Royal Comedy Soul Festival Tour, 2003.

Awards: *Bean Soup Times,* Funniest Female Stand up on DVD, for Funniest Female in a TV Series, 2005.

Hip hop describes a broad range of urban youth culture, including rap music, graffiti art, break dancing, and fashion. Though hip hop is closely identified with African-American youth, other youth of color, especially Latino youth have been central to creating it. Simmons' *Def Comedy Jam* brought a confrontational and spontaneous hip-hop consciousness to standup comedy and featured young African-American comedians performing outrageous, and often obscene, comedy acts. The fresh, uncensored nature of *Def Comedy Jam* appealed to audiences and won the show the U.S. Comedy Arts Festival Freedom of Speech Award in 2006.

Givens quickly became one of the most popular performers on *Def Comedy Jam,* earning the nickname, "Queen of Comedy." Taking her material from the issues in her life, she wrote constantly, always making sure that her hard-hitting and bawdy jokes had a serious and constructive point. Targeting such issues as sex discrimination, abusive relationships, and celebrity culture, Givens punctuated her biting observations with her trademark line, "I'm such a f***in' lady!" She used her own rough language as fuel for her comedy, as when she mimicked a self-righteous preacher who chastised her for her foul mouth only to reveal his own hypocrisy. "Whenever I get on stage, I try to teach through my word," she said in an October 2004 interview with Gezus Zaire of the Cleveland, Ohio, *Call and Post.* "It's always message-laced and I hope that...I make you laugh and think."

Givens' success on *Def Comedy Jam,* on tour, and on the DVD releases of the program led to more job offers. She made guest appearances on several TV series, including *Martin, Moesha,* and *The Steve Harvey Show,* and, in 1998, got a recurring role on the Tracey Ullman comedy/variety program *Tracey Takes On.* Also in 1998, she was cast in her first film role in *The Players Club,* directed by rapper Ice Cube. In 1999, she fulfilled her childhood dream of perform-

ing on radio when she returned home to Chicago to co-host the *New Howard "Crazy" McGee and Adele Givens Morning Show* on WGCI.

In spite of the success of Givens and a number of other African-American female comedians, comedy—especially black comedy—continued to be dominated by men. In 2000, Givens, along with comedians Mo'nique, Sommore, and Laura Hayes, set out to change that reality. During the 1990s, African-American entertainment promoter Walter Latham had produced a hugely successful comedy tour called The Kings of Comedy, featuring many of the most popular black comics in the industry, including Bernie Mac, Chris Tucker, D. L. Hughley, and Martin Lawrence. In 2000, Latham produced The Queens of Comedy Tour, featuring the four female comedians and their hilarious routines.

The Queens of Comedy played to sold-out houses throughout the United States, and Latham brokered a deal with the cable network Showtime to make a film of the show. The Showtime *Queens of Comedy* debuted on January 27, 2001, receiving the year's highest ratings for any network special. Along with boosting their careers, the Queens of Comedy became a place of friendship and support for the women on the tour.

Given's has continued to hone her act and develop her career, performing in the Platinum Comedy Series for HBO and being the only woman comic on the 2003 Crown Royal Comedy Soul Festival Tour. In 2005, she was cast in the Queen Latifah film, *Beauty Shop.* The same year she was nominated for a Platinum Mic Stand-Up Award at the Black Entertainment Television Comedy Awards.

Givens continues to perform her thought-provoking, in-your-face style of comedy at clubs and festivals throughout the country. Though she loves performing, she is deeply aware of her responsibility as an artist and is conscientious about choosing roles and material that are respectful both of herself and her audiences. "I'm from the west side of Chicago and ... I know how to hustle and survive without compromising my principles," she told the *Bean Soup Times.* A poet as well as a comedian, she has gradually added spoken word, or poetry performance, to her act. Givens is married, and she adopted her brother's sons when he was unable to raise them. Her role as a mother has made her even more determined to perform material aimed at making the world a better place for her children. When not on the road, Givens lives with her family in Kentucky, the place where she felt safe as a child.

Selected works

Films

The Player's Club, 1998.
Beauty Shop, 2005.

Television

Def Comedy Jam, 1992-97.
Tracy Takes On, 1998-99.
The Hughleys, 2001-01.
Comedy Central Presents: Adele Givens, 2002;

Sources

Books

Littleton, Darryl. *Black Comedians on Black Comedy: How African Americans Taught Us to Laugh.* Applause Theater and Cinema Books, 2006.

Periodicals

Call & Post (Cleveland, Ohio), October 21-28, 2004, p. 7; June 29-July 5, 2006, p. 2B.
Chicago Defender, February 8, 1990, p. 21.
Chicago Sun-Times, November 4, 1999, p. 47; February 3, 2000, p. 41; March 1, 2000, p. 49.
Essence. September 1993, pp. 84-9.
Jet, January 22, 2001, p. 32; June 2, 2003, p. 44.
Milwaukee Journal Sentinel, June 17, 1996.
Seattle Times (Seattle, Washington), October 27, 2000, p. I12.

On-line

"Friday Comedy: Adele Givens," *National Public Radio: Tavis Smiley Show,* www.npr.org/templates/story/story.php?storyId=1496551 (July 6, 2007).
"Giving Props to BET, Love to Chicago and Inspiration to the World," *Bean Soup Times,* www.beansoup-times.com/Adele_Givens.htm (March 6, 2007).
"Interview with Adele Givens," *AOL Black Voices,* http://blackvoices.aol.com/black_entertainment/movies_features_reviews_trailers/festivalcircuit/2006-abff-interviews-ty-hodges (March 6, 2007).

—Tina Gianoulis

Malcolm Gladwell

1963—

Author, speaker

Celebrated in *Fast Company* magazine as a "rock star, a spiritual leader, a stud," and named to *Time*'s list of the "100 Most Influential People" in 2005, Malcolm Gladwell is perhaps the hottest nonfiction author of the 2000s. Gladwell is the author of two bestsellers: *The Tipping Point,* which explored how trends, ideas, and products "tipped" into phenomena of much greater importance, and *Blink: The Power of Thinking without Thinking,* which examines the wisdom and folly of snap decisions. Gladwell's mixed-race background played a significant role in shaping *Blink,* for the genesis of the book came when the light-skinned Gladwell grew his hair out into an Afro style and was suddenly stopped far more frequently by the police. "The theme of the book," he explained to Rebecca Caldwell of the Toronto *Globe & Mail,* "is that what goes on in the first two seconds is really important in that those kinds of judgments are capable of being extraordinarily good but are also capable of being so screwed up and so biased that they can throw us off the track entirely."

Gladwell was born in England in 1963, but grew up in the Ontario, Canada, community of Waterloo, where his father taught mathematics at the local university. His father was British and white, while his mother Joyce was a native of Jamaica and black. She became a psychotherapist, but had also authored a memoir about being a young black woman in Britain and Jamaica during the 1950s. Like his two brothers, Gladwell was encouraged to read in the television-free home. At the age of age 16 he won a writing contest for an essay in which he interviewed God; not long after, he started his own (shortlived) 'zine, a journal of opinion.

Hired at the New Yorker

Gladwell studied history at the University of Toronto, and had a brief career as an advertising copywriter before landing a job at the *American Spectator,* a conservative political journal, before moving on to the *Washington Post* in 1987 as a reporter. Over the next nine years he moved up at the paper to become its science writer and then New York City bureau chief. In 1996 he was lured away from the *Post* by Tina Brown, the then-editor of the prestigious weekly magazine *The New Yorker.*

Gladwell soon carved out at niche for himself at the *New Yorker* with articles that offered explorations of the curious, unexplained phenomena of everyday life, such as 1999's "Six Degrees of Lois Weinberg," in which Gladwell explored how it was that certain people seem to know everybody. In this article, he traced the long career of the Chicago gadabout of the title, who was also the mother of one of his friends. Both Lois and Jacob Weinberg seemed to have vast networks of friends and were continually introducing people to one another. To explain this, Gladwell looked into the social-science experiment from a generation earlier era that yielded the phrase "six degrees of separation"— that everyone in the world is connected to one another by a chain of six other people—and posited that people like Lois and Jacob were natural "connectors" of others.

At a Glance . . .

Born on September 1, 1963, in England; raised in Elmira, Ontario; son of Graham (a professor) and Joyce (a psychotherapist) Gladwell. *Education:* Trinity College, University of Toronto, BA, history, 1984.

Career: Worked as an advertising copywriter and then in the editorial department of the *American Spectator,* mid-1980s; *Washington Post,* reporter, science writer, and New York City bureau chief, 1987-96; *New Yorker* magazine, staff writer, 1996–.

Awards: *Time* magazine, "100 Most Influential People," 2005.

Addresses: *Office*—c/o *The New Yorker,* 4 Times Square, New York, NY 10036; c/o Author Mail, Little, Brown, 1271 Avenue of the Americas, New York, NY 10020. *Web*—www.gladwell.com.

Sometimes, Gladwell's articles turned popular assumptions on their head, as in "The Talent Myth," which tracked the rise of expensive management-consultant firms like McKinsey & Company in corporate America. Many Fortune 500 companies hire consultants to come in, analyze operations, and make recommendations. Noting that such consultant firms hire the cream of the crop from among graduates of the Ivy League and the top-tier graduate business schools, Gladwell showed how disastrously wrong these talented thinkers could be for a company. He used the example of Enron, the Texas energy-trading company whose lengthy list of financial misdeeds and corporate mismanagement had managed to escape the McKinsey consultants who had conducted some 20 separate projects at Enron and were billing it $10 million a year for their services. Perhaps, intimated Gladwell, hiring the top talent out of America's best schools wasn't the silver bullet it was thought to be.

Found His Own Tipping Point

Many of the *New Yorker* staff writers specialize in a particularly field—John Cassidy on finance, Atul Gawande on medicine—but Gladwell's articles began to define a niche of their own, one summed up by *Fast Company* journalist Danielle Sacks as "an idea-driven narrative, one focused on the mundane rather than the bizarre. It takes you on a journey in and out of research through personal, social, and historical moments, transports you to a place you didn't know you were going to end up, and changes the way you think about

an idea." These thoughtfully crafted essays landed Gladwell a book contract with Little, Brown for $1.5 million, which another journalist rounded out to a payout of around $5,376 per page for each of the 279 pages of *The Tipping Point: How Little Things Can Make a Big Difference.* Published in 2000, the title was taken from his 1996 *New Yorker* article about why the crime rate in New York City had dropped so dramatically in the past 20 years. The "tipping point" refers to the method by which certain things—ideas, violent crime, consumer fads—suddenly seem to take over for a while, almost like an infectious-disease epidemic. These phenomena, Gladwell explains, indeed share some characteristic elements with viruses.

In *The Tipping Point,* Gladwell explains that certain goods or trends seem to catch on via word of mouth, sparked by a small group of trend-setters he calls "mavens" who have influence in one area. Their enthusiasms are passed on to "connectors"—the people like Lois Weisberg—who transfer ideas between groups. Finally, persuaders Gladwell calls "salespeople" ensure that the trend, idea, or product in question spreads like the proverbial wildfire. The book is peppered with scores of anecdotes, such as the story of the Aeron chair, whose manufacturer was advised to kill the product because its design was so universally loathed when it first came onto the market, yet the desk chair went on to become a bestseller. "It's hard not to be persuaded by Gladwell's thesis," noted a reviewer of the book in *Business Week.* "Not only does he assemble a fascinating mix of facts in support of his theory—from the impact of Paul Revere to a rash of suicides in Micronesia—but he also manages to weave everything into a cohesive explanation of human behavior."

Like the Aeron chair, *The Tipping Point* took time to catch on, but eventually became a *New York Times* bestseller. It also led to a lucrative secondary career for Gladwell as a marketing expert whose public-speaking fee for corporate events soared to $40,000. The "tipping point" became a widely used catchphrase for a while, even uttered by U.S. Secretary of Defense Donald Rumsfeld in a press conference about the war in Iraq. In his book, however, Gladwell notes that he did not coin the phrase, but credits rather Thomas Schelling, a Nobel prize-winning economist. Schelling's theory originally referred to the point when white homeowners would begin selling their homes when enough black families moved in.

Target of Racial Profiling

Conscious or subconscious racism also played a role in the genesis of Gladwell's next book, *Blink: The Power of Thinking without Thinking.* The idea for the book began when Gladwell decided to let his hair grow after keeping it short much of his adult life. Because of his mixed race, he was fair-skinned but his hair soon grew into a rather exuberant Afro. "The first thing that started happening was I started getting speeding tickets," he told Sacks in the *Fast Company* interview. "I wasn't driving any faster than I was before, I was just getting pulled over way more." Once, police even targeted him as a suspected rapist. These events, combined with the highly publicized shooting death of an unarmed Guinean immigrant in New York City in 1999, began to weigh heavily on Gladwell's mind. Amadou Diallo was shot 41 times in front of his Bronx apartment building by four police officers who were looking for another suspect; Diallo had panicked, ran into the lobby, but then reached for his wallet; officers assumed it was a weapon, and opened fire.

Published in 2005, *Blink* examines how and why the human mind makes snap decisions, which seem to rely on a hunch or a subconscious "feeling." Traditional wisdom holds that these quick judgments are inferior to a more careful, reasoned analysis in coming to a conclusion, but Gladwell argues that most decisions we make are based on our subconscious and occur in just a fraction of a second. *B* book examines this process, once again providing anecdotes of when this "rapid cognition" or what Gladwell calls "thin-slicing" succeeds, such as the case of a tennis coach who knows instinctively when one of his players is about to double-fault in a match, or the art historian who can recognize a fake in an instant—yet both are dumbstruck when trying to explain how they know these things.

Blink also contains compelling tales of when snap judgments do not succeed, such as the case in the seven seconds before Diallo was shot. "I think of the Diallo chapter as the culmination of the entire book," Gladwell told Angela Ards in *Black Issues Book Review*. "It's where I want the reader to end up: understanding that what they may have written off as a criminal act by a group of outlier cops was in fact a product of beliefs and tendencies that ALL of us have, in some sense, unless we take specific steps to correct ourselves." In his book, Gladwell does not specifically address race, but does bring up some compelling statistics about how we react to physical attributes in others. For example, 58 percent of chief executive officers of the top U.S. corporations are six feet or taller, but only 14 percent of the male population in America reaches that height. "I chose things like height because I felt that they were more subtle and more acceptable ways of getting people to take unconscious bias seriously," he explained in the interview with Ards.

Blink's reviews were mixed—many in the scientific community judged his theories harshly—but the book once again became a bestseller and even reinvigorated sales of *The Tipping Point*. "What Gladwell is saying in *Blink* is often less compelling than the facts he uses to back himself up," wrote Lev Grossman in *Time*. "Who doesn't know that tall, good-looking people get preferential treatment? But Gladwell's analysis of the political career of Warren G. Harding—who was a lousy President but (apparently) a hot, hot man—is mesmerizing."

Gladwell's dominance of the *New York Times* bestseller book rankings for much of 2005 and 2006 placed him in the ranks of black authors like Toni Morrison, Alice Walker, and Terry McMillan, each of whom enjoyed months on the same lists in the 1980s and early 1990s, a feat that had not been repeated since. But it was his mother's memoir that served as the most profound influence on his own work. Originally published in 1969, *Brown Face, Big Master* was reissued by MacMillan Caribbean in 2004. "Her book was the first book I ever remember reading closely, and it really inspired me," he told Ards in *Black Issues Book Review*. "She is a beautifully simple and clear writer. There is no wasted motion or unnecessary word, and that's the way I try to write as well."

Selected writings

Books

The Tipping Point: How Little Things Can Make a Big Difference, Little, Brown, 2000.
Blink: The Power of Thinking without Thinking, Little, Brown, 2005.

Sources

Periodicals

Black Issues Book Review, November-December 2004, p. 64; July-August 2005, p. 20.
Business Week, March 20, 2000, p. 19.
Fast Company, January 2005, p. 64.
Globe & Mail (Toronto, Canada), January 10, 2005, p. R1.
New Yorker, July 22, 2002.
New York Times, March 20, 2000; February 5, 2006.
Time, January 10, 2005, p. 57.

On-line

Gladwell.com, www.gladwell.com (July 4, 2007).

—Carol Brennan

Cuba Gooding Jr.

1968—

Actor

Gooding, Cuba, Jr., photograph. Vince Bucci/Getty Images.

When Cuba Gooding, Jr., delivered his nearly evangelical Academy Award acceptance speech for his performance in the 1996 film *Jerry Maguire*, audiences cheered for the young actor's unexpected catapult to stardom. However, like most overnight successes, Gooding's was the result of several years of wallowing in the dregs of Hollywood productions. Despite a resounding triumph in the gripping 1991 drama *Boyz N the Hood*, Gooding quickly found himself with ample talent and credentials but limited outlets. "[T]he truth of the matter is that he is a young black actor," wrote one critic for the Mr. Showbiz Web site, "and after the handful of good roles generally available for black actors is divvied up among [actors] Denzel Washington, Laurence Fishburne, and Wesley Snipes, there aren't many challenging roles left for the Cuba Gooding, Jrs. of today's Hollywood." Nonetheless, a heavy reserve of moxie and a genuine charm boosted Gooding back into a pole position.

Persevered Despite Hard Times

As the son of Cuba Gooding, the lead vocalist for the successful R&B group The Main Ingredient, Cuba Jr. and his brother Omar were both romanced by the entertainment world at an early age. However, shortly after relocating his family from the Bronx, New York, to Los Angeles, California, to accommodate his own career, the elder Gooding forfeited a family life and abandoned his children in 1974. While Gooding Jr.'s subsequent home life was anything but stable—he was in and out of four Southern California high schools—the fledgling entertainer remained a model of positivity, and even managed to become class president at several of his schools.

After several years of acting as well as dancing in school talent shows, Gooding began to make inroads to a proper career. At the age of 16, he made a fairly auspicious professional debut as a member of singer Lionel Richie's breakdancing entourage at the 1984 Olympics. Returning to the small stage, Gooding joined the cast of a production of the play *Li'l Abner*, which caught the eye of a talent agent who was also the parent of one of Gooding's peers. Under the guidance of his new agent, Gooding soon bagged modest but promising spots in television commercials for Sprite

At a Glance . . .

Born on January 2, 1968, in the Bronx, NY; son of Cuba Gooding (singer); brother of Omar Gooding (actor); married Sara Kapfer (elementary school teacher), 1994; children: Spencer, Mason (sons), Piper (daughter).

Career: Olympic Games, breakdance performer, 1984; actor, 1986–.

Awards: Academy Award, Best Supporting Actor, American Comedy Award, Funniest Supporting Actor in a Motion Picture, and Critics Choice Award, Best Supporting Actor, all for *Jerry Maquire*, 1996; Hollywood Walk of Fame Star, 2002; NAACP Image Award, 2004, and Camie Award, 2005, for *Radio*.

and Bugle Boy Jeans before making his television debut as a supporting character on the gritty police drama *Hill Street Blues*.

Cast by Singleton for Success, but Faltered

In spite of his initial promise, Gooding found that his avenues of opportunity were limited without formal acting lessons. After enhancing his skills with a personal trainer, Gooding built up his resume with several made for television films, as well as with his big screen initiation, a small but meaty comic bit in the Eddie Murphy vehicle *Coming to America*. However, it was not until he auditioned for first time director John Singleton's *Boyz N the Hood* that Gooding's acting abilities truly passed muster with both critics and audiences. As Tre Styles, an amiable teenager struggling to escape his gang infested environment, Gooding found himself riding the crest of one of the year's most acclaimed films. He was given kudos by *New York Times* film critic Janet Maslin for giving Styles a "gentle, impressionable quality that is most affecting." At the first major juncture of his career, it seemed that Gooding had found the touchstone to serious dramatic opportunities.

Unfortunately, the next several years were less of a gateway towards stardom and more of backward steps towards obscurity. Although Gooding's performances themselves were consistently up to par, he was either buried in lesser supporting roles, as in the 1991 military nailbiter *A Few Good Men*, or confined to banal box office duds, such as the widely panned boxing film *Gladiator*, released in 1992, or the dismal action comedy of 1993, *Judgment Night*. *Lightning*

Jack, a dud released in 1994, may have been Gooding's low point, but his adept performance as a deaf mute did bring to surface the comic flair that would blossom later in *Jerry Maguire*. Even the impressive *Losing Isaiah*, a poignant 1995 film involving a custody battle, failed to regain Gooding the footing he deserved, as the film received limited distribution. Only four years after *Boyz N the Hood*, it seemed that Gooding's career had bottomed out.

In the meantime, Gooding's otherwise lackluster series of roles had allowed him to afford a stable family life, quite the opposite of his negligent father. He married Sara Kapfer, then an elementary school teacher whom Gooding had been dating since high school, in 1994. The couple had three children.

Peaked with Jerry Maguire

Gooding had grown tired of his mediocre castings, no matter how lucrative, and in 1995 began courting director Cameron Crowe for a role in his upcoming film, *Jerry Maguire*. To land the part, the determined Gooding went on an intensive training program to beef up for the role of professional football player Rod Tidwell. With characteristic verve, Gooding even dropped his pants at a casting call when asked whether he was shy of onscreen nudity. Duly impressed with the actor's much needed energy, Crowe and producer James Brooks quickly tapped Gooding for the role.

When the romantic comedy *Jerry Maguire* was finally released in 1996, an almost unequivocal rush of commercial and critical approval lifted Gooding from his period of stagnation. Given a rich, witty script, a three-dimensional character, and a high profile star— Tom Cruise—to work with, Gooding was able to turn out a world-class performance that expertly fused brash comedy with dramatic conviction. "Show me the money," a line culled from a hilarious exchange between Gooding and Cruise, became a national catch phrase, and the film headed box office lists for weeks on end.

The overall reviews of the film were positive, but ultimately it was Gooding who received the highest honors. In addition to a Golden Globe Award nomination, Gooding received the Academy Award for Best Supporting Actor of 1996. At the awards ceremony, the actor delivered a vibrant, genuine acceptance speech that ranked among the most moving in the history of the Oscars. Soon, Gooding was being approached for other high-caliber parts.

Searched for Success after Academy Award

Although Gooding purports to suffer from intolerable seasickness, in 2000 he landed the starring role of the heroic Navy master diver, Carl Brashear, who earned his qualification even with a crippling injury to his leg, in *Men of Honor*, featuring Robert De Niro and Carl Lumbly. "I'm more proud of *Men of Honor* than any film I've ever made. You don't have to get too theatrical about his life to present a great story, it's compelling just as it is," Gooding reflected to the *Sacramento Observer*. Chris Vognar of the *Dallas Morning News* wrote that it was Gooding's "best role since *Jerry Maguire*," adding that "Gooding is by turns intense, prideful and jovial." Gooding appeared in a second blockbuster naval feature, *Pearl Harbor*, as Petty Officer Dorie Miller in 2001. That same summer he was seen as Owen Templeton in Jerry Zucker's zany summertime flick, *Rat Race*, followed the next year by another farce, *Snow Dogs*, which topped more than $80 million at the box office.

Despite his inability to win more awards, Gooding appreciated the control he had over his career. "And now I really can take more responsibility, because there is the freedom for me now, and a plethora of different projects for me to choose from," he told Prairie Miller of *Star Interviews* in 2002. "But when I first started out, hey, I got my SAG card with Thug Number Three on a TV show. I wasn't saying, you know, I don't feel I should start my career off stabbing nobody. Hey, I was stabbing and I had jeans on, and I was running. And I would cut you! And then from that, I did this role, and that role. And it wasn't because I decided that I should be, you know, a street kid. No, it was because those were the jobs that I got. And as an actor, that's how my career started. You have to take what you're given, and just shine in that role. Become that character, you know?"

After appearing in a few critically and popularly successful films, however, Gooding had a hard time finding roles as solid as those that brought his earlier success. In *Boat Trip*, he played a straight man surprised to find himself on a cruise surrounded by mainly homosexuals; it was a box office flop. The role earned him a Razzie Award nomination for worst actor in 2004. Some critics wondered if Gooding's trouble finding quality work came from his blind pursuit of money, yet others granted him more empathy: "I think Cuba saw himself as an actor who wanted to play characters, despite the fact the script wasn't up to par, or the project wasn't up to par," *Dirty* director Chris Fisher remarked to Lewis Beale of the *New York Times*. "He still believed in playing those characters." Gooding did take on a variety of different roles. He played a talent agent in *The Fighting Temptations*, featuring Beyonce Knowles, and the film won an NAACP Award. Gooding portrayed a mentally challenged man who never went anywhere without his wireless radio in *Radio* in 2003. For his performance of the character, which was based on a real man named James Robert Kennedy, who was featured in *Sports Illustrated* in 1996 for his work assisting a high school football team, Gooding won a NAACP Image Award for best actor in 2004.

Gooding even took on roles in small independent films. In *Dirty*, he played a corrupt L.A. police officer. In *Shadowboxer*, he played an assassin and earned a nomination for the Outstanding Lead Actor in a Motion Picture award at the Black Movie Awards in 2006. In 2007, his comic appeal was exploited in Eddie Murphy's *Norbit*, as the scheming fiance of Norbit's childhood sweetheart, and as Eddie Murphy's replacement in the sequel to *Daddy Day Care*, *Daddy Day Camp*. Gooding explored his darker side as the notorious criminal Nicky Barnes, a drug dealer who was sentenced to imprisonment for life in 1977 but released into the federal witness protection program in 1998 after becoming a government witness and helping to convict scores of drug dealers, in *American Gangster*. Gooding was slated to tap his dramatic instincts in the upcoming films *Harold*, in which he would portray a friendly high school janitor who befriends an outcast student, and *Hero Wanted*, in which he would play a bank robbery victim who recovers from his near fatal injuries to seek revenge. Though Gooding had yet to regain the critical acclaim of his *Jerry Maguire* role, he seemed close. Director Lee Daniels noted in 2006 in the *New York Times* that he thought that such success may be "just a role away" for Gooding.

Selected works

Films

Coming to America, 1988.
Boyz N the Hood, 1991.
Gladiator, 1992.
Lightning Jack, 1994.
Losing Isaiah, 1995.
Outbreak, 1995.
Jerry Maguire, 1996.
What Dreams May Come, 1998.
Instinct, 1999.
Men of Honor, 2000.
Pearl Harbor, 2001.
Rat Race, 2001.
Snow Dogs, 2002.
Boat Trip, 2003.
The Fighting Temptations, 2003.
Radio, 2003.
Dirty, 2005.
Shadowboxer, 2005.
Daddy Day Camp, 2007.
Norbit, 2007.
What Love Is, 2007.

Sources

Periodicals

Afro-American Star, October 11, 2003, p. B1.
Dallas Morning News, November 10, 2000.
Jet, September 22, 2003, p. 58.
Los Angeles Times, January 3, 1997, p. F4.
New York Times, July 12, 1991, p. C1; February 19, 2006, p. 2.20; March 4, 2007, p. 1.27.

Philadelphia Weekly, March 28, April 3, 2007, p. 43.
Rolling Stone, August 8, 1991, p. 78.
Sacramento Observer, November 15, 2000, p. E7.

Sports Illustrated, October 27, 2003, p. 28.
Star Interviews, February 4, 2002, p. 1.

—Shaun Frentner and Sara Pendergast

Juanita Long Hall

1901-1968

Singer, actor, music director

The first African-American woman to win a Tony Award, singer and actor Juanita Long Hall became most famous for stage and film roles in which she played Asian characters. According to many critics, she "stole the show" in her portrayal of Bloody Mary in the musical *South Pacific,* for which she won the Tony Award in 1950. Hall also enjoyed a long and distinguished career as a concert artist and nightclub singer.

Hall was born in 1901 in Keyport, New Jersey. Her mother died during Hall's infancy, and the girl was raised primarily by her grandmother, who encouraged her interest in music. As a child, Hall sang in church choirs and became fascinated by Negro spirituals, which she heard performed at a revival meeting near her home. "The whole quality of the singing grabbed hold of me," she recalled in remarks quoted in *Notable Black American Women.* Hall knew by then that she would pursue a career as a singer.

At age 14 Hall began teaching singing at Lincoln House in East Orange, New Jersey. In her teens she married an actor, Clement Hall; the marriage ended in divorce and Hall did not marry again. She moved to New York City and studied orchestration, harmony, theory, and voice at the Juilliard School of Music. She also took private lessons in voice and acting.

Hall did choral work and spent many years appearing in minor stage roles before achieving stardom. She began working with the Hall Johnson Choir in the 1920s, becoming a soloist and serving as assistant director until she formed her own choral group, the

Juanita Hall Choir, in 1936. This choir, which operated for five years as a Works Progress Administration (WPA) group, gave more than 5,000 performances, including thrice-weekly radio concerts broadcast on WNYC and a concert at the 1939 World's Fair in New York City. Hall also opened a private voice studio.

Hall's stage debut came in 1928, with a role in the Ziegfeld production of *Show Boat.* In the 1940s the singer appeared in several productions, including *The Pirates, Deep Are the Roots*, and *St. Louis Woman*, in which she had a solo number, "Racin' Forms." Though Hall received rave reviews for her performance in *St. Louis Woman,* her breakthrough role did not come until 1949, when Richard Rodgers and Oscar Hammerstein II, who had heard her sing the year before in an audition for the revue *Talent 48* cast her in their musical, *South Pacific.* She played Bloody Mary, an Asian woman who sells souvenirs on a Pacific island where U.S. naval personnel are stationed during World War II. A smash hit, the show ran for more than five years on Broadway, and many of its songs—including "Bali Hai," sung by Hall—became international standards. *South Pacific* won the Pulitzer Prize for drama and nine Tony awards. In addition to Hall's award for best performance by a featured actress, the show won for best performances in all the other acting categories as well. When *South Pacific* was made into a film in 1958, Hall again played Bloody Mary. Oddly, however, her songs for the film were dubbed by Muriel Smith, who had played the role in a London production.

At a Glance . . .

Born on November 6, 1901, in Keyport, NJ; died on February 29, 1968, in Bayshore, NY. married Clement Hall (divorced). *Education:* Attended Juilliard School of Music.

Career: Singer in stage productions, New York, NY and traveling, 1928-1958; Hall Johnson Choir, New York, NY, soloist, 1920s-1936, assistant director, 1931-1936; founder and director, Juanita Hill Choir, 1936-1941; performer in nightclubs, 1950-1962; film actor and concert artist.

Awards: Antoinette Perry (Tony) Award and Donaldson Award, Best Performance by a Featured Actress in a Musical, *South Pacific*, 1950; Bill "Bojangles" Acting Award, 20th Century Fox Appreciation Award, and Box Office Film Association Award, for film *South Pacific*, 1958; Laurel Award, top female supporting performance, for film *Flower Drum Song*, 1962.

The success of *South Pacific* established Hall, at age 49, as one of the leading black performers on Broadway in the 1950s. According to the *Dictionary of American Biography* (*DNB*), a newspaper columnist reported that Hall was so famous that the post office delivered letters to her addressed simply "Bloody Mary, N.Y.C." When *South Pacific* was in its second year, Hall received a salary increase and she "switched from whiskey to champagne to enjoy life," as quoted in *DNB*.

In 1954 Hall starred in "The Story of Ruby Valentine," the first radio program broadcast on the National Negro Network. Later that year she played Madame Tango, the owner of a West Indian bordello, in the 1954 musical *House of Flowers*, which starred Pearl Bailey and Diahann Carroll. In 1958 Hall appeared in another Rodgers and Hammerstein musical, *Flower Drum Song*, playing a Chinese woman, Madame Liang. She also played this role in the 1961 film version of the musical, for which she won the Laurel Award for top female supporting performance.

In addition to her stage and film work, Hall maintained a busy vocal performance schedule through the 1950s and 1960s. She appeared in several top nightclubs, including the Café Society in New York, and the Saint Moritz and the Flamingo in Las Vegas. She also performed at Chicago's Black Orchid and at The Flame in Detroit, and was seen on popular television variety shows, including *Philco Television Playhouse*, *The Ed Sullivan Show*, *The Perry Como Show*, and *The Today Show*. In concerts, Hall loved to perform the spirituals that had affected her so profoundly as a child.

She was also interested in the blues, having been influenced by the music of Bessie Smith and Billie Holiday, and in 1949 made a recording that included four blues lyrics written for her by poet Langston Hughes. In the late 1950s, she recorded a full album, *Juanita Hall Sings the Blues*. Supporting her on this recording were jazz luminaries Coleman Hawkins on tenor sax and Doc Cheatham on trumpet. According to album notes on the Concord Music Group Web site, the "authenticity of her [blues] renditions" on this recording was a "revelation."

By the 1960s Hall's career had started to fade and her health was in decline. But she was able to appear on stage in 1966 in *A Woman and the Blues*, a tribute blues singers Billie Holiday and Ethel Waters. Hall spent her final years in poverty after an investment in a New York City restaurant, The Fortune Cookie, failed. Her friends and family arranged for her to live in an actors' home in New Jersey and then on Long Island, where she died in 1968.

Hall is remembered as a consummate professional and a thoughtful colleague. "I think everyone who had anything to do with her loved her," wrote Richard Rodgers, as quoted in *Notable Black American Women*. "As an actress, she was…a joy to work with."

Selected works

Films

Miracle in Harlem, 1948.
South Pacific, 1958.
Flower Drum Song, 1961.

Plays

Show Boat, 1928.
Green Pastures, 1930.
The Pirates, 1942.
Sing Out, Sweet Land, 1944.
The Secret Room, 1944.
Deep Are the Roots, 1945.
St. Louis Woman, 1946.
Mr. Peebles and Mr. Hooker, 1946.
S.S. Glencairn, 1948.
Moon of the Caribees, 1948.
South Pacific, 1949.
House of Flowers, 1954.
Flower Drum Song, 1958.

Sources

Books

Dictionary of American Biography, Supplement 8: 1966-1970, American Council of Learned Societies, 1988.
Notable Black American Women, Book 1, Thomson Gale, 1992.

Periodicals

Jet, April 10, 2006, p. 24.
New York Times, February 15, 2003.

On-line

"Juanita Hall," *African American Registry*, www.
aaregistry.com/african_american_history/1274/

Juanita_Hall_great_singer_great_actress (June 26,
2007).

"Juanita Hall," *Concord Music Group,* http://con-
cordmusicgroup.com/artists/?name=Juanita+Hall
(June 26, 2007).

—E. M. Shostak

Larry Leon Hamlin

1948-2007

Actor, association executive

Often dressed head to toe in purple, Larry Leon Hamlin was a hurricane-strength force on the stage of black theater. He was the vision, the fury, and the power behind the National Black Theatre Festival, the world's largest gathering of black theater professionals. Every other summer since 1989, the festival has been drawing thousands of actors, directors, producers, poets, filmmakers, and fans to Winston-Salem, North Carolina, for a week of performance, practice, and parties. Hamlin started the festival, as he once said, to help revive and unify black theater. He succeeded. "I think that black theater needed me," Hamlin told *Contemporary Black Biography* (*CBB*). "Of course, I needed it as well." Hamlin's work, according to Brian McLaughlin of *Black Masks,* resulted in a festival that became "one of the most historic and culturally significant events, not only in the history of Black theatre, but in American theatre."

Fell in Love with the Theater

Born on September 25, 1948, Larry Leon Hamlin was the second of four children of Annie and Charles Hamlin. He grew up in Reidsville, North Carolina, about 45 minutes from Winston-Salem, deep in tobacco country. His father worked for the American Tobacco Company, his mother was a housewife, and according to North Carolina's *The News & Record*, Hamlin was "the first generation off the factory floor." He landed on the stage. Hamlin told *CBB* that he fell in love with the theater the moment he uttered his first line in a first-grade play. "Once I got back to class, I

immediately wanted to be back on the stage, so I raised my hand and asked if I could go to the bathroom" he told *CBB*. Back in the auditorium Hamlin continued, "I saw the stage and was so happy. I ran down to the stage and put my arms around the footlights. They were hot, really hot, but I hugged them." He embraced theater from that day on.

"My mother really supported my acting when I was a child," Hamlin told *CBB*. "She would work with me on my lines and help with delivery." Hamlin acted throughout childhood but after high school, he gravitated north and ended up majoring in business at Rhode Island's Johnson & Wales University. "After graduation I had to think about what I wanted to do for the rest of my life," Hamlin told *CBB*. "I thought about it and went all the way back to that experience I had when I was five, and I said, 'Of course, acting. That's what I love.'" Hamlin promptly enrolled in theater classes at Brown University and joined the school's theater company. "I've been focusing on my acting ever since," he told *CBB*.

There were very few black theaters in the country in the mid-1970s. Hamlin, with characteristic vision and a heavy dose of self-confidence, set about fixing that. He formed his first company, Star Theater Productions, while he was still in Rhode Island. However, the South was calling him back. "Eventually I had to go home so I came to Winston-Salem because my family had settled there," he told *CBB*. Again, he found that there was no local black theater. "In fact, not in the whole state of North Carolina," he told *CBB*. So with $2,000, Hamlin founded the North Carolina Black Repertory Company in 1979. He served as the company's executive and artistic director—a post he still held into 2004. He also acted, directed, and wrote plays. Like all small theaters, the company struggled. Over the years, it produced several local shows, launched national tours, and even took performances to the Caribbean. Much of the company's success was due to Hamlin's electric personality. Whether standing onstage, speaking about the state of black theater, or asking for donations, Hamlin's personal style oozed a can-do attitude that made people want to say "yes."

Inspired to Form Festival

In the mid-1980s Hamlin wrote an article about the state of black theater in the South. "As I was interviewing these different theater companies, I saw so much pain and frustration," he told *CBB*. "They didn't have money, didn't have good management, they couldn't put on the shows they wanted." He continued, "I began to wonder what was happening in the other parts of the country. And it was the same—pain, frustration. Then

I looked around in New York and saw that black theaters were closing at such a rate that I figured by the millennium they'd disappear." Hamlin decided something had to be done. "I didn't see anyone else doing it," he told *CBB*. He came up with the idea of a national black theater conference. "There were some successful companies out there, and I thought if we could share our experiences, we could build a core of black theater companies that could work together and develop an agenda for all of us," Hamlin told *American Visions*.

With a budget of $500,000 the National Black Theatre Festival debuted in 1989. "The first one we decided not to call a conference," Hamlin told *CBB*. "Conference sounds so boring. So we called it a festival. That sounds like a party. A celebration." A chance meeting with Maya Angelou at an airport bar gave the festival a needed boost of celebrity. "Most of the people I talked to thought I was crazy," Hamlin told the *Winston-Salem Journal*. "She said she would support my dream, as it were." Angelou signed on as the festival's first chairperson and brought along friend Oprah Winfrey as a celebrity guest. The star power worked. Over 10,000 people showed up to see 30 performances by 17 of the country's top black theater companies. Theater professionals took part in workshops on topics from raising money to producing new works. *The New York Times* wrote, "The 1989 National Black Theatre Festival was one of the most historic and culturally significant events in the history of black theatre and American theatre in general." Hamlin had struck a long-neglected nerve and revealed a hidden cultural resource. "At first I thought there were only about 60 or 70 black companies in the country," Hamlin told *CBB*. "I found out there were over 250. We didn't know about each other. We had never had an occasion to get together."

Subsequent festivals, held every two years, grew exponentially on all fronts. In 1991 the number of performances jumped to 45 performances and the workshops doubled. Celebrities flocked to Winston-Salem to take part, including black theater royalty Ossie Davis and Ruby Dee, who signed on as that year's chairpersons. By 1993 performances were up to 76. In 1995 international troupes joined in the festivities, coming from Africa, the Caribbean, and Latin America. Over 20,000 guests endured the North Carolina heat to see them perform. The prestige of the festival also grew. 1997 saw the premier of renowned playwright August Wilson's play, *Jitney*. By 1999 corporate heavy hitters had signed on as sponsors, including US Airways, Sara Lee Corporation, and R.J. Reynolds Tobacco Company. They were needed as the festival's budget had tripled to $1.5 million. The 2001 and 2003 festivals featured over 100 performances apiece and drew upwards of 50,000 guests each. By that time the festival had also added an awards gala, a film festival, poetry jams, a market, and true to its founding vision, dozens of workshops. "There's something going on morning, noon, and night," Hamlin told the *Winston-Salem Journal*.

Festival Surged in Popularity

The theme of the 2001 was "Black Theater, Holy Ground," which nicely summed up the way the festival had come to be viewed by those in the black theater community. "It's one of the greatest things we have going," actor Bill Cobbs told the *Winston-Salem Journal*. "In terms of having an opportunity to network and interact with people in the world of theater, it is a great thing." "It is so culturally significant to all of us, whether you are a nationally respected artist or some little theater practicing in a church basement," producer Ernie McClintock added. "It's a focal point for black cultural expression." It is also a focal point for celebrities. People like Denzel Washington, Sidney Poitier, Cicely Tyson, Angela Bassett, Leslie Uggams, Malik Yoba, and Malcolm-Jamal Warner are regulars year after year.

The festival also became a boon for the city of Winston-Salem, jam-packing hotels and restaurants and bringing in an estimated $11 million over a five-day period. "It obviously has a multimillion-dollar impact on the city," Gayle Anderson, the president of the Greater Winston-Salem Chamber of Commerce, told the *Winston-Salem Journal*. "But more important is the image we create of Winston-Salem as a cultural center. The fact that it is African-American theater is unique. We couldn't pay for all the publicity that this generates." Winston-Salem's mayor, Allen Joines, also hailed the importance of the festival, and gave direct credit to Hamlin. "This festival has brought international recognition to Winston-Salem, and I think Mr. Hamlin's work has really made it successful," Joines told the *Winston-Salem Journal* in 2002. "His personal perseverance has been key to the festival's success."

As the founder, artistic director, and producer of the festival, Hamlin's name became synonymous with the National Black Theatre Festival. Dressed in purple—his favorite color and the official color of the festival—Hamlin served as the festival's number one promoter, cheerleader, and fundraiser. For each festival he planned dozens of workshops, wooed hundreds of celebrities, screened thousands of plays, and raised hundreds of thousands of dollars. "I sleep very, very little," he told *CBB* in 2004. "For years I didn't sleep at all. Now I am starting to think that maybe I should get at least three hours a night." Ask anyone in black theater, anyone in Winston-Salem, and they will tell you his sleeplessness paid off. The *Winston-Salem Journal* noted, "Hamlin has been praised as a visionary who built a nationally recognized black-theater festival in a Southern city that many New York and Los Angeles actors would never visit." However he has not been without critics who have claimed that his over-the-top personality has wreaked financial and logistical havoc. In 2001, on the eve of the seventh festival, Hamlin

dismissed those critics. "If I did not know how to handle money this would have ended in 1989," he told the *Winston-Salem Journal*.

Hamlin was recognized for his work on behalf of black theater with dozens of awards, including a prestigious NAACP award for community service. However his biggest honor was an invitation to the White House from President and Mrs. Bill Clinton. "I wasn't even aware that he knew I existed," he told *CBB*.

Worked to the End

As 2004 came to a close, Hamlin was intensely planning the 2005 festival, scheduled to be "marvtastic"—a word Hamlin coined. "It is marvelous and fantastic, but what it means to me is there is nothing greater than this," he told *CBB*. The six-day festival was indeed "marvtastic." With 40 productions, it attracted nearly 60,000 people and an estimated $15 million to Winston-Salem. As he prepared for the next festival, Hamlin continued to run the North Carolina Black Repertory Company, writing plays, and of course, acting. He also had another big idea brewing—the National Black Theatre Hall of Fame and Museum. "There is a major need for it," he told *CBB*. "And it doesn't look like anyone else will do it, so here I go again."

Despite his ongoing enthusiasm for his work, Hamlin's health declined. Just before the 2007 festival opened, Hamlin died at the age of 58 on June 6, 2007, in his home in Pfafftown, North Carolina. His family attributed his death to a long-term illness, but did not disclose details. Hamlin did not die without recognizing the value of his life's work. Relating how much his hard work paid off since the first festival, Hamlin told Linda Armstrong of the *New York Amsterdam News* in 2005: "As I look back now over the things that have happened since…I am so proud." Those who worked alongside him found him an inspiration. The festival continued in his absence in 2007, and the Marvtastic Society, formed in 2003, pledged to continue the festival into the future. Cheryl Oliver, the acting interim director of the 2007 event, hoped that the festival would serve as Hamlin's legacy, according to the *Greensboro News & Record*. At Hamlin's memorial service in Winston-Salem more than 1,000 people, many wearing Hamlin's favorite purple color, gathered, but as the *Winston-Salem Journal* related, they were "in no mood to mourn." The service exuded a "the-show-must-go-on spirit," which boded well for Hamlin's life's work to live on in the enthusiasm and hard work of others.

Sources

Periodicals

American Visions, April-May, 1995.

Black Masks, August/September 2005, p. 7.

Cincinnati Enquirer, August 19, 2001.

Greensboro News & Record, June 7, 2007, p. A1.

News & Record, (Piedmont Triad, NC), August 31, 2001; August 24, 2003.

New York Amsterdam News, July 14-20, 2007, p. 22.

New York Times, August 8, 2003, p. E1; June 8, 2007, p. B7.

Winston-Salem Journal (Winston-Salem, NC), August 1, 1999; June 12, 2001; July 29, 2001; August 1, 2001; August 7, 2001; May 18, 2002; July 1, 2003; August 12, 2003; August 6, 2005, p. B7; June 14, 2007, p. 1.

On-line

The National Black Theatre Festival, www.nbtf.org (July 10, 2007).

Other

Additional information for this profile was obtained through an interview with Larry Leon Hamlin on November 9, 2004.

—Candace LaBalle and Sara Pendergast

Ben Harper

1969—

Singer, songwriter

Harper, Ben, photograph. AP Images.

Singer-songwriter Ben Harper came into the national spotlight in the 1990s as a retro 1960s-type folksinger, with songs such as "Like a King," which protested the Rodney King beating while referring at the same time to the legacy of Martin Luther King, Jr. He also appeared onstage singing his own adaptation of Maya Angelou's "And Still I Rise" without accompaniment, with his fist raised in the air. It soon became evident that Harper could do more than write earnest protest songs and strum an acoustic guitar, however. In the years since the release of his first album, Harper has been called the heir to Bob Marley as well as Jimi Hendrix. He has performed quiet and reverent gospel songs, covered hard-rocking tunes by Led Zeppelin, and played 1970s funk, as well as acoustic blues. Harper's versatility has become a hallmark of his powerful career. "The fact that I even exist in the record industry is outrageous, because everyone said I couldn't do it," Harper related to John Kreicbergs of *Pitch-Weekly*. "All the labels said, 'No, it's not this, it's not that, it's not the other thing.' But man, I've been doing it so wrong for so long, it's now become a style."

Grew Up Surrounded by Music

Harper was born October 28, 1969, in Pomona, California, and was raised in the Inland Empire region 50 miles east of Los Angeles. It is no wonder that Harper is able to draw from so many sources for his musical inspiration. His grandparents Charles and Dorothy Chase opened a music store in 1958 called the Claremont Folk Music Center. His grandfather played the lute and his grandmother played the guitar. Harper's parents were also musically inclined. His mother, Ellen, sang and played guitar while his father, Leonard, played the drums. Harper grew up in an environment saturated with many different types of music as well as books and different instruments from all over the world. When he was a teenager Harper listened to hip-hop, but his musical compass had already been set: he would play the music that he had grown up with, American roots music.

In his late teens Harper began to drift away from rap music and move toward the roots of today's popular music: the blues. He began to play Robert Johnson and

Son House, key figures in the formation of the Delta Blues tradition from the 1920s. It was this reverence for the old traditional forms of music that led him to his trademark sound, which comes from playing bottleneck slide guitar.

Harper told Jas Obrecht of *Guitar Player* about the influence of the early blues masters on his development as an artist: "I'd play those records at night, and then I'd go to school and hear them in my mind. The music that I was brought up with puts me in a trance, and that's the channel to the spirit of my music. I woodshedded on the bottleneck for years, putting in hours and hours a day to where morning would turn to night. I did that from the time I was 18 to 20. I was really trying to learn Robert Johnson tunes...Mississippi John Hurt just hit me like a truck, and that was something I had to play and be a part of. Then Taj Mahal called me up."

Harper had been playing acoustic blues sets in and around Los Angeles from the time he was 16 years old. At one of his shows, blues legend Taj Mahal noticed the serious young man playing the lap slide guitar and invited him on tour. In 1992 Harper appeared on the television show *Austin City Limits* as part of Mahal's band and collaborated with him on the soundtrack for *The Drinking Gourd*, a biography of Harriet Tubman. But Harper continued to play mostly the small local coffee shops with his vintage Weissenborn guitar, a completely hollow instrument handmade in the 1920s by Herman Weissenborn. Harper's childhood friend and producer J. P. Plunier was able to arrange meetings with Los Angeles record companies on the strength of the buzz surrounding "Like a King," but Harper's protest song scared some record executives away. In an article on the website of the American Society of Composers, Authors, and Publishers, Harper told Randy Grimmett about his meeting with the head of Virgin Records: "We were advised not to play 'Like a King' because it made the other A&R people nervous. So, of course, we get to the meeting and it's the first song I play. It turned out to be the song he liked most."

From that meeting Harper and Plunier received money to make a six-song demo, which turned into Harper's first album, 1994's *Welcome to the Cruel World*. The acoustic-based album was very different from the music that dominated the airwaves in the last gasp of the grunge era. But it was exactly that community that was most attracted to Harper's music. He and his band, The Innocent Criminals, began a marathon tour playing solo shows and warming up at the concerts of more well-known acts.

Gained Popularity and Grew Artistically

Harper told Jeffrey Pepper Rodgers of *Acoustic Guitar* magazine about one of his typical early shows: "I'll never forget opening up for P. J. Harvey—she invited us to tour with her. I'd sit down with an acoustic Weissenborn in front of 12-year-old girls with black eyeliner packed in the front row, looking up at me going, 'What in the hell is he playing?' But by the third or fourth song, the heads would start to nod, and then it would be on, you know. We never got stoned or anything like that—not yet."

It was during this ceaseless touring that the band worked on material for Harper's next release, 1995's *Fight for Your Mind*. Harper's song "Look Like Gold" also garnered some radio airtime. The record also yielded a two-year worldwide tour that found Harper traveling the globe to spread his music. Harper and his band toured throughout the United States and also in Europe and places like Turkey and New Zealand. While on the road Harper wrote material for his next album, which was released in 1997 and called *The Will to Live*. This record proved to be somewhat of a departure for Harper, as it featured a harder, more electric sound, especially on the record's single, "Faded," which featured a grinding electric guitar over Harper's hushed vocals. Harper was now playing with the heavyweights of the music industry such as Pearl Jam, Dave Mathews Band, and the Fugees, as well as blues and soul icons like John Lee Hooker and Ray Charles. He headlined at the HORDE Festival and played at the legendary Montreux Jazz Festival.

It was this variety of influences that led to the next album, *Burn to Shine*, which was released in 1999. On this record Harper fully spread his musical wings, showing his quiet spiritual side in "Two Hands of a Prayer," and from there going to the light and playful "Steal My Kisses," which attracted significant radio airplay. He went all electric on the album's title track and on "Forgiven," and ventured into the realms of reggae, soul, and even ragtime jazz on "Suzie Blue." Harper told Rodgers of *Acoustic Guitar* about his musical progression: "I do have to say that playing and expressing myself on electrics of late is renewing my focus and enthusiasm and excitement about acoustics. If I played only acoustic for my entire life, I would get bored. So for my own musical growth, I need to venture out into other worlds of music and sound."

Remained Committed to Music and Performing

Harper's versatility was showcased on 2001's *Live from Mars*, a two-disc concert recording. One disc features his acoustic music, including a soulful rendition of Marvin Gaye's "Sexual Healing," and the other disc features his more hard-edged music. Though *Live from Mars* was met with critical acclaim, Harper's life took a turn from the touring and recording cycle that he had known for the past six years. Harper's name began to appear in the gossip columns as much as it did in the music section of the newspapers. Late in 2001 it was reported that Harper had divorced his wife, Joanna, and bought a house in Los Angeles with actress Laura Dern. The couple married in 2005.

In the early 2000s Harper took time to found his own record label—Inland Emperor Records. His first artist, who had also appeared on selected recordings throughout Harper's four studio albums, was Patrick Brayer, the man who had given Harper his first paid gig. Brayer was the man who organized the Starvation Café series of concerts. The local concert promoter paid the stunned 16-year-old Harper half of the gate, which at that time was $75.

Harper enjoyed a growing fan base as he continued touring and recording, releasing a new album each year from 2003. In 2004 he collaborated with the gospel quartet, the Blind Boys of Alabama, to produce the Grammy-Award-winning album *There Will Be a Light,* and recorded *Live at the Apollo* with them on tour. Though his record sales increased dramatically since 1997, with his 2006 album *Both Sides of the Gun* reaching number seven on the Billboard charts, he remained focused his ability to perform his music live. He even tried to translate the power of live performance to his 2007 studio album, *Lifeline*; Harper and his band the Innocent Criminals gathered in a Paris recording studio immediately following an extensive tour to record the album in just seven days. Harper explained the benefit of recording in such a manner to Jonathan Cohen of *Billboard.com*: "I had always wanted to make a record directly coming off of a tour. It just makes sense. You've got all your best equipment and your musical abilities are never as sharp or as heightened as when you've been consistently on the road."

Harper's obsession with perfecting his music revealed itself as his ultimate goal in interviews over the years. Harper had told Lisa Wilton of the *Calgary Sun* in 2000: "I'll never be a rock star and I'll never care to be. It doesn't interest me. It's not me being a rock star, it's me being perceived as a rock star. There's a difference. I feel no physical, spiritual, psychological or egotistical

connection to that term at all. My commitment and discipline is in writing songs and playing them well live." Even as the crowds thronging to see his live performances swelled and his popularity, especially in France and Australia, approached "superstar status," according to BBC Radio, Harper remained true to his word: his music remained his focus, not his fame.

Selected discography

Albums

Pleasure and Pain, Cardas Records, 1992.
Welcome to the Cruel World, Virgin Records, 1994.
Fight for Your Mind, Virgin Records, 1995.
The Will to Live, Virgin Records, 1997.
Burn to Shine, Virgin Records, 1999.
Live from Mars, Virgin Records, 2001.
Diamonds on the Inside, Virgin Records, 2003.
There Will Be a Light, Virgin Records, 2004.
Live at the Apollo, Virgin Records, 2005.
Both Sides of the Gun, Virgin Records, 2006.
Lifeline, Virgin Records, 2007.

Sources

Periodicals

Calgary Sun, August 22, 2000.
Guitar Player, September, 1997.
PitchWeekly, June 5, 2003.
New York Post, 2002.
New York Times, June 18, 2007, p. E1.
Voice (London, England), March 22-26, 2006, p. 6.
Washington Post, September 12, 2006, p. C14.

On-line

"Awards for World Music 2007: Ben Harper," *BBC Radio,* www.bbc.co.uk/radio3/worldmusic/a4wm-2007/2007_ben_harper.shtml (July 23, 2007). *Ben Harper*, www.benharper.net (July 10, 2007).
"Ben Harper Sends Out a 'Lifeline' in August," *Billboard.com,* www.billboard.com/bbcom/news/article_display.jsp?vnu_content_id=1003581298 (July 23, 2007).
"Ben Harper: Will = Power," *American Society of Composers, Authors and Publishers,* www.ascap.com/musicbiz/harper.html (July 23, 2007).
"Next Generation Blues," *Acoustic Guitar*, www.acousticguitar.com/issues/ag88/CoverStory.shtml (July 22, 2007).
"Talking Head," *Perth Now,* www.news.com.au/perthnow/story/0,21598,21440848-5005381,00.html (July 23, 2007).

Other

Pleasure and Pain (documentary film), by Danny Clinch, 2000.

—Michael J. Watkins and Sara Pendergast

Kimberly N. Holland

19(??)—

Sports agent, business executive

When Olympic silver medalist Terrence Trammell persuaded her to act as his agent in negotiating a sports contract, Kimberly N. Holland found her calling. As one of very few African-American women sports agents, Holland was able not only to help young athletes navigate the complex world of professional and amateur athletics, but also to provide an example of honesty, integrity, and respect, both to her clients and to other young women who aspired to a career in sports law. Holland found that sports law enabled her to serve her religious principles and her community.

Determined to Pursue a Law Career at an Early Age

Kimberly Novella Holland was born in Norfolk, Virginia. When she was three years old, she, her sister, Sabrina, and her mother Joyce moved to Washington, D.C., where her mother married a police officer named Don S. Sauls. Sauls would become not only young Kimberly's stepfather, but also the man she considered her true father. During the later years of Holland's childhood, Joyce Sauls worked as a unit secretary at the city's prestigious Columbia Hospital for Women.

The Sauls lived in a largely black neighborhood in the nation's capitol city. Even though, she was raised as a Baptist, Kimberly attended local Catholic schools, chosen for their academic excellence and disciplined structure: St. Thomas Moore for grade school and All Saints Academy for high school. Holland's parents were watchful and protective of their children, driving them

to school and scheduling after school activities to keep them busy and out of trouble. Holland achieved good grades and involved herself in student government as well as many other school programs, including becoming editor of the yearbook and co-captain of the cheerleading squad. She was also an expressive girl who liked to discuss and debate, prompting her parents to suggest that she become a lawyer. Because she liked the idea of solving problems and making peace between conflicting parties, Holland decided at a young age to become not just a lawyer, but a judge.

When she was in the eighth grade, Holland also developed an interest in modeling. Tall, thin, and attractive, she attended classes at the internationally known John Casablancas Modeling and Career Centers. She found work as a model in high school and in college. She also earned extra money working part-time babysitting and clerking in a shoe store.

After graduating from All Saints Academy, Holland returned to her Virginia birthplace to attend the historically black Norfolk State University. She earned her bachelor's degree in political science, a common pre-law major. While in college, Holland began exploring different areas of law, hoping, as she related to *Contemporary Black Biography* (*CBB*), that the God she worshiped would make it clear to her which direction she should take. Following her childhood ambition, she worked as an intern in judges' offices and other types of law offices, from personal injury to criminal law, but did not find the work as satisfying as she had hoped. After graduation, she returned home to Washington, D.C., to work in the offices of Massachusetts democratic

At a Glance . . .

Born Kimberly Novella Holland on February 25, 19(??) in Norfolk, VA; married 1996 (divorced 2006). *Education:* Norfolk State University, BA political science, 1992; Regent University, JD, 2002.

Career: LaFace Records, paralegal, 1994-96; Ernst and Young, executive consulting assistant, 1996-99; Icon Management, president, chief executive officer, and sports agent, 2002–.

Memberships: Alpha Kappa Alpha sorority.

Addresses: *Office*—3455 Peachtree Road, Suite 500, Atlanta, GA 30326.

Senator Edward M. Kennedy starting in 1992. Though she found the work interesting, she left after two years. The values of the political arena clashed with her own deeply held spiritual values, and she continued to feel that she had not found the work she was meant to do.

Energized by Entertainment Law

While she was at college, Holland had become aware of another area of law practice when, after emceeing a campus concert, she was offered an ongoing job by the concert promoter. Working as a personal assistant to the entertainers, Holland enjoyed meeting such performers as Whitney Houston, Bobby Brown, Boyz II Men, and Babyface, and she began to feel that entertainment law might be the right field for her. Though she continued to investigate other areas of law, she eventually accepted a job offer with Allan Haymon Productions, one of the biggest promotion companies in the world. The company was based in Atlanta, Georgia, and Holland moved to Atlanta, excited at the prospect of working in the entertainment field. Once in Atlanta, however, she decided not to accept the position at Allan Haymon and took a job instead at LaFace Records, a successful music company formed during the 1990s by musicians Antonio Reid and Kenneth Edmonds. The name LaFace is a combination of Reid's and Edmonds' stage names, "LA" and "Babyface." Holland worked as a paralegal, or legal assistant, for LaFace's legal affairs department.

After leaving LaFace Records, Holland married and took what she felt was a more stable job as an executive consulting assistant with the prestigious accounting firm of Ernst and Young. After three years there, she decided it was time to fulfill her lifelong dream of entering law school. Still devoutly religious, Holland wanted to attend a law school that was founded on

Christian principals. She chose Regent University School of Law in Virginia Beach, Virginia, and began attending classes in the fall of 1999.

During her last year of law school, Holland stumbled on still another kind of legal career. Terrence Trammell, her then brother-in-law and a talented track athlete, was dissatisfied with his sports agent and asked Holland to replace him. (At the time, Holland used her married name, Kimberly N. Trammell professionally.) She refused at first, saying that she had no experience and little interest in sports, but Trammell was persistent and persuasive. He had confidence that Holland could perform well as a sports agent, and, after many prayers, she finally agreed to give it a try.

As Holland began to pursue her career in entertainment law, she herself was pursued by track and field athletes who had heard of her through Trammell. She began to consider the idea of opening her own agency. She had never before considered starting her own business, and the idea of being on her own was a bit frightening. However, she had not found the career she believed God intended for her in any of the law offices where she had worked. She wanted to do work that she could be proud of, and the idea of being her own boss appealed to her. As a sports agent, she would not only use her legal education, but she could help young athletes achieve their goals and protect their careers. As one of a very small number of female black sports agents, she could provide an example of integrity and self-confidence to athletes and other agents. Finally, Holland felt that she had found the work she was meant to do, and it seemed appropriate that it took courage and faith to make the leap to do it.

In 2002, she got her sports agent license from the U.S.A. Track and Field Association and the International Association of Athletics Federation and opened her business, Icon Management, Inc. She did not advertise or recruit; all of her clients were referred to her by word of mouth. By 2004, Icon Management had a roster of 11 world-class track and field clients, including Olympic gold medalist Shawn Crawford. The company opened a new facility in the Buckhead area of Atlanta, and Holland hired a new assistant, her youngest sister. In 2007, Holland was on a panel at the first University of Virginia School of Law Symposium on Sports and Entertainment Law.

Trusted by her clients and respected by her colleagues, Holland has become a successful sports agent, but she has not abandoned her interest in entertainment law and still considers creating an artists division of Icon Management, Inc.

Sources

Periodicals

Atlanta Tribune, July 2005, p. 12.
Ebony, June 2005, p. 164.

On-line

"First Virginia Sports and Entertainment Law Symposium," *University of Virginia School of Law,* www.law.virginia.edu/pdf/sports_law_07.pdf (July 2, 2007).

Other

Information for this profile was obtained through an interview with Kimberly Holland, April 30, 2007.

—Tina Gianoulis

Willie Hutch

1944-2005

Songwriter, producer, and singer

Many different people have been credited over the years with creating the classic "Motown sound," from the studio musicians who can be heard on scores of recordings to Motown founder Berry Gordy himself. Meanwhile, lurking behind the scenes are the likes of Willie Hutch, the songwriter, producer, and performer who wrote, produced, and arranged dozens of Motown hits over a career spanning more than 20 years. During his time at Motown during the label's "golden age," Hutch worked with such stars as Michael Jackson, Diana Ross, Marvin Gaye, Smokey Robinson, and Junior Walker. Hutch's own recordings have been sampled countless times in recent years by contemporary performers who have been drawn to the soulful soundtracks he created during the 1970s "blaxploitation" era in film.

Willie McKinley Hutchinson was born on December 6, 1944, in Los Angeles, California. When he was a small child, he moved with his mother and three siblings—two brothers and a sister—to Dallas, Texas, where they lived with his grandmother and an aunt. As a youth, Hutch showed considerable musical promise. He immersed himself in gospel, jazz, and rhythm and blues, and learned to play several instruments. While still a student at Booker T. Washington High School in Dallas, Hutch formed his own doo-wop band, called the Ambassadors, and he began writing his own songs for the group.

After high school, Hutch joined the U.S. Marines, with whom he served a two-year tour of duty. When his military service was over, he resettled in Los Angeles with the intention of forging a career in the music industry. He did not have to wait long to break into the music business. He released his debut single, "Love Has Put Me Down," in 1964. The following year, Hutch met a photographer named Lemonte McLemore. McLemore was in the process of forming a vocal group built around two former Miss Bronze America titlists. The group was to be called the Versatiles. Popular singer Johnny Rivers signed McLemore's group to a contract, under the condition that they change their name to the Fifth Dimension. As their debut single, the Fifth Dimension chose to release a song written by their new friend Hutch, called "I'll Be Loving You Forever." Hutch went on to write several more songs for that group, and he co-produced their 1967 hit album *Up, Up and Away*. On the strength of that album, the Fifth Dimension went on to become one of the best-selling musical acts of the era.

With his foot—as well as the rest of his body—firmly in the door of the music industry, Hutch was ready to launch his own career as a performing artist. In 1969 he signed with the RCA record label and released his first solo album, *Soul Portrait*. He would go on to release 16 more albums by the end of his career.

Hutch's biggest career breakthrough came in 1970. Hal Davis, a prominent producer for Motown Records, called Hutch in the middle of the night desperate for help. The Jackson 5 was scheduled to record a new song the next morning, but Motown honcho Berry

At a Glance . . .

Born Willie McKinley Hutchinson on December 6, 1944, in Los Angeles, CA; died on September 19, 2005, in Duncanville, TX; children: six. *Education:* Booker T. Washington High School, Dallas, TX. *Military service:* U.S. Marines.

Career: The Ambassadors (doo-wop group), founder; recording artist, 1964-2005; RCA label artist, 1969-70; music arranger, 1970-2005; staff writer/producer, Motown Records, 1971-94.

Gordy was unhappy with the material in its present state. Davis needed Hutch to rework the song into a form that would meet with Gordy's approval. Hutch worked through the night and delivered the finished song by 8:00 in the morning. He was then summoned into the studio right away to arrange the vocals. The song, "I'll Be There," was recorded on schedule. Featuring the 12-year-old Michael Jackson on the lead vocal, it became Motown's best selling hit up to that time, reaching to top of the both the pop and R&B charts in the United States and reaching number four in the United Kingdom.

Having come through in a big way for Gordy and Davis, Hutch was quickly hired to arrange some other Jackson 5 songs, and soon after he was signed on by Motown as a full-time staff writer and producer. He was with Motown during the label's heyday, working over the next two decades with such superstars as Smokey Robinson, Marvin Gaye, Diana Ross, Michael Jackson, and Aretha Franklin. In addition to his work for Motown, Hutch had a lasting impact on the movie industry. He wrote the soundtracks for two iconic blaxploitation films of the early 1970s: *The Mack* (1973) and *Foxy Brown* (1974). Blaxploitation refers to a 1970s genre of low-budget, violent pictures aimed at a black, urban audience. These movies featured funk/soul soundtracks, and had themes that often involved cool, urban African-American heroes turning the tables on corrupt white establishment figures.

In the hip-hop generation, blaxploitation films found a new audience that identified with the brutal violence and ambiguous morality of the genre. Consequently, the music and songs Hutch had written in the early 1970s gained a new popularity more than 20 years later. Pieces of Hutch's soundtrack for the *Mack* were sampled by a number of hip-hop artists, including Biggie Smalls, Lil' Kim, and Moby. The Chemical Brothers, a British electronic music duo, not only sampled Hutch's song "Brother's Gonna Work It Out"

from the *Mack* soundtrack—creating a United Kingdom rave anthem in the process—but they made the original "Brother's Gonna Work It Out" the title track on a DJ mix album. Another track from the *Mack* was featured in the 2005 film *Hustle & Flow,* a winner at the Sundance Film Festival.

Hutch recorded several more solo albums with Motown, before jumping ship for the rival Whitfield record label in the late 1970s. By 1982 he was back at Motown, recording his own albums and writing and producing for others musicians. His song "In and Out" was a modest dancefloor hit in 1982, and he scored a minor hit in 1985 with the song "The Glow" from the soundtrack to the movie the *Last Dragon.* Hutch continued to work as a producer for Motown into the 1990s. In 1994 he moved back to Dallas, where he continued to record and perform when he felt like it, while royalties from his old hits and samples used in new hits generated a very comfortable income. In 1998 Motown released *The Very Best of Willie Hutch,* a compilation of Hutch's best work over his long career with the label. Hutch released his final album, *Sexalicious,* in 2002.

Hutch died in Texas on September 19, 2005, at the age of 60, leaving behind six children, ten grandchildren, one great-grandchild, and legions of saddened music fans. On February 8, 2007, many of the recording industry's biggest celebrities gathered to celebrate Hutch's life and art and perform some of his music at a gala tribute event at the Biltmore Hotel in Los Angeles. Proceeds from the event, called "From the Heart," were given to the Booker T. Washington High School for the Performing and Visual Arts and the American Society of Young Musicians.

Selected discography

Singles

"Brother's Gonna Work It Out," Motown, 1973.
"Slick," Motown, 1973.
"Sunshine Lady," Motown, 1973.
"If You Ain't Got No Money," Motown, 1974.
"Get Ready for the Get Down," Motown, 1975.
"Party Down," Motown, 1976.
"Shake It, Shake It," Motown, 1977.
"We Gonna Party Tonight," Motown, 1977.
"All American Funkathon," Motown, 1978.
"What You Gonna Do After the Party," Motown, 1978.
"In and Out," Motown, 1982.

Albums

Soul Portrait, RCA, 1969.
Seasons for Love, RCA, 1970.
Fully Exposed, Motown, 1973.

The Mack (soundtrack), Motown, 1973.
Foxy Brown (soundtrack), Motown, 1975.
Mark of the Beast, Motown, 1975.
Ode to My Lady, Motown, 1975.
Color Her Sunshine, Motown, 1976.
Havin' a House Party, Motown, 1977.
In Tune, Whitfield, 1979.
Midnight Dancer, Whitfield, 1980.
In & Out, Motown, 1983.
Making a Game Out of Love, Motown, 1985.
The Last Dragon (soundtrack), Motown, 1985.
From the Heart, GGIT, 1994.
The Mack Is Back, Midwest, 1996.
Sexalicious, GGIT, 2002.

Sources

Periodicals

Guardian, October 4, 2005, p. 32.
Sacramento Observer, June 12, 2002, p. E5.
Times (London), September 27, 2005, p. 60.

On-line

"From the Heart: In Memory of Willie Hutch," *Willie Hutch: A Tribute to the Man, the Music, and the Art,* www.williehutch.org/bio.php (March 5, 2007).

—Bob Jacobson

Charles H. James III

1959(?)–

Business executive

When Charles H. James III became CEO of his family's West Virginia-based food distribution company, he inherited the nation's oldest black-owned business. James's great grandfather, Charles H. James, had begun the business back in 1883 when segregation and racism were still the order of the day. Peddling fresh eggs and produce from a bedraggled backpack, he eventually moved up to a mule-drawn wagon and finally to a warehouse. Over the decades, James' descendents grew the company and by the mid-1960s it was a million-dollar business. "Each generation of my family has created a bigger and better company," James told the *Los Angeles Times.* "All my forefathers are my heroes—but especially my great-grandfather. When you consider what he did in his time, I really have no excuses." Indeed, James has employed no excuses. During the more than two decades he has led the firm, he has set an aggressive pace for growth. "I've never viewed this company as a local business selling food in Charleston," he told *Black Enterprise.* "I always saw it as a base from which to build an international food distribution empire." In pursuing this goal, he has driven the C. H. James Company to its current position as a national leader in food distribution and a major player in the fast-food industry. In 2006, C. H. James was counting some $60 million in sales, a success that aptly reflected his family's 124-year legacy of entrepreneurial success.

Charles Howell James III was born in the late 1950s and raised near the Charleston, West Virginia base of his family's business, then called C. H. James and Company. He grew up helping his father with tasks from driving trucks to making phone calls to "candling" eggs, a process of looking inside the shell of an egg with a candle to ensure the freshness of the yolk. Though his three sisters Sheila, Stephanie, and Sarah went on to pursue careers outside of the family business, James recalled to *Black Enterprise,* "As a child growing up in West Virginia, I always knew I would someday work with my father." At Morehouse College in Atlanta, George, James studied history and business. Upon graduating in 1981, he worked for two years as a banker in Chicago.

In the 1950s, James' father, Charles H. James II had earned a Masters of Business Administration (MBA) from the prestigious Wharton School of Business and James III followed in those footsteps. His two years at the University of Pennsylvania-based school were a training ground for his future takeover of the family firm. His Wharton master's thesis chronicled his family's three generations of entrepreneurial success. After graduating in 1985 he was offered very lucrative banking jobs with Chase and Citicorp in New York City, but he had already made the decision to go home. "I felt like the base was here to build on," he told the *Charleston Daily Mail.* "I was proud of what my family had done, and it's the American dream to own a business." He added, "I considered it an honor to work in the family business."

Even before he graduated from Wharton, James had begun to contribute to company's coffers. By the 1980s, C. H. James had begun to stagnate. Competition from national supermarket chains and discount food wholesalers had limited their food delivery service

At a Glance . . .

Born in 1959(?), in West Virginia; married, Jeralyn; children: three; *Education:* Morehouse College, 1981; University of Pennsylvania, Wharton School of Business, MBA, 1985.

Career: Continental Illinois National Bank and Trust Co., Chicago, IL, banking associate, 198(?)-83; C.H. James & Co., Charleston, WV, management, 1985-88; president and CEO, 1988–; North American Produce, CA, CEO, 1992-99; Produce Online, Charleston, WV, CEO, 1999-2000; PrimeSource FoodService Equipment Inc., Dallas, TX, CEO, 2001-03; C. H. James Restaurant Holdings, CEO, Deerfield, IL, 2003–.

Memberships: Commerce Bank, Charleston, WV, board member; Morehouse College, Trustee; West Virginia Economic Development Authority, treasurer; University of Charleston, trustee; Charleston Area Medical Center, board member.

Awards: U.S. Department of Agriculture, Minority Contractor of the Year Award, 1988, 1989 and 1990; Small Business Association Mid-Atlantic Region, Minority Small Businessman of the Year, 1990; Morehouse College, Bennie Leadership Award, 2001; Dow Jones, Award for Entrepreneurial Excellence; Office of the Governor, Distinguished West Virginian Award.

Addresses: *Office*—C. H. James Restaurant Holdings LLC, Deerfield Executive Center, 1020 N. Milwaukee Avenue, Ste. 360, Deerfield, IL 60015. *Web*—www. chjamesco.com.

to local hospitals and restaurants in a ten-county region and sales had leveled off to just above $4 million. During his business studies, James learned of a government program that allowed minority-owned business to skip the competitive bidding process for government contracts. During Christmas break from classes, he helped his father fill out the necessary paperwork and a year later, the firm started landing government contracts. This would be the key to the future of the company. "I realized that we wouldn't grow by remaining a local distributor," James told the *Los Angeles Times*. "I always considered the government business a means for building enough revenue to expand to the national level."

James joined C. H. James full-time in 1985 working alongside his father, the then-CEO. James continued to pursue government contracts and worked on revising the company in general. When the elder James retired in 1988, James became CEO at age 29. He promptly modernized the firm's business practices. He introduced the company's first mission statement, rewrote job descriptions, streamlined operations, created training programs, and introduced productivity incentive programs. Overall employee response was positive. "Chuck allows people to become more involved in the company and the decisions that are made. That makes you feel more responsible for your job and the outcome," the firm's comptroller told *Black Enterprise*. James also landed lucrative contracts with the Department of Veterans Affairs, the Department of Agriculture, and the Department of Defense. The results were impressive. Over the next five years, the company had an average annual sales increase of 38 percent, reaching $18 million per year by 1992. Prestigious small business awards started to line the walls of the company and *Black Enterprise* named C. H. James "Company of the Year" for 1992.

Some business leaders might have been happy with continuing this trend but James wanted more. "Chuck is always aggressive," a local Charleston banker told *Black Enterprise*. "He prefers to spend more time working on larger scale projects that are going to make more money in the long run." After divesting 49 percent of the local business, he used the funds to purchase a controlling stake in North American Produce, a California-based distributor responsible for delivering produce to 2,000 McDonald's restaurants nationwide. James invested $1 million in equipment and increased productivity 40 percent. With C. H. James now positioned as a holding company, sales for 1999 exceeded $31 million. James sold his interests in North American in 1999 and joined the internet boom just long enough to turn a profit of $16 million in one year with his start-up, ProduceOnline.com.

In 2001, C. H. James Holding purchased a controlling interest in PrimeSource, a Dallas-based company that delivered restaurant equipment to over 27,000 fast-food restaurants including Pizza Hut, KFC, and Taco Bell. As CEO, James took the company to $140 million in revenues in 2003, but again he chose to sell his interests in the company. In 2004 he joined forces with Goldman Sachs's Urban Investment Group to form C. H. James Restaurant Holdings, and they soon purchased 37 Burger King restaurants in Chicago. Within three years, they bought six more, making James one of Burger King's largest franchisees and its largest African-American franchisee. In 2006, sales reached nearly $60 million. His continual purchase and sale of businesses has prompted some to call James a 'serial entrepreneur,' a term he has rejected. Instead, he has consistently reflected his success back on family tradition. "This is what really defines our family," he told *Black Enterprise*. "It is truly an honor to be able to do what I do, and hopefully have something to pass on to the next generation." As he entered his third decade of leading the company, he planned to maintain his family's track record of success long enough for his three sons to become the fifth generation to inherit the family business.

Sources

Periodicals

Black Enterprise, June 1992, p. 142; May 2000, p. 116; June 2001, p. 46; June 2003, p. 165; February 2005, p. 36.

Charleston Daily Mail, July 7, 1992, October 4, 1988.

Los Angeles Times, June 1, 1997, p. D1.

On-line

C. H. James Companies, www.chjamesco.com (July 3, 2007).

—Candace LaBalle

Avery Johnson

1965—

Professional basketball coach, basketball player

Johnson, Avery, photograph. AP Images.

In 2005, Avery Johnson became the eighth head coach of the Dallas Mavericks franchise in the National Basketball Association (NBA). Although he had no experience as a coach beyond youth basketball and was best known as an NBA player, he proved to be something of a prodigy. He took over as head coach during the 2004-05 season, and he steered the club to the finals of the NBA championship tournament during his first full season in 2005-06. Beyond his concrete measures of ability, Johnson also had intangible marks of charisma that were so important in marketing-heavy professional sports: simply put, Johnson was fun to watch. Amateur video-makers posted short films of his antics on the YouTube on-line video site, and video views of "The Little General" numbered as high as the hundreds of thousands.

From Substitute to Starter

A native of New Orleans, Avery Johnson was born on March 25, 1965, and the Louisiana accent that flavored his instructions to players became an integral part of his appeal. From the start, on the basketball court, he made up in hustle for what he lacked in stature. Attending St. Augustine High in New Orleans, he grew slowly; although he reached an adult height of five feet, eleven inches, he was only five feet three as a high school senior. "When you first saw him, you wondered if he could play basketball," St. Augustine coach Bernard Griffith told Lars Anderson of *Sports Illustrated.*

Johnson's high school career was anything but illustrious. "I was the 14th man on a 14-member team," he recalled to Anderson. "I was the backup to the backup's backup." Despite his meager average of 1.1 points per game, however, Johnson became part of the starting lineup when St. Augustine competed in and won the 1983 Louisiana state high school championships after the team's starting point guard was suspended. College scouts were in the crowd, and Johnson snared an athletic scholarship from New Mexico Junior College.

Playing for one season there, and for another at Cameron University in Lawton, Oklahoma, Johnson won a scholarship back home in Louisiana, at Southern University in Baton Rouge, part of the Southwest Athletic Conference or SWAC. He grew over his college career from five feet three to five feet eleven, and his list of on-court accomplishments grew. In both of his two years as a guard at Southern, he led the National Collegiate Athletic Association in assists. His NCAA Division I records for most assists in a single game, highest single-season assist average, and highest career assist average still stood in 2007. Some of his greatest accomplishments, though, came in the area of leadership. "AJ kept all the kids straight," Southern coach Ben Jobe told Anderson. "When I had AJ, we never had guys breaking into Coke machines, breaking curfew. AJ is what you need if you want a guy who has character."

Trained for Success

Johnson was short for the NBA, even playing at the position of guard. His record as a shooter was modest, and he was not picked in the NBA draft after graduating from Southern with a degree in psychology in 1988. That was a setback that would have ended the careers of most players, but, he told Anderson, "I just

wasn't ready to stop playing. If I wasn't good enough to be a pro, so be it, but I was going to find out myself." He began a gym routine that even at the end of his career would see him training for five hours every afternoon, and he signed on for the summer with the Palm Beach Stingrays of the United States Basketball League. That fall, he joined the Seattle SuperSonics as a free agent.

That began an NBA career that was spotty at times but that steadily built as Johnson worked on his game. He remained with the Supersonics, getting into games mostly as a substitute, and was traded in the fall of 1990 to the Denver Nuggets only to be dumped by Nuggets coach Paul Westhead in an airport on Christmas Eve. Another unkindly timed blow came in 1991, after he signed as a free agent with the San Antonio Spurs and agreed to serve as a groomsman at the wedding of teammates David Robinson. At the wedding reception, he was given the pink slip by San Antonio assistant coach Gregg Popovich. The news was a sour note in an otherwise good year; Johnson had gone home to New Orleans to marry his wife, Cassandra, earlier that year. The couple went on to raise two children, Christianne and Avery Jr.

Johnson bounced back with a free-agent signing in Houston, but the Rockets too dropped him at the end of the 1991-92 season. He spent another year with San Antonio in 1992-93. By this time Johnson seemed headed for the fate of an NBA journeyman who saw action only occasionally in the later stages of a game, but close observers, including Popovich (who had been promoted to San Antonio general manager), noticed that his hard work was beginning to pay off. With The Golden State Warriors in 1993-94, he cracked the starting lineup as a guard after an injury to star shooter Tim Hardaway, breaking into season double figures with an average of 10.9 points per game. His points-per-game average increased in each of his first seven seasons in the NBA, and his season field-goal percentage, at first an anemic 35 percent, hovered around the 50 percent mark by the mid-1990s.

Popovich brought Johnson back to San Antonio for the 1994-95 season, and Johnson remained there until 2001. The stability did his game good as he notched five more seasons with points-per-game averages in double digits. He narrowly missed that mark in 1999 with 9.7 points per game, but that year he had the satisfaction of making a shot that clinched the Spurs' first title in franchise history. The energetic Johnson acquired a fan base of his own and a nickname, "Taz," to go with it.

A popular figure in the San Antonio community, Johnson participated in many charitable activities and won the Spirit of Philanthropy Award from the Nonprofit Resource Center of Texas in 1999, as well as *USA Weekend* magazine's Most Caring Athlete award. He had a standing group of 25 tickets for Spurs games that he donated to underprivileged area children. Many of Johnson's off-court activities were motivated by his Christian faith, and he liked to say that the perfect day involved two "B's"—Bible study and biking. A member of Antioch Baptist Church in San Antonio, he played a role in efforts to construct a new church school there.

Developed Leadership Qualities

On the court, Johnson began to develop leadership qualities—and they were of an unorthodox kind. He was famous among his teammates for pre-game pep talks that combined basketball and Scripture in roughly equal proportions. One, delivered before a game against Golden State during the successful 1998-99 campaign, delved into the military conflicts described in the Old Testament Book of Joshua. Joshua, Johnson related, sent only a small part of his Israelite army to attack the small town of Ai, thinking it would be easily conquered. "Do you know what happened?" Johnson warned (according to Anderson). "They got busted in the mouth!"

After he left the Spurs in 2001, Johnson's playing career wound down. He spent part of the 2001-02 season with the Denver Nuggets and then moved to the Dallas Mavericks in a mid-season trade in February of 2002. Traded to Golden State, he spent the 2003-04 season there and then signed with Dallas as a free agent once again in September 9, 2004. He did not take the field for the 2004-05 season, retiring as a player in October of that year with an average of 8.4 points per game over 1,054 games. He was the all-time leader in assists among Spurs players and ranks 28th in NBA history in assists.

From the time he joined the team, however, the Mavericks had other things in mind for Johnson than just some late-game sub slots. Having already assisted the club's coaching staff during playoff runs in 2002 and 2003, he was hired as an assistant coach for the 2004-05 season. The high-powered but somewhat unfocused Mavericks offense entertained fans but failed to propel the Mavericks to a coveted NBA finals spot. Johnson, as assistant coach, brought a new intensity to the Mavericks' game. "Suddenly," assistant coach Del Harris told Jack McCallum of Sports Illustrated, "we had this guy with all this energy running up and down the court with the guys, hooting and hollering on every play. Nellie [head coach Don Nelson] and I would just fill in the blanks whenever we had to. Avery's voice became the voice the players knew."

So it came as no surprise when, on March 19, 2005, Mavericks owner Mark Cuban elevated Johnson to the position of head coach after Nelson's resignation. What was a surprise was how quickly the novice coach succeeded. The Mavericks under Johnson closed out the 2004-05 seasons by winning 16 of their last 18

games. The following season showed that the performance was no fluke as the Mavericks advanced to the NBA finals for the first time in team history and nearly won the championship, going out to a 2-0 lead before falling to the Miami Heat. Johnson won 66 of his first 82 games as head coach, demolishing the previous record over that stretch by a four-win margin.

Johnson attributed his success to the long period of hard knocks he had endured as a player. Not particularly popular among Mavericks players, he was credited with sharpening the games of several of them, in particular center Dirk Nowitzki. "You know, in this situation, everybody feels that I got this job so suddenly," Johnson observed to David Aldridge of the Philadelphia Inquirer. "But this is my 18th year in the NBA, so whether it's as a player or a coach or combined, you know, this is 18 years in basketball, after playing a thousand and something games, when I wasn't necessarily invited to the party, all right? I had to kind of come in through the back door."

Johnson was named NBA Coach of the Year for 2005-06. In the 2006 NBA All-Star Game, he was named coach of the Western Conference Squad. He brought the Mavericks to the playoffs once again in 2006-07, but the team was shocked in the first round as the Golden State Warriors defeated the Mavericks in six games. Fans still found the charisma of the hard-driving Johnson, dubbed the "Little General," an endless source of fascination. Amateur video of Johnson surfaced frequently on YouTube and other Internet sites, with a short clip of Johnson inadvertently (and obliviously) elbowing forward Josh Howard in the groin while signaling officials for a quick substitution garnered more than 250,00 viewings on YouTube as of mid-2007. The Mavericks, under their new coach, looked like consistent championship contenders, and, noted McCallum, "in a sporting culture desperate for the unvarnished and the unexpected, he was a frequent, high-pitched source of both. Rest assured there are more Avery Moments to come."

Sources

Books

Reach Beyond the Break: The Avery Johnson Story, A&D Communications, 2002.

Periodicals

Fort Worth Star-Telegram, April 29, 2007.
Houston Chronicle, April 21, 2007, p. 7.
Men's Health, May 2007, pp. 164-170.
Philadelphia Inquirer, June 10, 2006.
Sporting News, May 6, 2005, p. 14.
Sports Illustrated, July 7, 1999, p. 44; December 25, 2006, p. 78.

On-line

"Avery Johnson," *Dallas Mavericks Official Website,* www.nba.com/coachfile/avery_johnson/index.html-?nav=page (July 6, 2007).
"Family Never Far from Johnson's Mind," *Dallas Morning News,* www.dallasnews.com/sharedcon tent/dws/spt/basketball/mavs/stories/050107dnspoavery.3896ea3.html (June 12, 2007).
"Player Profile: Avery Johnson," *National Basketball Association,* www.nba.com (April 28, 2007).

—James M. Manheim

Doris W. Jones

1914(?)-2006

Dance instructor, choreographer

Though she had never seen a black ballet dancer at the time, Doris W. Jones was so fascinated by ballet as a young girl that she decided she would make it her life's work to provide classical dance training to children of color. Denied such training herself, she studied on her own and established the Jones-Haywood School of Ballet in Washington, D.C., in 1941. The school taught thousands of students and graduated several distinguished alumni, including Broadway star Chita Rivera. In 1961 Jones cofounded the Capitol Ballet, an integrated company that helped to provide roles for black dancers. Admired as a passionate teacher, Jones played a central role in breaking down race barriers in the world of ballet.

Jones, the daughter of a butcher and a homemaker, was born in the second decade of the twentieth century in Malden, Massachusetts, and grew up during the Great Depression. From an early age, she loved dance. She was a talented tap dancer and longed for formal dance training after high school, but college was beyond the family's means. So Jones made appointments to audition at local dance studios. When she would arrive and the teachers saw that she was black, though, they made it clear that she would not be accepted into their training programs. She often heard this disappointing news in the room where other aspiring students were performing, so she would watch closely to learn as much from them as she could. She also got every book she could find about ballet, teaching herself from what she had seen and read.

Jones found a job teaching dance to students at summer camps in Massachusetts. Her tap dance talents were so impressive that she was invited to go on tour with Bill "Bojangles" Robinson, the African-American dancer who played a central role in popularizing this art form. But she was not able to take this opportunity, since her parents felt she was too young to go on the road. Eventually Jones was able to persuade one of the dance schools that had rejected her to let her teach tap there, in exchange for ballet lessons. She also taught students in her own studio, which she established in a part of her parents' house.

After a brief marriage that ended in divorce, Jones moved to Washington, D.C., in 1940 at the suggestion of one of her students, Claire Haywood. The women became partners with a plan to establish a dance studio. Without enough money to jump start the venture, Jones worked at the Bureau of Engraving to make ends meet during her first years in the city. The Doris W. Jones School of Dance started in a spare room at the YMCA in Northeast Washington in 1941 and moved to several temporary locations before settling in 1950 at a permanent site on Georgia Avenue. At its permanent location, Jones and Haywood renamed their business as the Jones-Haywood School of Ballet.

Jones worked hard to give her students excellent training and a wide exposure to the arts. She invited guest teachers, including George Balanchine of the New York City Ballet, to the school and pushed talented students to pursue further training. "Thank God she was my teacher," said Chita Rivera in a *Washington Post* article by Sarah Kaufman. "She was really my foundation. I could not be whatever I am today without

At a Glance . . .

Born in 1914(?) in Malden, MA; died on March 21, 2006, in Washington, DC; married Tusker Crowsson (divorced).

Career: Bureau of Engraving, Washington, DC, 1940-1942(?); Doris W. Jones School of Dance (renamed Jones-Haywood School of Ballet), Washington, DC, founder and director, 1941-2006; Capitol Ballet Company, founder, 1961; Jones-Haywood Youth Dancers, founder, 1980.

Awards: Dr. Martin Luther King, Jr. Medal for Outstanding Service in Human Rights; Metropolitan Theatrical Society, Mainline to Stardom award.

Miss Jones." As Rivera explained, Jones instilled in her students the expectation of excellence and the understanding that inner discipline was required to achieve it. "It makes your body strong when you're taught properly," she noted, "but it also makes you strong spiritually, and gives you hope to keep going, when you're taught to be great." In her autobiographical Broadway show, *Chita Rivera: The Dancer's Life*, Rivera played Jones in a scene that dramatized how the influential teacher took Rivera to New York to audition for Balanchine. Rivera and another of Jones's students won scholarships to the New York City Ballet's School of American Ballet, becoming the only two students of color in the organization at that time. Other distinguished alumni of the Jones-Haywood School of Ballet, which is now part of the African-American Heritage Trail, include Sylvester Campbell, premier danseur of the Royal Netherlands Ballet Company; Elizabeth Walton of the Paul Taylor Dance Company; Hinton Battle, a Tony Award winning dancer who, like Rivera, went on to study under Balanchine; and Sandra Fortune Greene, who in 1973 became the first black American woman to enter an international ballet competition, according to the *New York Times*.

In 1961 Jones and Haywood founded the Capitol Ballet, an integrated company associated with their school. The company performed classical works such as *Swan Lake*, as well as original pieces choreographed by Jones. The Capitol Ballet became known for its nontraditional approach, such as putting tap dance to the music of Johann Sebastian Bach. Financial difficulties forced the company to shut down in 1983, but it reopened in 1988 with a dance honoring Rosa Parks, whose refusal to give her bus seat to a white passenger in Montgomery, Alabama in 1955 inspired the Civil Rights Movement.

After Haywood's death in 1978, Jones continued running the school and the company on her own. She also served as choreographer for the Washington Opera Society and the Washington Civic Opera. In addition, Jones served as director of the Washington, D.C., Public Schools Dance Program. "I never want that door shut again in the face of any black youngster," she emphasized in remarks quoted in a *Washington Post* article by Patricia Sullivan.

Jones's health deteriorated in her later years. She suffered with breast cancer, diabetes, and arthritis so severe that it made it difficult for her to use her hands. Nevertheless, she remained actively involved in the Jones-Haywood School. Confined to a wheelchair, she sometimes had herself carried down from her living quarters above the studio so that she could observe classes. Even after becoming bedridden, she would ask teachers to bring students upstairs to her bedside, where she would watch their technique and give them critiques and encouragement. As a former teacher at the school described it to Kaufman, the students "would go up on pointe, do a couple of pirouettes, and she would give corrections like, 'Your back's not right,' or 'Bring up those knees.'"

Jones, who died in on March 21, 2006, received the Dr. Martin Luther King, Jr. Medal for Outstanding Service in Human Rights, and the Mainline to Stardom award from the Metropolitan Theatrical Society. Jones was a "remarkable figure, quite a visionary," according to Washington Ballet artistic director Septime Webre, quoted in Sullivan's article. "She was like Johnny Appleseed, and developed a wonderful school which trained generations of wonderfully talented dancers."

Sources

Periodicals

Dance, July 2006.
Negro History Bulletin, January-September, 1996, p. 13.
New York Times, April 4, 2006, p. A21.
Washington Post, March 23, 2006, p. B8; March 23, 2006, p. C1.

On-line

"Doris Jones," *The History Makers*, www.thehistory-makers.com/biography/biography.asp?bioindex= 620&category=artMakers (July 19, 2007).
"Jones-Haywood School of Ballet," *African American Heritage Trail Database*, www.culturaltourismdc. org/ (July 19, 2007).

—E. M. Shostak

Leon Kintaudi

1949(?)—

Physician

Dr. Leon Kintaudi, also known as Ngoma Miezi Kintaudi or Leon Ngoma M. Kintaudi, was the medical director of non-profit healthcare organizations and projects in the Democratic Republic of Congo (DRC). He worked tirelessly to reestablish basic healthcare in the war-torn country. Between 1998 and 2006 an estimated four million people died in the DRC, either as a direct result of the fighting or from disease and malnutrition. Kintaudi was named a 2005 Global Health Hero at the *Time* Magazine Global Health Summit in New York City in November of 2005.

Ngoma Miezi (Leon) Kintaudi was born 150 miles from Kinshasa in Zaire, now the DRC. As a teenager Kintaudi watched helplessly as his father died of acute appendicitis because there was no doctor at the local hospital. He determined he would become a physician. As his country sank into turmoil, Kintaudi's family sent him to study in the United States.

Kintaudi worked his way through college, graduating from the University of La Verne in La Verne, California, in 1974 with a double major in biology and chemistry. After earning his medical degree Kintaudi entered private practice. Later he worked in a public health clinic in Los Angeles. Yet as he started his career in the United States, Kintaudi focused on how he might help his own country. His country erupted in civil war during the 1990s, and Kintaudi witnessed his country's struggle firsthand when he returned to visit his mother, who had refused to leave. In a University of La Verne commencement address, quoted on the *Santé Rurale*

(SANRU) Web site, Kintaudi told his audience: "My dream was always to be part of something that would make an impact on the country of my birth."

So in the mid-1990s, at a time when droves of physicians from sub-Saharan Africa were emigrating to Europe and North America, Kintaudi moved back to Kinshasa. Initially he ran a medical residency program for the Eglise de Christ au Congo (ECC-DOM), an association of the major Protestant churches in the DRC. Fully one-half of the 40 doctors that Kintaudi trained in his first class left the country, unwilling to make do on a $30-per-month salary. Eventually Kintaudi also became director of the ECC's Department of Medical Services, with responsibility for 80 hospitals and more than 400 clinics.

In 2000 Kintaudi and the ECC approached the U.S. Agency for International Development (USAID) for help rebuilding the DRC's shattered healthcare system. They received a five-year $25-million grant to be administered by Interchurch Medical Assistance, Inc. (IMA), a nongovernmental organization based in the United States. Kintaudi became director of the SANRU III Basic Rural Health Program, a collaborative effort of the ECC, IMA, and Programme de Santé Rurale to establish 56 decentralized health zones across the country. Another 17 ECC-managed health zones were funded by the World Bank. Additional funding was obtained through the Global Fund, corporate donors, and the development agencies of American churches. In general, a single health zone served 100,000-

At a Glance . . .

Born Ngoma Miezi Kintaudi in 1949(?) in Zaire (now the Democratic Republic of Congo). *Education:* University of La Verne, CA, BS, biology and chemistry, 1974; MD; MPH. *Religion:* Church of Christ.

Career: Los Angeles, CA, physician in private practice and at a public health clinic, 1980-1995(?); Eglise de Christ au Congo (ECC), Kinshasa, Democratic Republic of Congo, director of medical residency, 1995(?)–, Department of Medical Services, director, 1996(?)–; SANRU Rural Health Program, Kinshasa, DRC, medical director, 2000–.

Memberships: Ecumenical Pharmaceutical Network (EPN), Nairobi, Kenya, director.

Awards: La Verne University, honorary doctorate, 2005; Time Global Health Summit Hero Award, 2005; United Nations Humanitarian Award, 2005.

Addresses: *Office*—Director, SANRU Rural Health Program, ECC-DOM (The Protestant Church of Congo), 75 Ave. de la Justice, Kinshasa, DR Congo.

150,000 people with a hospital and approximately 20 clinics run by nurses.

In addition to supporting and improving rural hospitals and clinics, Kintaudi coordinated religious, governmental, non-governmental, and corporate partners in numerous other efforts. These included the establishment of local community development groups, the training of village health and hygiene workers and traditional birth attendants, and the health education of local residents.

As of 2005, due to the efforts of Kintaudi and his collaborators, 80 percent of the children in the health zones were receiving vitamin A and vaccinations against childhood diseases, up from 27 percent in 2001. Tuberculosis detection rates jumped significantly. Hundreds of thousands of insecticide-treated bednets were distributed as part of the battle against malaria. HIV/AIDS was being addressed through education, screening, testing, counseling, and treatment. Thousands of healthcare workers and community volunteers were being trained to practice preventative and curative medicine in the most remote regions of the country. More women received family planning assistance, prenatal care, and attended childbirth. Many of the health zones obtained potable water for the first time.

Through the ECC-DOM and SANRU III, Kintaudi directed the training of thousands of doctors, nurses, and healthcare administrators and helped create the school of public health at the State University at Kinshasa. But the fight to retain trained medical personnel continued.

Kintaudi conducted collaborative research assessing the effectiveness of public-health initiatives in rural Africa. He presented his findings at pan-African and international meetings of professional organizations, including the American Public Health Association. He endorsed a 2004 letter to the British medical journal the *Lancet* that called for an all-inclusive program to halt the sexual transmission of HIV/AIDS in sub-Saharan Africa.

Kintaudi became a recognized spokesperson for the ongoing efforts to bolster health care in the DRC. He told the Time Global Health Summit in 2005: "I am but one man standing before you today to be recognized as a global health hero, but I turn around and see thousands of Congolese heroes behind me, linking arms, linking hands with a vast network of partners around the globe that are caring for Congo." In addition to addressing the Health Summit, Kintaudi spoke to students at the Columbia University Medical School and School of Public Health. Along with other members of the SANRU leadership, he made a presentation to the Global Health Council in Washington, D.C. By 2007, Kintaudi had become especially well known for his work on behalf of women and children in the DRC.

Selected works

Presentations

(With P. Derstine and F. Baer) "Faith-Based Co-Management of Health Zones and Umbrella Projects in DR Congo," American Public Health Association, 2004.
(With F. Baer) "The DR Congo Experience in Health System Development and Management," Christian Connections for International Health Conference, 2005.
"Caring for Congo," TIME Global Health Summit, November 1-3, 2005, *SANRU,* http://sanru.org/news/global_health_summit_pix.htm.
"FBOs and the Ministry of Health in DR Congo," *Global Health Council,* 2006, www.globalhealth.org/images/pdf/conf_2006/presentations/b5_kintaudi.pdf.

Sources

Periodicals

Lancet, November 27-December 2, 2004, pp. 1913-1915.
Time, November 7, 2005, p. 95.

On-line

"Kintaudi Named Global Health Hero by TIME Magazine," *SANRU,* http://sanru.org/news.htm (July 18, 2007).

"Kintaudi Speaks at TIME Magazine Global Health Summit," *IMA World Health,* www.interchurch.org/news/article.php?articleid=48 (July 17, 2007).
"TIME Global Health Summit Heroes," *Time,* www.time.com/time/2005/globalhealth/transcripts/110205heroes.pdf (July 17, 2007).
"Time Magazine Honors ULV Alumnus Dr. Leon M. Kintaudi as a Global Health Hero," *University of La Verne: Voice,* www.ulv.edu/ur/alumni/voice-pdf/2006-winter-spring.pdf (July 17, 2007).

—Margaret Alic

Debra L. Lee

1954—

Media executive

Already one of the most powerful women in media, in 2006 Debra L. Lee became the chairman and chief executive officer (CEO) of Black Entertainment Television (BET), a multi-billion-dollar conglomerate. During her first two decades at BET, Lee's responsibilities steadily increased as she prepared to succeed Robert L. Johnson, founder of the most prosperous black business in American history. As CEO Lee set out to significantly expand the network's programming while remaining faithful to its core demographic of 18-34-year-olds and deflecting ongoing criticism of its violent and misogynist music videos.

Studied Law

Little in Lee's background suggested her future as a media mogul. The youngest of three children of Richard M. and Delma L. Lee, Debra Louise Lee was born on August 8, 1954, in Fort Jackson, South Carolina. Her mother worked as a hospital clerk and her father was an Army tank driver. The family moved often. Lee told Patricia Sellers of *Fortune* magazine: "My dad never set boundaries for me as a girl. When I moved to Greensboro, N.C., in the sixth grade, they elected me class president because no one else wanted it. It was a terrifying experience and set the tone for the rest of my life." In a 2006 interview on the *BET* Web site, Lee related her parents' advice: "You should always be the best you can be at whatever you decide to do. Get the best education you can; go to the best school you can; and reach for the stars." Lee did.

Intending to become a journalist, Lee studied political science at Brown University. Influenced by the Black Power movement, she focused on Asian politics and communist ideology. As she told the *New York Times* in 2006: "It was the 70's, we were more militant then." Lee graduated from Harvard with dual degrees in law and public policy. She told the *Seattle Times:* "One thing Harvard Law does is teach you that you can change the world, and I knew I wanted to do that, it was just a question of how." Although Lee had prepared herself for a career with the federal government, she decided to wait rather than work in the Republican administration of President Ronald Reagan.

After a year as a U.S. District Court law clerk, Lee spent five years at the elite corporate law firm of Steptoe & Johnson. BET, America's first black-owned cable network, was one of her clients. She jumped at Johnson's offer to create the company's legal department. In 1986 BET was an unknown company with only 80 employees and cable television had not yet arrived in Washington. Lee's colleagues warned her that she was leaving the fast track. But Lee told Sellers: "I believed in the mission. I had grown up with brands like Ebony and Motown. And I grew up in the segregated South...so a black-owned business was really important to me."

Grew with the Network

Almost from her start as vice president and general counsel, Lee was being groomed as Johnson's successor. As BET grew into a media conglomerate, Lee's

At a Glance . . .

Born Debra Louise Lee on August 8, 1954, in Columbia, SC; married Randal Spencer Coleman, 1985 (divorced); children: Quinn Spencer, Ava. *Education:* Brown University, AB, political science, 1976; Harvard University, JD, 1980, John F. Kennedy School of Government, MPP, 1980.

Career: U.S. District Court, Washington, DC, law clerk, 1980-81; Steptoe & Johnson, Washington, DC, attorney, 1981-86; Black Entertainment Television (BET), Washington, DC, vice president/general counsel, 1986-92, executive vice president of legal affairs, publishing division president, general counsel, corporate secretary, 1992-96, vice president for strategic business development, 1995; BET Holdings, Inc., Washington, DC, president/COO, 1996-2005, president/CEO, 2005-2006, CEO/chairman, 2006–.

Selected memberships: Alvin Ailey Dance Theater, board of directors; Eastman Kodak Co., board of directors; Girls Inc., national board of directors, co-founder and chair of Washington, DC chapter; Marriott International, board of directors; Revlon, Inc., board of directors.

Selected awards: Turner Broadcasting System, Tower of Power Trumpet Award, 2000; National Association of Minorities in Communications, Quasar Award, 2003; National Cable and Telecommunications Association, Idell Kaitz Vanguard Award for Leadership, 2003; *Ebony* Magazine, Madame C. J. Walker Award for best exemplifying the entrepreneurial spirit of the pioneering Black businesswoman, 2005; New York Women in Film and Television, Muse Award, 2005.

Addresses: *Office*—BET Holdings, Inc., One BET Plaza, 1235 W St NE, Washington, DC, 20018-1211.

proudest moment.

In 1996 Lee became president and chief operating officer, in charge of BET's day-to-day operations during a period of major expansion. The company added event productions, theme restaurants, a men's clothing line, a financial services division, and new cable networks—BET Jazz, BET Gospel, and BET Hip Hop. BET International broadcast jazz to Europe and Africa. Its Web site became the number one Internet portal for black Americans. Under Lee's leadership BET programming moved beyond hip-hop videos and reruns, with original movies, concerts, documentaries, late-night talk shows, and news and public affairs. At a time when most broadcast and cable networks were stagnant, BET experienced year after year of audience growth and record ratings. Viacom bought the company for $3 billion in 2000, making Johnson America's first black billionaire.

BET gained a reputation for public service under Lee. She was responsible for the annual BET Walk of Fame that raised money for the United Negro College Fund. She led BET's "Black America Saves" initiative, a financial-planning assistance and education program. BET's Rap-It-Up campaign became the nation's largest HIV/AIDS initiative aimed at blacks.

However BET continued to suffer from bad press. In 2000 a fired executive sued the network for $21 million, charging that Johnson and Lee had used corporate funds for personal purposes, evaded taxes, and used illegal accounting methods. A 2004 biography of Johnson made public his personal relationship with Lee. With the 2001 firing of talk-show host Tavis Smiley, BET was again accused of not serving the best interests of the black community. In a July 2005 *Billboard* interview Lee addressed the issue of BET's music videos: "We also need to teach young people how to use the media and understand that these videos aren't necessarily portraying a lifestyle that anyone is supporting. People expect high standards from us.... If there are real issues, they come to me and we discuss the free speech aspect or whether something is so egregious that we're not going to put it on."

Succeeded Johnson as CEO/Chairman

In June of 2005 Lee was named BET president and CEO, set to become chairman in January of 2006 when Johnson retired. Johnson told the *Seattle Times*: "Debra has been the architect with me...of BET's success. She has held every senior strategic position in the company. She has helped define the company and she's helped direct the company." That year BET sold its book business, launched home-entertainment and mobile divisions, and arranged to

responsibilities grew too. While awaiting the birth of her first child, Lee simultaneously directed the construction of BET's corporate headquarters, acted as its general counsel, and ran BET's publishing division. In 1991 Lee was responsible for taking BET public, making it the first black-owned company to be listed on the New York Stock Exchange. She called it her

sell BET brands through Wal-Mart. Lee planned to move BET into filmmaking and to take the company global.

Lee began to overhaul BET programming, pushing for more original productions, reality shows, stand-up comedy, news, and information. One of her first moves as CEO was to hire filmmaker Reginald Hudlin as president of entertainment. She told Ken Parish Perkins of the *Chicago Defender* that she would "challenge him to breed a creative first culture. There are great stories out there that need to be told, and we must challenge the old ways of thinking." Lee eliminated infomercials, added an animation division, and launched *Meet the Faith*, a weekly discussion program on political and social issues from a moral and spiritual perspective. In 2007 Viacom announced that it would increase BET's budget for original programming by 30-50% annually.

However BET's ratings declined dramatically whenever it tried to introduce more highbrow programming. In July of 2005 Lee announced that BET was canceling its nightly newscast. She told Perkins: "We always hear, 'All you guys are interested in is making money.' We're a business. That's what we do." In 2006 *Lil' Kim: Countdown to Lockdown*, a reality show that followed the rapper as she prepared to go to prison, became the highest-rated series in BET's history.

In a *Billboard* interview in July of 2005 Lee addressed the paucity of black women in the corporate world: "It's not that I run into discrimination every day. It's always there, but it's not like it was 25 years ago. However, there's still a lot to be done…. There just needs to be more women executives in general. I just hope the numbers increase. The more women who can prove we can do it, the more opportunities there will be."

Selected writings

Periodicals

"Show Opened Door to Radical Dialogue: Remembering *Roots*," *TelevisionWeek*, January 22, 2007, p. 23.

Sources

Periodicals

Advertising Age, April 11, 2005, pp. B8-12.
Billboard, July 2, 2005, p. 21; October 29, 2005, pp. 28, 30, 32.
Broadcasting & Cable, June 8, 1998, p. 70.
Cable World, February 6, 2006.
Chicago Defender, August 4-6, 2006, p. 11.
Current Biography, June 2006, pp. 44-49.
Essence, February 2006, p. 134.
Fortune, October 16, 2006, p. 180.
New York Beacon, January 19-25, 2006, p. 29; March 30-April 5, 2006, p. 23.
New York Times, January 10, 2006, p. E1.
Seattle Times, February 17, 2006, p. E3.

On-line

"Debra Lee Assumes Helm of Black America's Network," *BET.com,* www.bet.com/News/debra_lee.htm (July 16, 2007).
"Fierce and Fabulous: Up Close with Debra Lee," *BET.com,* www.bet.com/Community/FierceandFabulous.htm (July 16, 2007).

—Margaret Alic

Kingsley Leggs

196(?)—

Singer, actor

Kingsley Leggs dedicated himself to a career in musical theater because he found performing fun and exciting. From his earliest experiences in the chorus of high school musicals, Leggs had been aware of the theater's ability to captivate and transport audiences. When he discovered African American theater in the early 1980s, he found a more deeply personal reason to remain in the theater—to make sure that black writing, black music, and black experience remained onstage where audiences of all colors could learn from it. As he grew as an actor and singer, he became determined to find, in each character he played, a powerful message to communicate, so that, in addition to being entertained, his audiences might be inspired as well.

Encouraged by Teacher

Leggs was born in the Midwestern city of St. Louis, Missouri, a major port on the Mississippi and a gateway between the Eastern and Western United States. When he was a teenager, his family moved to the St. Louis suburb of Normandy where Leggs attended Normandy High School. There he played snare drum in the school band, joined choral groups, and began performing in plays. His voice teacher Paul Mabury was strict and demanding, but he believed in his students' ability to succeed, and that confidence inspired Leggs to work hard to improve his performance skills.

Mabury's affection and encouragement gave Leggs the confidence to audition for roles on stage. It was while singing in the chorus of a Normandy High School production of the Rogers and Hammerstein musical

Carousel that Leggs realized he wanted to make the theater his career. "I just thought, 'This is the most fun thing I've ever done in my life,'" he told Ruth Ezell in an interview on St. Louis' public television channel, "People actually do this and make money. I want to do this."

After his graduation from Normandy High School, Leggs followed his mentor Paul Mabury to Benedictine College in Atchison, Kansas. Mabury taught in Benedictine's music department, and Leggs majored in music, studying and training in classical singing. He planned to become an opera singer, as he performed in college concerts and in summer productions at Atchison's Municipal Theater. However, after his graduation from Benedictine in 1983, he returned to St. Louis, where he found a group of artists who would change his career direction.

St. Louis' Twenty-Third Street Theater had been founded in 1976 by producer/director Ron Himes to showcase works by and for African Americans. The theater company began as a touring group which traveled to local college theaters and festivals. By the time Leggs joined, it had established a home theater in a former St. Louis church. The Twenty-Third Street Theater soon became the St. Louis Black Repertory, or the Black Rep. The company's mission—to provide a space for the creative expression of African Americans in order to educate audiences about black culture and create social change—captivated Leggs. For almost a decade, Leggs worked with the Black Rep, appearing in many productions, including *Ain't Misbehavin'*, *Blues in the Night,* and *Five Guys Named Mo.*

Reached Broadway

During the early 1990s, Leggs went on tour with a musical revue. The group performed in Chicago, and Leggs fell in love with the Midwestern metropolis and the exciting theatrical opportunities there. He remained in Chicago for several years, continuing to perform, and soon auditioned for a touring company production of the Tony-award winning musical *Miss Saigon.* Leggs landed a part in the chorus, but while he was waiting for the tour to begin, he received a life-changing call. Several actors had dropped out of the Broadway production of *Miss Saigon,* and the producers offered Leggs a role in the New York show. He accepted, and the name Kingsley Leggs made its first appearance in a Broadway playbill.

Following his run on Broadway, Leggs went on tour with *Miss Saigon,* first in the United States, then in the United Kingdom and in Asia. He also toured with other plays, including *Forbidden Hollywood, It Ain't Nothing But the Blues.* In *Ragtime,* in which he took the leading part of Coalhouse Walker, Leggs earned complimentary reviews for the warmth and sympathy he brought to the role. His long run in *Ragtime* introduced Leggs to one of the biggest challenges of live theater: repeat performances. Unlike film acting, in which only one good performance needs to be preserved on film, theater actors must repeat their demanding performances eight times a week, often for many weeks in a row. His classical training contributed to his strong singing voice and commanding stage presence. It also helped him to concentrate his energy and focus his attention so that he could deliver a sincere and fresh performance

Cast in The Color Purple

In 2000, Leggs' powerful work in *Ragtime* was honored with a nomination for the LA Stage Alliance's Ovation Award in the category of Best Actor in a Musical. In 2003, he received another nomination for his role in *Dreamgirls.* The same year, he auditioned for a role in a new musical production, based on Alice Walker's Pulitzer-prize winning 1982 novel *The Color Purple.* Leggs got the role and was chosen to go to Atlanta, Georgia, to workshop the new play. Workshopping a theatrical production means that the cast and creators work together through discussion and improvisation to develop a show that works well onstage. *The Color Purple* is the powerful story of Celie, a poor, Southern, African American woman who survives and triumphs after many painful experiences, especially at the hands of the men in her life. Leggs was cast in the role of Mister, Celie's abusive husband.

After extensive pre-production work, *The Color Purple* opened at Atlanta's Alliance Theater on September 9, 2004. Though the show received mixed reviews, it did well enough that a group of producers, including media celebrities Quincy Jones and Oprah Winfrey, began working on a New York production. In December 2005, *The Color Purple* opened on Broadway, with Kingsley Leggs in the role of Mister. As it had in Atlanta, the play drew a mixed critical response, but it was an immediate hit with audiences, drawing large numbers of black theatergoers, who did not traditionally attend Broadway musicals. In 2006, the show received thirteen nominations for Broadway Audience Awards, including one for Kingsley Leggs. Though Leggs did not win the award, the show won five Audience Awards, including Favorite New Broadway Musical.

The role of Mister allowed Leggs to do what he enjoyed most about theater, to delve deep within a character to find something uplifting to the human spirit. Mister begins as an abusive, almost evil, man who ignores his children and dominates his wife. However, as the play progresses, Mister loses everyone and everything in his life. Alone and despairing, he finally finds his humanity. Leggs thoroughly enjoyed the opportunity to create the complex character of Mister, both the menacing anger and the anguish that leads to his redemption. Throughout his career, Leggs had felt that art should have an empowering message. He had tried to express that principle in all of his work, and the role of Mister was especially satisfying.

Found More Work on Stage

Leggs remained with *The Color Purple* until November 2006, when he left to pursue other projects. He has continued to perform in a wide variety of regional productions, including *Two Gentlemen of Verona* at Baltimore's Centerstage, and *The Full Monty* at the Gateway Playhouse on Long Island. In addition to working in plays, he has also continued to develop his singing career, and in August 2006 he performed in a solo concert, which included a tribute to song-and-dance icon Sammy Davis, Jr., at the Triad Theater on Manhattan's west side. He has maintained his connection to the Black Rep, and in June 2006, he returned to St. Louis to host that theater's yearly Woodie Awards show.

Leggs married fellow actor Dawn Stern in 1992. Though the life of a theater actor means a good deal of time on the road, Leggs hopes eventually to make a home with his family in Los Angeles.

Selected works

Plays

Miss Saigon, Broadway.
The Color Purple, Broadway.

Sources

Periodicals

Back Stage West, February 19, 1998, p. 8.
Los Angeles Times, December 26, 1997, p. 41.

On-line

"The Color Purple: Kingsley Leggs Video Diary," *Oprah.com,* www.oprah.com/presents/2005/purple/video/video_leggs.jhtml (July 10, 2007).
"Kingsley Leggs," *Internet Broadway Database,* www.ibdb.com/person.asp?id=405710 (July 19, 2007).
"Kingsley Leggs," *KETC: St. Louis Public Television,* www.ketc.org/productions/productions_livingSTL_videoArchive.asp (July 19, 2007).
"'Mister' Comes Home to Emcee the 13th Annual Woodie Awards," *Black Repertory Theater,* www.theblackrep.org/site/index.php?option=com_content&task=view&id=85&Itemid=134 (July 19, 2007).

—Tina Gianoulis

Mark Mallory

1962—

Politician

In 2005, Mark Mallory became the first African American to be elected mayor of Cincinnati, Ohio, under a new system in which voters chose their city leader by direct ballot. Mallory had little experience in municipal leadership, but had forged an impressive career representing his hometown in Ohio's state house and senate over the past decade. The Democrat came from a family with deep roots in Cincinnati and with a long legacy of public service. "I need everyone in the city to take pride in our city," Mallory asserted in his inaugural speech, according to the City of Cincinnati's Web site for the Mayor's Office. "Everyone must focus on solutions rather than problems. Everyone should consider the needs of the city and know that each and everyone of us are part of making this city great."

Born April 4, 1962, Mallory is a lifelong resident of Cincinnati and grew up in a politically active family. The doorbell of the Mallory home in the West End neighborhood frequently rang with community leaders and ordinary citizens hoping to speak to Mallory's father, William Sr., a public school teacher who was elected to the Ohio state house in 1966 and served there for the next 27 years. When Mallory was nine years old, his father began to take him to Columbus, the state capital, on days that he was out of school. "I would seat him at a committee table with the representatives," William Mallory told Margo Pierce of *Cincinnati CityBeat,* "and I would deliberately go out of the room and come back and I would say, 'Look, I didn't leave you here to chew gum. What'd they talk about while I was gone?' Just to make him alert."

Mallory graduated from the city's Academy of Math and Science and went on to earn a Bachelor of Science degree in administrative management from the University of Cincinnati. He worked for city library system in various management posts before deciding to run for his father's seat in the state house when the senior Mallory announced his retirement. After winning that 1994 election, he was reelected two years later, but in 1998 made a run for a seat in the Ohio senate, and won that race by ousting the Republican incumbent. He was reelected in 2002, but limited to two consecutive four-year terms by law.

Like his father, who had served as Democratic majority leader in the state house for almost 20 years, Mallory quickly emerged as a leader in the senate. He served as assistant leader of its Democratic caucus and then became the assistant minority leader. Though the Democrats were in the minority in the upper house, he managed to win passage for an impressive number of bills. One of those was purely symbolic, but signed into law in a solemn ceremony on Constitution Day, September 17, 2003: a resolution that finally ratified the 14th Amendment to the U.S. Constitution 135 years after Congress sent it to the states for approval. This Amendment defined U.S. citizenship and guaranteed equal protection under the law to all persons, not just citizens, living in the United States. Mallory's resolution was a mere formality to correct a technical glitch—one Ohio General Assembly had ratified it back in the 1860s, yet that vote was rescinded by their successors—but its ratification in 2003 was an important symbolic gesture. "Ohio has made some terrible mistakes in the past," *Dayton Daily News* writer William Hershey quoted Mallory as saying at the ceremony. "This afternoon we took an opportunity to correct those mistakes."

At a Glance . . .

Born April 4, 1962, in Cincinnati, OH; son of William L. Mallory Sr. (a politician); married. *Education:* University of Cincinnati, BS, 1993(?). *Politics:* Democrat.

Career: Hamilton County Public Library, manager of graphic production department, and of security department, 1993-94(?); Ohio State General Assembly, representative, 1994-98; Ohio State Senate, senator, 1999-2005; Cincinnati, mayor, 2005–.

Memberships: 4C for Children Advisory Council, board of trustees; the Friars Club, board of trustees; Ronald McDonald House of Cincinnati, advisory board; Students in Free Enterprise, advisory board.

Awards: Meryl Shoemaker "Legislator of the Year" award, 1998; Correctional Education Association, Excellence in Correctional Education award, 1999; National Association of Social Workers, Legislator of the Year award, 2001; Ohio Association of Election Officials, Wolfe Award of Excellence, 2002; Ohio Library Council, Andrew Carnegie Award, 2003; Ohio Community Corrections Association, Legislator of the Year award, 2003.

Addresses: *Office*—Mayor's Office, 801 Plum St., Rm. 150, Cincinnati, OH 45202-1979.

With the end of his career in the state senate nearing, Mallory entered the Cincinnati mayor's race of 2005. Over the past several decades, voters in the city had chosen only their city council, which then elected a mayor from amongst themselves. After 1987, the council candidate with the highest number of votes became mayor. In 1999, the city implemented a new system whereby candidates were directly elected in a municipal election, but political infighting remained a hallmark of Cincinnati City Hall, and the problems worsened after the city erupted in riots in April of 2001 after the shooting death of a black man by a police officer—the 15th such death in six years.

A third political party, the Charter Party, had dominated Cincinnati city politics for several decades, but there had long been a shortage of Republican candidates willing to run for municipal office. In the Democratic primary in September of 2005, Mallory and David Pepper Jr.—son of the former chief executive officer of Procter & Gamble, one of the area's largest employers—received the highest number of votes and

faced off on the general election. Pepper was a city council member and campaigned on his experience in city government. "Mallory has clearly staked out a position as a politically experienced outsider," noted *Cincinnati Post* writer Barry M. Horstman, "one familiar with the city's litany of problems but whose fingerprints cannot be found near any of them by virtue of having served in Columbus, not City Hall." The final vote on November 8, 2005, was close, with Mallory winning with 51.8 percent, compared to the 48.2 percent that Pepper garnered. Mallory became the first mayor in more than 70 years who had not served on Cincinnati's city council, and was the city's first African-American leader to be elected under the new system.

Mallory resigned from his seat in the state senate and was sworn in as mayor on December 1, 2005. During his first year in office, he added more police officers to street patrols, made cuts in property tax rates, and increased regional cooperative efforts with officials across the Ohio River in Kentucky and Indiana. He also launched what he called the "Young Professionals' Kitchen Cabinet" to keep younger working families and singles from leaving the city. "You are among the most energetic people in this city," he told the advisory board at its first meeting in October of 2006, according to *Cincinnati Post* journalist Joe Wessels. "It only makes sense to reach out and try to get information from you about how to keep you here and about how to reach out and attract more people to this city."

The Cincinnati mayor is not the only Mallory who followed their father into a career in politics or government service. The mayor's brother, William Jr., is a municipal court judge, while another, Dale, serves as a state representative, and a third, Joe is a civic leader in nearby Forest Park. They were undoubtedly inspired by their father's career as a public servant, but their mother was a formative influence, too, as Mallory recalled in the interview with Pierce for *Cincinnati CityBeat.* "I don't care what you do in life but you have to do something," were her words to her six children, Mallory said, "and you need to do something that's going to make me proud."

Sources

Periodicals

Cincinnati April 2006, pp. 90-219.
Cincinnati CityBeat, May 11, 2005.
Cincinnati Post, September 23, 2005, p. A10; May 16, 2006, p. A1; October 18, 2006, p. A1; December 25, 2006, p. A2.
Dayton Daily News, September 18, 2003, p. B3.

On-line

"Mayor's Biography," *City of Cincinnati—Meet the Mayor,* www.cincinnati-oh.gov/mayor/pages/-3052-/ (July 6, 2007).

—Carol Brennan

Theresa Maxis

Religious leader, educator

1810-1892

The co-founder of the Sisters, Servants of the Immaculate Heart of Mary, an order of Roman Catholic nuns devoted to education, Theresa Maxis was an important figure in the development of Catholic education in the American Midwest. The extent of her contributions, however, has been largely obscured by church authorities. Maxis was apparently a charismatic figure who was gifted at motivating a growing religious community on the American frontier. But she encountered resistance from the white male Catholic hierarchy, motivated at least partly by racial and sexual discrimination. Key aspects of Maxis's background were later excised from church histories.

Maxis was born Marie Almaide Maxis Duchemin in 1810 in Baltimore, Maryland. Her father, Arthur Howard, was a white military officer of British citizenship. Maxis's mother, Marie Annette Maxis Duchemin, was a biracial woman, a nurse, who had come from the island of Santo Domingo (from the French-speaking part that is now Haiti) in 1793 as a girl, with a white French family named Duchemin; Maxis's material grandparents had died in the slave revolts that shook the Caribbean in the 1790s. Maxis grew up with light skin and an ability to pass as white if she chose to do so. She recalled at the end of her life that, at age eight or nine, she stood at a doorway at the Howard house watching the man whom she had been told was her father, although he may not even have known that she existed.

As a young woman of mixed racial background in Maryland, which permitted slavery at the time, Maxis's prospects were not bright. Yet she succeeded in getting a good education at a boarding school operated in the home of two women from Haiti, Elizabeth Lange and Marie Magdalen Balas. Maxis learned to speak French, English, and Latin, and she became conversant with other subjects, ranging from mathematics to needlework. At age 19, Maxis joined with Lange, Balas, and another woman named Rose Boegue, to form a new congregation called the Oblate Sisters of Providence; they intended "to consecrate themselves to God, and to the Christian education of young girls of colour," according to *Building Sisterhood: A Feminist History of the Sisters, Servants of the Immaculate Heart of Mary*. The Oblate Sisters of Providence may have been the first Catholic congregation composed specifically of women of African descent.

Mother Died in Cholera Epidemic

Several factors combined to push Maxis toward a path of spiritual leadership. One was a cholera epidemic that struck Baltimore in 1832 and claimed the life of her mother, who had volunteered her nursing services at the almshouse of the Oblate Sisters. Another was the decision of the growing congregation of Afro-Caribbean women to choose Maxis as general superior in 1842, replacing the ailing male leader, a sympathetic priest named Nicholas Joubert. A third set of experiences that impressed Maxis as a young woman was the intensification of white racism in Baltimore in the decades preceding the Civil War. The women of the Oblate Sisters were harassed, and white mobs threw rocks through the windows of the small school they had

At a Glance . . .

Born Marie Almaide Maxis Duchemin, 1810, in Baltimore, MD; changed name to Mary Theresa Maxis, Monroe, MI, mid-1840s; died on January 14, 1892, in West Chester, PA. *Education:* Boarding school for Caribbean refugees, Baltimore, MD. *Religion:* Roman Catholic.

Career: Oblate Sisters of Providence congregation for Catholic women of color, co-founder, 1829, general superior, 1842; Sisters, Servants of the Immaculate Heart of Mary, co-founder, Monroe, MI, 1845, superior, 1852-59; IHM missions, Pennsylvania, nun, 1859-67; Grey Nuns Convent, Ottawa, ON, Canada, nun, 1867-85; West Chester IHM Motherhouse, West Chester, PA, nun, 1885-92.

Awards: Michigan Women's Hall of Fame, inducted 2001.

established. It became harder for the school to attract students, and the Sisters were forced to take in washing and sewing in order to make ends meet.

Alone with no family ties, and having endured frightening experiences, Maxis (in the words of historian Marita-Constance Supan, writing in *Building Sisterhood*) "developed a strong reliance on God's Providence and a parallel inclination to clutch life's reins in her own hands through decisive action." When two Belgian-born priests came to Baltimore in 1843 and discussed plans for a new Catholic school in what was then the wilderness of southeastern Michigan, Maxis saw her chance. The two priests were Peter Paul Lefevere, the Bishop of Detroit, and Belgian national, Louis Florent Gillet. Gillet was a member of a sect called the Redemptorists that emphasized personal forms of devotion and worship—something that fit perfectly with Maxis's own attitudes.

The exact sequence of events that led Maxis to Michigan is unclear, but in 1845 she left Baltimore for the ten-day overland journey to Monroe, Michigan, where Gillet had already settled and had begun celebrating Mass with the area's spread-out Catholic worshippers. Maxis decided that she could leave racial discrimination behind by concealing her African descent, and though she brought one of her Oblate companions, Anne Constants Shaaff, to Michigan, she rejected another because her skin was too dark. Known up to that time as Marie Therese Duchemin (or as Mother Marie Therese), she became Mary Theresa Maxis.

Lived in Log Cabin

Gillet and Maxis excitedly made plans for the new religious community and school, which grew slowly but attracted young women from neighboring communities who wanted to join and serve as teachers. At first the school was intended to serve French-speaking girls in the still heavily French-speaking area; later the language of instruction changed to English. The community became the Sisters of Providence; later it was renamed the Sisters, Servants of the Immaculate Heart of Mary. The sisterhood's school was called St. Mary's. The first residence of the new sisterhood was a log cabin. Maxis recorded the community's experiences in a diary called the Monroe Motherhouse Chronicles, recalling (as quoted in *Building Sisterhood*) that "[t]he roads were often so bad that they [the sisters] were in danger of falling at each step; this, however, for them was a recreation, for they considered themselves fortunate in not breaking their legs or necks: this must be told to testify the truth, and show the power of grace."

Maxis was the community's de facto leader even when Lefevere sent figureheads from Detroit. As one sister quoted in *Building Sisterhood* wrote, "As Mother Theresa was the first, she was looked on as *the* one to whom to go, although Sister Alphonsine was appointed superior." Maxis herself became the community's superior in 1852. "I think she must have carried some African influences with her…in the way she relied on the whole community to discern where the spirit was moving," Detroit religious leader Rev. Marsha Foster Boyd, who produced a one-woman play about Maxis in 2007, told David Crumm of the *Detroit Free Press.* Maxis's own ecclesiastical superiors, however, were never entirely comfortable with her independent attitudes, and later in the 1850s she and her Monroe sisterhood became embroiled in conflict.

What first began to cause problems was the Redemptorist sect's withdrawal of financial support from the Sisters in 1855. The reasons were apparently purely financial—the school was losing money—but the cutoff angered Bishop Lefevere, and part of his anger was directed toward Maxis, who was strongly sympathetic to Redemptorist ideas. He appointed a new leader for St. Mary's, the Rev. Edward Joos, who had recently immigrated from Belgium and spoke English poorly. Maxis was undaunted. She and a group of other Sisters once hitchhiked by carriage to a mass being celebrated in Erie, on the Ohio line, after fund shortages prevented them from engaging transportation of their own. The portrait of Maxis that emerges from her writings and letters is one of a woman with boundless energy, always thinking about new projects.

One of those projects was a new Redemptorist mission in Reading, Pennsylvania, which Maxis had been invited to organize by Redemptorist Philadelphia bishop John Neumann. Lefevere initially gave Maxis permission to make the trip, but a request for a return visit prompted a serious clash with Joos, who conveyed the bad news of Lefevere's refusal. Joos wrote in a letter to Lefevere (quoted on the Sisters, Servants of the Immaculate Heart of Mary Web site) that Maxis had exploded in anger. "'I am not,' she said [Joos wrote], 'astonished; we have known since long that no one take interest in the Convent, and so all the Sisters know; therefore I have no confidence any longer neither in the Bishop, nor F. Hennaert, nor you, and so you may write the Bishop who can give me my demission.'"

Cut Off from Community

Lefevere angrily complied, sending Maxis to Pennsylvania on a permanent basis, splitting the new Pennsylvania missions off from the original Monroe community, and forbidding her to have any further contact with the other Sisters at St. Mary's—a rule that many disregarded as Maxis successfully convinced them to follow her. In addition to internal Catholic politics, Lefevere was clearly motivated by the racism of his time. He knew of Maxis's racial background from his previous visit to Baltimore, and he wrote to a Pennsylvania associate (as quoted in *Building Sisterhood*) that Maxis had "all the softness, slyness, and low cunning of the mulatto."

The Sisters' two new missions in Pennsylvania flourished, but Maxis was troubled by what she saw as her role in the splitting of the congregation in two. She wrote repeatedly to Lefevere trying to heal the wounds, but her letters were never answered. Finally, in 1867, she decided to go into voluntary exile as a way of removing herself as a potential source of conflict. She lived in Ottawa, Canada, at the Grey Nuns Convent, from 1867 to 1885, petitioning repeatedly but unsuccessfully for readmission to the Monroe community. In 1885 she returned to Pennsylvania and lived at an Immaculate Heart of Mary convent, the West Chester IHM Motherhouse, until her death on January 14, 1892.

By that time, histories of the Immaculate Heart of Mary sisterhood were already being rewritten to expunge Maxis's name: it was thought that the revelation of her mixed-race background would hurt fundraising, and her name was actually erased from documents that contained it and could not be concealed in any other way. Maxis lived on in the memories of the women who

knew her, but Joos, who was fictitiously elevated to the role of founder of the Sisters, Servants of the Immaculate Heart of Mary, intervened late in life to prevent the writing of a biography of Maxis, and threatened to reveal her racial background. The Sisters grew into an influential organization that went on to found the University of Detroit, but the rediscovery of the group's true origins did not occur until the late 20th century, when members of the congregation uncovered Maxis's letters and sought to reconstruct her story. The Sisters, Servants of the Immaculate Heart of Mary recognized Maxis as their founder only in 2000. The following year, she was elected to the Michigan Women's Hall of Fame.

Sources

Books

Gannon, Margaret, ed., *Paths of Daring, Deeds of Hope: Letters by and about Mother Theresa Maxis Duchemin*, Congregation of the Sisters, Servants of the Immaculate Heart of Mary, Monroe, MI and Scranton, PA, 1992.
Sisters, Servants of the Immaculate Heart of Mary, *Building Sisterhood: A Feminist History of the Sisters, Servants of the Immaculate Heart of Mary*, Syracuse University Press, 1997.

Periodicals

Detroit Free Press, March 28, 2007.
Lansing State Journal, October 26, 2001, p. B1.

On-line

"Our Co-Founders: Louis Florent Gillet and Theresa Maxis," *Congregation of the Sisters, Servants of the Immaculate Heart of Mary,* www.ihmsisters. org/www/About_Us/History/founders.asp (July 31, 2007).
"IHM: Mother Theresa Maxis," *Congregation of the Sister, Servants of the Immaculate Heart of Mary,* http://ihmnew.marywood.edu/2.OurHistory/2IH-MTheresaMaxisDuchemin.html (July 26, 2007).
Oblate Sisters of Providence, www.oblatesisters.com (July 26, 2007).

—James M. Manheim

Audra McDonald

1970—

Actress, singer

Audra McDonald is one of the American theatre's outstanding performers. Within the span of only a few years, McDonald picked up four Tony Awards in the featured (or supporting) actress category for her work in *Carousel* in 1994, *The Master Class* in 1996, *Ragtime* in 1998, and *A Raisin in the Sun* in 2004. In his review of *Carousel*, David Richards of the *New York Times* called McDonald "the real find of this production" adding that she has a "welcomingly open manner …a vigorous voice and a ready sense of comedy." In 2007, when McDonald landed her

McDonald, Audra, photograph. Laura Cavanaugh/UPI/Landov.

sixth Tony Award nomination, *Broadway.com* contributor Robert Sandla observed that Audra McDonald had become "the kind of Broadway star that Hollywood used to make movies about." Yet Broadway stardom was only part of McDonald's career; she also maintained a thriving concert singing and recording career and landed a part in the ABC network *Grey's Anatomy* spin-off *Private Practice*.

Enrolled at Juilliard

McDonald was born in Berlin, Germany, in 1970, while her father was stationed there with the U.S. Army, and grew up in Fresno, California. Her mother

worked as an administrator at California Polytechnic State University in San Luis Obispo, and her father, finished with his military service, was a high school principal. Musical talent runs in the family. Her parents are both trained musicians, and her aunts have toured with a gospel-singing group. McDonald joked with Barry Singer of the *New York Times* that if she had not shown musical ability as a child "I probably would have been sent back." McDonald's professional career began at age nine when she began participating in shows at Roger Rocka's Music Hall, a Fresno dinner theatre that showcases young performers. As a teenager she participated in Music Hall productions of *Hello, Dolly!*, *A Chorus Line*, *Grease*, and had the lead role of Dorothy in *The Wiz*. After high school at the Roosevelt School of the Performing Arts in Fresno, McDonald enrolled at the prestigious Juilliard School of Music in Manhattan. At Juilliard, McDonald focused her studies on voice and did not take any classes in the school's highly regarded drama division. Because of her lack of formal training in drama, McDonald is especially pleased when her acting is praised, particularly her sense of comedy. "Comedy is difficult for me. I'm good at suffering and dying…. I haven't done much comedy professionally, and I've never really had acting lessons," McDonald told Glenn Collins of the *New York Times*.

Broadway was always McDonald's first love and she was unhappy at the classically oriented Juilliard. "It wasn't me," McDonald said of Juilliard to Singer. "I had danced around the room singing to Barbra Streisand. That's what I wanted to do." Mental stress caused McDonald to take a break from her studies at Juilliard. While away from school she landed a part on Broadway in the chorus of *The Secret Garden*, a musical version of the beloved children's story by Frances Hodgson Burnett. McDonald then toured with the national company of *The Secret Garden*. She eventually went back to Juilliard and finished a bachelor's degree in 1993. McDonald credits her Juilliard training with providing her with a greater sense of discipline and with a prestigious credential that draws notice. "I think people will certainly pay a little more attention to you, just because you've got Juilliard on your resume. That certainly helps to get the door opened a little bit," McDonald explained to Chris Haines of *Tony Awards Online*.

McDonald auditioned several times before being cast in a much-ballyhooed production of *Carousel* at the Lincoln Center in 1994. The project was a restaging of a highly praised production of the classic Rodgers and Hammerstein musical done at London's National Theatre in 1992. Reviews in New York were mostly favorable, and McDonald was singled out as one of the stellar performers. Brian Kellow in *Opera News* wrote that "Audra Ann McDonald works wonders with the part of Carrie Pipperidge; she also sings well." Stefan Kanfer in *The New Leader*, among the minority of critics who did not like the overall production, had only good words for McDonald, saying that she "possesses great warmth and purity of tone. She also reveals a comic gift." The character of Carrie Pipperidge, a mill worker in a nineteenth-century Maine town, is not a specifically African-American part and there was some criticism of the non-traditional casting of McDonald, and of opera star Shirley Verrett in the role of town matriarch Nettie Fowler. "Is this a color-blind New England town?…Or are we not supposed to notice hue and ethnicity? In that case, why was the multiracial policy given ceaseless self-congratulatory publicity in London and New York?" wrote Kanfer. McDonald dismisses the race issue. "It's a universal story, with universal music and lyrics…If these people are concentrating on the fact that I'm black …well, there's nothing I can do about that," she told Collins.

Earned Awards, Worked with Legends

McDonald won the Tony, Drama Desk, Outer Critics Circle, and Theatre World awards for her work in *Carousel*. She recalls her acceptance of her first Tony Award as a blur. "The only thing that really stuck out in my mind was when I got up there and I looked in the audience, I thought, 'Oh, my God, I have to talk. How am I going to do this?' I looked down and saw Carol Channing just beaming up at me. I thought, 'That is just the sweetest face I've ever seen.' And then I was fine," McDonald said to Haines.

Terrence McNally's play *Master Class* is a fictional depiction of a "master class" for three aspiring opera singers conducted by legendary opera star Maria Callas. In the Broadway production, Callas was portrayed by Zoe Caldwell and McDonald played Sharon, a talented, attractive student mercilessly bullied by the great diva. McDonald was hesitant to try out for the part of Sharon, which requires an impressive delivery of a demanding aria from Verdi's *Macbeth*. She was so frightened of the aria, a piece so challenging that even Callas herself sang it only a few times in her career, that she canceled her first audition. A week later McDonald's agent called to say the part was still open and suggested she make another attempt. She did so and, despite her lack of confidence, came through with flying colors. "She has got it all. She has such natural ability, she doesn't even realize it," *Master Class* director Leonard Foglia said of McDonald to Susan King of the *Los Angeles Times*. *Master Class* opened on Broadway in November 1995. Robert Brustein of the New Republic said the part of Sharon was "powerfully sung and acted by Audra McDonald."

The most valuable aspect of *Master Class* for McDonald was working with Zoe Caldwell, one of the theatre's most admired actresses. "She is just it for me," McDonald said of Caldwell to Kipp Cheng of *American Theatre*. "She's such a force of nature, on and offstage. She is like my touchstone. A ruby-red gem I touch and I get my energy. I learned so much from Zoe." McDonald picked up a second Tony award for *Master Class*, this time for best featured actress in a play. Despite her success as Sharon in *Master Class*, a role that was basically an acting assignment that called for singing, McDonald continued to consider herself primarily a singer. "I've always felt that I am a better actress when I'm singing than I am when I am just speaking. I think it's because I'm more comfortable singing. What I am trying to do as an actress is to bring that abandonment that I find in singing, in line with the choices that I make as an actress. I don't judge myself as much while I'm singing as I do while I'm acting," McDonald said to Haines.

Impressed with Ragtime Role

Among the most highly touted productions to come to Broadway in the 1990s, *Ragtime* is a musical version of E.L. Doctorow's bestselling 1975 novel about New York at the turn of the century. The sprawling plot concerns three sets of characters: a prosperous white family living in pleasantly suburban New Rochelle; black musicians in Harlem creating the new musical style called "ragtime;" and Jewish immigrants struggling in poverty on the teeming Lower East Side. McDonald's character, Sarah, a young black washer-

At a Glance . . .

Born Audra Ann McDonald on July 3, 1970, in Berlin, Germany; daughter of Stanley McDonald, Jr., and Anna McDonald; married Peter Donovan; children: Zoe Madeline. *Education*: Juilliard School of Music, BA, 1993.

Career: Singer and actress, 1979–.

Awards: Tony Award for Best Featured Actress in a Musical, Drama Desk Award, Outer Critics Circle Award, and Theater World Award, for *Carousel*, 1994; Tony Award for Best Featured Actress in a Play, Los Angeles Ovation Award, for *The Master Class*, 1996; Tony Award for Best Featured Actress in a Musical for *Ragtime*, 1998; Tony Award, Drama Desk Award, Outer Critics Circle Award, for *Raisin in the Sun*, 2004; Drama Desk Award for *110 in the Shade*, 2007.

Addresses: *Office*— c/o *Private Practice*, ABC, Inc., 500 S. Buena Vista Street, Burbank, CA 91521.

woman who abandons her illegitimate child, is the thread that weaves the different characters together. To the disappointment of many theatergoers, McDonald's part, though important plot-wise, was relatively small (she dies in the first act and comes back only as a ghost figure in the finale). She did get a powerful solo number, "Your Daddy's Son," and shared a duet, "Wheels of a Dream," with the lead male character, ragtime pianist Coalhouse Walker, Jr., played by Brian Stokes Mitchell.

The ebullient and sensitive McDonald associated with Sarah's emotionalism. "She's very impulsive. Very, very, impulsive. Sarah does not think before she acts. That comes really easy to me," McDonald explained to Haines, adding that "I think the challenge with Sarah, is that she's so innocent. And she's so young in her thinking, and in her way of viewing the world. I don't consider myself to be as innocent and as young in the way I view the world. I try to wipe off the grittiness of the way I view the world and look at it through a crystalline point of view like Sarah's."

Produced by the Canadian company, Livent, Inc., *Ragtime* came to New York in December 1997, after playing for a year in Toronto. An album of songs from the musical was made by the Toronto cast (including McDonald) even before the show had been seen by any audience. This unusual situation allowed *Ragtime* to open on Broadway as a known quantity and a proven success that could survive in regional productions even

if it failed in New York. Happily, the musical was a smash hit. Michael Tueth of *America* wrote that "*Ragtime: The Musical* creates a kaleidoscope whose brilliant colors glitter against a constantly threatening darkness," adding that the cast offers "some of the finest voices in American musical theater today," including the "operatic richness of Audra McDonald." John Lahr of the *New Yorker* called McDonald "outstanding" and praised *Ragtime* as "a kind of theatrical watershed: an awesome pyrotechnical display of theatrical craft and showmanship..a big, brave passionate gamble, not just with cash but with content, and it brings the American musical back to its roots as populist commercial entertainment." Written by composer Stephen Flaherty and lyricist Lynn Ahrens, with a book by *Master Class* playwright Terrence McNally, *Ragtime* won Tony Awards for Best Score and Best Book, but lost in the Best Musical category to the Disney-produced spectacle *The Lion King*. McDonald won her third Tony for *Ragtime*, her second in the Best Featured Actress in a Musical Category.

Career Blossomed Beyond the Stage

While McDonald remained a rising star on the stage— she won a fourth Tony Award in 2004 for her part in *A Raisin in the Sun* and was nominated for a her sixth Tony Award in 2007 for her role as Lizzie Curry in *110 in the Shade*—she also branched out to record solo albums and appear on television and in film. On her debut solo recording, *Way Back to Paradise*, released in the autumn of 1998, McDonald sang 14 songs by promising young musical theatre composers, including Adam Guettel, Jason Robert Brown, Ricky Ian Gordon, and Michael John LaChiusa. Originally McDonald and her producers considered using "standard" songs by Harold Arlen. When the idea to do untested material was suggested McDonald became excited about taking a chance and quickly warmed to the notion. As she told Singer, "When it's music that fills my soul, there's just no fear." Her subsequent albums featured her two-octave vocal prowess with more songs from musical theater, helping to increase her appeal among theatergoers. *How Glory Goes* featured a mix of theater standards and new songs, while *Happy Songs* offered a variety of songs from the 1930s and 40s. With her fourth album, *Build a Bridge,* in 2004, McDonald broadened her appeal by singing pop songs from such balladeers as Burt Bacharach, Elvis Costello, Rufus Wainwright, Randy Newman, and John Mayer. *Harvard Crimson* reviewer Kyle L.K. Auley found it "hard to imagine a better album to bring her to the masses."

McDonald had landed various film roles since 1998, including parts in *Cradle Will Rock* in 1999, *It Runs in the Family* in 2003, and *Best Thief in the World* in 2007, but none of these parts launched her public appeal as greatly as her work in television. McDonald positioned herself yet again to attract the attention of a broader audience when she accepted the role of Dr. Naomi Bennett on the spin-off of ABC's popular melodrama *Grey's Anatomy,* a new program called *Private Practice.* An honored veteran of the stage, McDonald seemed poised to earn more accolades in the entertainment industry. "I think her future is huge," noted *Master Class* and *Ragtime's* writer Terrence McNally to Susan Freudenheim of the *Los Angeles Times.*

Selected works

Albums

Way Back to Paradise, Nonesuch, 1998.
How Glory Goes, Nonesuch, 2000.
Happy Songs, Nonesuch, 2002.
Build a Bridge, Nonesuch, 2006.

Films

Seven Servants, 1996.
Object of My Affection, 1998.
Cradle Will Rock, 1999.
It Runs in the Family, 2003.
Best Thief in the World, 2004.

Plays

The Secret Garden, 1992.
Carousel, 1994.
The Master Class, 1995-96.
Ragtime, 1996.
Henry IV, 2003.
A Raisin in the Sun, 2004.
110 in the Shade, 2007.

Television

Private Practice, 2007.

Sources

Periodicals

America, March 28, 1998, p. 21.
American Theatre, July-August 1998, p. 26.
American Visions, June-July 2000, p. 14.
Christian Science Monitor, November 22, 2002, p. 20.
Los Angeles Times, June 20, 1995, p. F7; April 9, 2000, p. 8.
New Leader, April 11, 1994, p. 22.
New Yorker, February 2, 1998, pp. 79-80.
New York Times, March 25, 1994, p. C1; May 15, 1994, sec. 2, p. 5; November 6, 1995, p. C11; August 30, 1998, sec. 2, p. 5; September 25, 2006, p. E1.
Opera News, September 1994, p. 62; December 14, 1996, p. 52.
Washington Post, May 7, 2000, p. G1.

On-line

"Audra McDonald," *Internet Broadway Database,* www.ibdb.com/person.asp?ID=52250 (July 23, 2007).
"Audra McDonald in Concert," *National Public Radio,* www.npr.org/templates/story/story.php?storyId=7545256 (July 23, 2007).
"CD Review: Audra McDonald, 'Build a Bridge,'" *Harvard Crimson,* www.thecrimson.com/article.aspx?ref=514911 (July 23, 2007).
Tony Awards Online, www.tony.org/pantheon (August 1, 2007).

—Mary Kalfatovic and Sara Pendergast

Dwayne McDuffie

1962—

Comic book and cartoon writer, editor, publisher, producer

When Dwayne McDuffie was in high school, he wrote a film as a class project. Hearing his classmates laugh appreciatively as they watched his Super-8 film was all the encouragement McDuffie needed to launch him on a career path that led first to film school, then to becoming one of the most prolific and inventive writers in the comic book industry. Along with penning fresh and absorbing storylines for familiar comic characters from Spiderman to the Fantastic Four, McDuffie created his own highly original superheroes who would soon become classics in their own right.

Painfully aware of the absence of black faces and African-American stories in the world of U.S. comics, McDuffie joined forces in the early 1990s with a comic artist and a business expert to publish a more diverse line of comic books. Milestone Media, the company they formed, introduced a generation of children of color to a wide variety of superheroes who looked like them. After several years of publishing comics, McDuffie and Milestone both expanded their creative energies into television, creating shows that, like their heroes, smashed stereotypes and demolished prejudice with jaunty humor and a passion for justice.

Enjoyed Entertaining People

Dwayne Glenn McDuffie was born in Detroit, Michigan, on February 20, 1962, the son of Edna Earle Hawkins Gardner and Leroy McDuffie. He attended the Roeper School, a school for gifted children in the nearby Detroit suburb of Bloomfield Hills. It was while he was attending high school at Roeper that McDuffie

wrote a film for a class assignment and learned the satisfaction of entertaining an audience. After graduating from high school during the late 1970s, he earned his bachelor's degree at the University of Michigan in 1983, then moved to New York to attend New York University's Tisch School of the Arts. Though he did not graduate from the program, he learned many elements of visual storytelling and script production that would make him a skilled comic book writer.

While attending NYU in 1985 and 1986, McDuffie worked as a resident advisor for other students. In 1987, he was hired as copy editor for *Investment Dealers Digest*, a New York-based financial journal. After a short time there, he took a job as a special projects editor for Marvel Comics. Founded in 1939, Marvel was first known as Timely Publications, then Atlas, before taking its present name. As Marvel Comics, the company launched such popular comics as *Spiderman, Daredevil,* and *The Fantastic Four.* McDuffie began writing for Marvel, and soon found that comic writing was not so different from writing for films, since his stories were not narrated as in a novel, but "acted" by the drawn characters on the page. He loved the drama, the magic, and the endless possibilities of the comic universe, where superpowers were commonplace, and the characters had long, complex, and interconnected histories.

McDuffie had worked for Marvel for two years when he came up with an innovative idea for his own comic series. Comic fans are often exacting critics, and they demand that writers remain consistent to reality, as it exists within the comic universe. Keeping this in mind,

At a Glance . . .

Born Dwayne Glenn McDuffie on February 20, 1962, in Detroit, MI; married Patricia Younger, 1990; children: Angel, Avshalom. *Education:* University of Michigan, BA, 1983; attended New York University, Tisch School of the Arts.

Career: Marvel Comics, special projects editor, 1987-90; Harvey Comics, consultant, 1990; Milestone Media Inc, editor-in-chief, 1991-97; *Static Shock*, writer, story editor, 2000; *Justice League*, producer, 2001, editor, 2001, writer, 2002-06, story editor 2003-04; *Teen Titans*, writer, 2003; *What's New, Scooby-Doo?* writer, 2002.

Selected awards: Humanitas Prize, 2003; 11 Parents' Choice Awards.

Addresses: *Web*—www.dwaynemcduffie.com.

McDuffie became intrigued with the question of who cleaned up the mess when superheroes battled supervillains, leaving skyscrapers in ruins and city streets full of rubble. Perhaps inspired by generations of African Americans who had worked behind the scenes cleaning other people's messes, he invented a comic corporation called Damage Control. Part construction company, part engineering firm, and part insurance brokerage, Damage Control specializes in repairing the destruction caused when superpowers collide. The first Damage Control story appeared in a 1989 anthology comic titled, *Marvel Comics Presents.* The concept was immediately popular with readers and soon Damage Control had top billing in its own comic mini-series. Marvel published three different *Damage Control* mini series before ending the title in 1991. However, Damage Control executives still turn up occasionally as bit players in other Marvel stories.

Founded Milestone Media

In 1990, McDuffie left Marvel to work independently as a freelance comic writer. While working on stories for a variety of publishers, including Marvel, Valiant, and Harvey, he was hatching another bold idea. In 1992 he united with two comic artists, Denys Cowan and Michael Davis, and an expert in business, Derek T. Dingle, to found Milestone Media, a publishing company devoted to promoting diversity in comics. The owners of Milestone made a publishing agreement with comic giant DC Comics, gaining DC's wide distribution while keeping creative control and copyright ownership of all Milestone titles.

While still at Marvel, McDuffie had introduced several African-American characters into the Marvel universe, including Deathlok, the only black superhero at the time who had his own comic title. As editor in chief of Milestone, he created many memorable black superheroes, among them Static and Icon. *Icon* comics highlight the adventures of an extra-terrestrial who takes on the form of a black slave after his spacecraft crashes on earth. Surviving through many human generations, Icon becomes a superhero whose secret identity is Augustus Freeman IV, a conservative lawyer. Static is the superhero alter ego of Virgil Hawkins, a geeky high school student who, after being exposed to toxic chemicals, realizes he can control and throw static electricity.

Static comics proved so popular with readers that the WB network approached McDuffie and Milestone about creating an animated series based on Static's adventures. The resulting program, *Static Shock,* which debuted in 2000, aired 52 episodes and was one of WB's top Saturday morning cartoons for two seasons. After its initial run, the program was syndicated on the Cartoon Network, where it again gained high ratings. *Static Shock* was nominated for Emmy awards, Writer's Guild Awards, and Eisner Awards, and won McDuffie the prestigious Humanitas Award for an episode titled "Jimmy," condemning violence and the use of guns.

Working on *Static Shock,* McDuffie found that he enjoyed writing for television. He worked on other programs, bringing his originality and sense of fun to the classic cartoon shows, *Justice League, Teen Titans,* and *What's New, Scooby-Doo?* McDuffie's solid writing and his respect for both viewers and subject matter have drawn strong praise from both critics and fans. As Ayize Jama-Everett says on the *Code Z* Web site, "You can't watch a Dwayne McDuffie cartoon and think you're watching fluff. There isn't a character that he's involved with that doesn't have some compelling motivation. These aren't animated figures you're watching, they're people struggling with feelings and emotions."

In 1997 Milestone Media dropped its comic publishing division to devote itself to its television productions. In 2006, the company signed a contract with the Black Entertainment Television to form a BET animation department. The new department is slated to debut the network's first animated series in 2007, an adult action-adventure cartoon titled *Hannibal the Conqueror.*

McDuffie continues to be one of the most prolific writers in the world of comics and animation. In 2006, he returned to Marvel to work on a special edition comic of the classic *Fantastic Four,* and in 2007 he began writing for the DC comic *Firestorm.* Meanwhile, he continues to work on animated television programs, including an update of a Cartoon Network classic *Ben 10*, about a youth who discovers an alien device that allows him to become ten different superheroes, as well as a fresh take on the *Justice League*. One of the most important skills McDuffie brings to his work is his ability to add depth and complexity to bring a fresh approach to familiar characters and stories. Just the way a writer of more "serious" literature does, he offers both readers and viewers the opportunity to find their own experience in the lives of his characters, while at the same time providing escape, fun, and fantasy.

Selected works

Comics

Damage Control, Marvel Comics.
Deathlok, Marvel Comics.
Double Dragon, Marvel Comics.
Fantastic Four Special, Marvel Comics.
Giant Man, Marvel Comics.
Hellraiser, Marvel Comics.
Iron Man, Marvel Comics.
Marvel Super Heroes, Marvel Comics.
Blood Syndicate, Milestone Comics.
Hardware, Milestone Comics.
Icon, Milestone Comics.
Milestone Ultimate, Milestone Comics.
Shadow Cabinet, Milestone Comics.
Static, Milestone Comics.
Static Shock, Milestone Comics.
Worlds Collide, Milestone Comics.
Firestorm, DC Comics.
Fantastic Four, DC Comics.

Television, writer, editor, producer

Static Shock, 2000.
Justice League, 2001–.
Teen Titans, 2003.
What's New, Scooby-Doo? 2002.

Sources

Periodicals

Black Enterprise, November 1994, pp. 81-6.
Booklist, March 15, 2005, pp. 1302-4.
New York Times, October 8, 1989, p. 46.
Television Week, August 14, 2006, p. 9.

On-line

"Breaking In: Dwayne McDuffie on a Life in Comics and Animation," *Code Z,* www.codezonline.com/featurearticle/ (June 29, 2007).
"Damage Control," *Don Markstein's Toonpedia,* www.toonopedia.com/dcontrol.htm (June 29, 2007).
"Dwayne Glenn McDuffie," *Biography Resource Center,* http://galenet.galegroup.com/servlet/BioRC (June 29, 2007).
Dwayne McDuffie, www.dwaynemcduffie.com (June 29, 2007).
"Dwayne McDuffie," *Internet Movie Database,* www.imdb.com/name/nm0568336/ (June 29, 2007).
"Dwayne McDuffie on the Balance of Justice and Injustice," *Comic Book Resources,* www.comicbookresources.com/news/newsitem.cgi?id=10988 (June 29, 2007).
"Getting The FF Off Their Mcduffs," *Wizard Entertainment,* www.wizarduniverse.com/magazine/wizard/003231572.cfm (June 29, 2007).
"Pro File: Dwayne McDuffie," *Mac.com,* http://web.mac.com/dmcduffie/iWeb/Site/Marvel%20Pro%20File_files/Image37.png (June 29, 2007).
"Wordballoon: Dwayne McDuffie, Justified," *Digg,* http://digg.com/podcasts/wordballoon_the_comic_creators_interview_show/152206 (June 29, 2007).

—Tina Gianoulis

Elizabeth Nunez

1944(?)—

Author

The novels of Elizabeth Nunez examine the cultural unease that West Indian blacks like herself have experienced both at home in the Caribbean and as immigrants to an America deeply divided by racism. Her 2006 novel *Prospero's Daughter* was hailed by critics as a trenchant fictional exploration of the clashes between British and blacks in Trinidad, her native land. Elizabeth Schmidt, writing in the *New York Times Book Review,* called it a "gripping and richly imagined" work, while *Black Issues Book Review* critic Marjorie Valbrun praised it as "a rich story that moves back and forth easily between the past and the present, between reality and fantasy, and between falsely perceived truth and the truth that ultimately sets the characters free."

Nunez was born in Trinidad in the mid-1940s and grew up during the final years of the island's struggle for independence from Britain. As a young girl she won a scholarship to a prestigious academy established by colonial authorities. She then came to the United States at the age of 19. By 1967, she had earned her bachelor's degree in English from Marian College in Fond du Lac, Wisconsin. After a brief return to Trinidad, where Nunez found it difficult to find satisfying work, she returned to the United States to further her studies. She earned her doctorate in English from New York University, and entered academia in 1972. For much of her career she has taught at Medgar Evers College, founded in 1970 as a Brooklyn campus of the City University of New York (CUNY) system, where she has advanced to serve as distinguished professor and chair of the school's humanities department.

Debuted as Novelist in 1986

When the esteemed novelist John Oliver Killens became a writer-in-residence at Medgar Evers in 1981, he urged Nunez to join one of his writing workshops. One of her fellow students in the fiction seminar was Terry McMillan, who was working on what would become her 1987 debut novel, *Mama,* at the time. Nunez and Killens went on to organize the National Black Writers Conference at Medgar Evers College, which Nunez ran for 13 years following Killens's death in 1987. Nunez secured funding for the project from the National Endowment for the Humanities, the Nathan Cummings Foundation, and the Reed Foundation.

Nunez's first novel, *When Rocks Dance,* was published by Putnam in 1986 and featured a fantastical plot involving a voodoo ritual. A dozen years passed before its follow-up, *Beyond the Limbo Silence,* appeared. Its story recounts the journey of a young West Indian woman who arrives in the United States for college at the height of the civil-rights movement in the early 1960s, and her political awakening comes with the help of a young African-American man active in the struggle for equal rights. "Nunez integrates a wealth of Trinidadian culture into her tale," wrote Barbara Mujica in *Americas.* "Descriptions of music, folklore, customs, and foods enrich her narrative and make it a celebration of Afro-Caribbean traditions as well as a sad reminder of a difficult time in U.S. history."

Bruised Hibiscus, Nunez's third novel, won critical acclaim in 2000 for its exploration of interracial ro-

At a Glance . . .

Born in 1944(?) in Trinidad; naturalized U.S. citizen. *Education:* Marian College, Fond du Lac, WI, BA, English, 1967; New York University, English, PhD, 1972.

Career: City University of New York, Medgar Evers College, professor (now CUNY Distinguished Professor of English), 1972–; National Black Writers Conference, co-founder and director, 1986-2000; WBAI 99.5 FM, *Sunday with Writers,* host; CUNY TV, *Black Writers in America,* executive producer, 2000s–.

Memberships: PEN (chair, American Open Book committee).

Awards: Independent Publishers Book Award, for multicultural fiction, 1999; American Book Award, 2001 and 2002; Institute of Caribbean Studies, Outstanding Contribution to Literature Award, 2004.

Addresses: *Home*—Amityville, NY. *Agent*—Ivy Fischer Stone, Fifi Oscard Agency, 110 W 40th St, 16th fl, New York, NY 10018.

mance in Trinidad in the early 1950s. Its dual protagonists are Rosa and Zuela, childhood friends who meet again as adults when both are locked in abusive marriages. A *Publishers Weekly* review commended "the incantatory, authentic Trinidadian dialect with which Nunez deftly infuses the dark, devastating tale with spirit and heart," while *New York Times* reviewer Jana Giles asserted that Nunez's "substantial research results in illuminating and sometimes moving insights into the entanglements of race, class and gender in the heterogeneous and geographically limited society of Trinidad a half century ago."

Viewed Personal Loss through Male Viewpoint

Nunez's next tale, *Discretion,* finally moved away from the Caribbean settings of her earlier works, and featured her first male protagonist. Of the genesis for this 2002 story, Nunez explained to Denolyn Carroll of *Essence* that the fact that "women get their hearts broken" had long driven her fiction, and "I wondered whether men suffered the same torments of the heart." The story centers around Oufoula Sindede, a diplomat from an unnamed African nation trapped in a loveless marriage. Posted in Washington, he falls in love with

the wife of a colleague while on a visit to New York City. Initially he does not reveal to the woman, an artist named Marguerite, that he is married. Though for much of his life he has adhered to Western cultural values as a way to show disapproval of some of the less admirable aspects of his heritage, he does begin to rethink the concept of polygamy, which his culture condones. Writing in the *New York Times Book Review,* Sarah Towers found the work "refreshingly ambitious in its intellectual scope, and in Oufoula, who's a decent, thoughtful man, she's created a persuasive, sometimes deeply moving character, a man who remains haunted by his early betrayal by his mother, who left him and his father for another man."

The protagonist of Nunez's next novel, *Grace,* is also a man who suddenly finds himself confused by the institution of marriage after several uneventful years as a family man. In this case the character is Justin Peters, a Trinidad-born professor of literature in New York City who is married to an African-American woman. She leaves him one day, placing their union in jeopardy, and Justin struggles to understand the causes of her discontent and remain a presence in the life of his beloved young daughter. In the end, he finds some answers in the works of classic literature from the "dead white writers" that others in his English department urge him to reconsider in his course syllabi. "Nunez's skill as a writer and storyteller," noted Denolyn Carroll, this time writing in *Black Issues Book Review,* "is...evident in her portrayal of Justin's slow recognition of his own failings," and described this fifth novel from Nunez as a story that "speaks to our propensity for self-delusion that cripples our relationship with ourselves and with those we profess to care deeply about."

Nunez's 2006 work, *Prospero's Daughter,* earned her more critical accolades for its re-imagining of a classic Shakespeare play, *The Tempest.* The original plot centered on the scholarly Prospero, who was shipwrecked with his daughter on an island and finds there Caliban, a dark-skinned slave, and a sprite named Ariel. As the play begins, Prospero has jailed Caliban, whom he has spent several years educating, for what he believes to be an attempted sexual assault on Miranda. One of Shakespeare's most enduring and analyzed tales, *The Tempest* is widely considered an allegory on colonialism and its pitfalls. Nunez first encountered the play in the classroom of her private school in Trinidad, and she recalled in an article she wrote for *Black Issues Book Review* in 2006 that she felt a deep sense of shame at the time, for "even at 14, I cannot miss the parallels between my situation in a British colony and Caliban's. In both our cases, Europeans have come to our islands, and though surely they have laid claim to our land, they have given us much in return. I am proof of their beneficence, sitting in a classroom, getting an education they have been kind enough to provide for me."

Re-Imagined Shakespeare's Tale

Nunez revealed in the same article that throughout her academic career she had periodically revisited the play and considered different interpretations of the symbolism of Caliban and Miranda. Finally she decided to explore the issue herself in the novel form. *Prospero's Daughter* is set in the mid-twentieth century when a disgraced British physician, Philip Gardner, arrives with his infant daughter, Virginia, on an island off Trinidad's coast that is home to a colony of lepers and few others. The doctor takes over the home of an orphaned boy named Carlos. While he uses Carlos to carry on his medical experiments, he also tutors the boy alongside his own daughter. The two children develop a strong bond with each other and grow closer as they mature. The story begins in the early 1960s just as Gardner has jailed Carlos for what he termed improper behavior toward his now-teenaged daughter, Virginia. A British police official from Trinidad comes to investigate, and the story unfolds in flashback.

"Carlos's traditional education—even at the hands of a creep like Gardner—helps him grow and eventually challenge Gardner," noted Schmidt in the *New York Times Book Review*. "In this sense, Carlos's fate represents a plan for post-independence Trinidad; going backward, ignoring the traces of European influence isn't a realistic way to move forward." Nunez said that the four years it took her to write *Prospero's Daughter* marked a turning point in her life. The process, she told *Essence*, "helped me realize I can be a proud Caribbean person without having to apologize for being the beneficiary of a colonial system that inspired my love of classical literature." *Black Issues Book Review* named Nunez's book the Best Novel of the Year in 2006.

While spending the majority of her time writing, Nunez remained a mentor others. Continuing as a professor at Medgar Evers College, she also chaired the PEN American Center Open Book program and served as Chairman of the Board for the Center for Black Literature and the Friends of the Calabash International Literary Festival. She produced the 2004 Emmy-nominated series, *Black Writers in America*, a CUNY TV television program featuring interviews with prominent black authors. And served as host of *Sundays*

with Writers, a radio program for WBAI 99.5 FM. Whether writing her own works or working with with others, Nunez found her life revolved around books. Summing up her experience to eCaroh Communications writer Cedriann J. Martin, Nunez said, "I read books, I write books, I write about books."

Selected works

Books

When Rocks Dance, Putnam, 1986.
Beyond the Limbo Silence, Seal, 1998.
Bruised Hibiscus, Seal, 2000.
Discretion, One World/Ballantine, 2002.
Grace, One World/Ballantine, 2003.
Prospero's Daughter, Ballantine, 2006.

Sources

Periodicals

Americas, May 1999, p. 61.
Black Issues Book Review, March-April 2002, p. 30; March-April 2003, p. 43; March-April 2006, p. 24, p. 26.
Essence, April 1990, p. 36; March 2002, p. 104; April 2006, p. 72.
New York Times, April 9, 2000.
New York Times Book Review, March 10, 2002, p. 9; February 26, 2006.
Publishers Weekly, February 28, 2000, p. 59; January 20, 2003, p. 54; October 17, 2005, p. 39.

On-line

"Authors: Elizabeth Nunez," *Random House,* www.randomhouse.com/author/results.pperl?authorid=22421 (July 2, 2007).
"Book Talk with Caribbean Writers," *eCaroh Communications,* www.ecaroh.com/bmp/think/caribbean-writers.htm (July 2, 2007).
"Trinidad Author Recognized by ICS in DC," *Trinidad and Tobago Association of Washington, DC,* www.ttdc.org/tantan/features4.htm (July 2, 2007).

—Carol Brennan

Paula Patton

1975—

Actor

Patton, Paula, photograph. Sebastian Widmann/DPA/Landov.

Paula Patton grew up in Los Angeles, California, in the backyard of the movie business. Though she dreamed of acting in films and attended a high school that focused on the creative arts, she was too shy to consider acting a realistic career choice. Yet after she earned a college degree in filmmaking and began working behind the scenes in the movie industry, her desire to perform persisted. Deciding that she had to at least try to succeed as an actor, she took lessons and began auditioning. In a business where success often comes after years of painful rejection, Paula Patton was cast in a leading role in her third film. Patton's warmth and generosity on screen coupled with an enthusiastic willingness to work hard have endeared her to both filmmakers and audiences at the beginning of her acting career. Aware that, in her early 30s, she was already considered "old" by Hollywood standards, Patton refused to accept such limitations. In order to break down barriers of race, gender, and age, she applied the same determination that helped her overcome shyness and insecurity to become a breakout movie star.

Raised for Film

Born in 1975, the daughter of a lawyer father and a teacher mother, Patton grew up very close to the Twentieth Century Fox studios in Los Angeles. Inspired by the movies that were being made close by, she spent her childhood playing dress-up in the vintage gowns her mother bought for her at second-hand shops and putting on neighborhood productions. She attended Hamilton Magnet Arts High School, where she continued to perform in school plays. One of her favorite roles was the part of Abigail Williams, a girl whose schemes and lies are central to the plot of *The Crucible,* Arthur Miller's drama about a witch-hunt in Salem, Massachusetts.

The summer after her graduation from high school, Patton attended a summer film program at the University of Southern California, where she made two dramatic short films using a super-8 camera. That summer, she also heard that the Public Broadcasting System was seeking young aspiring filmmakers to participate in a new reality show, created and produced by Shauna Garr, who had previously produced pro-

At a Glance . . .

Born in 1975; married Robin Thicke, 2005. *Education:* University of Southern California, School of Cinematic Arts, BA, critical studies, 1997.

Career: *Howie Madel Show,* production assistant, 1998-99; Discovery Health Channel, *Medical Diaries,* producer, 2000; actor, 2005–.

Awards: Multicultural Motion Picture Association, Nova Award, 2006.

grams for the MTV cable network. More than 250 teenagers sent in letters and tapes, auditioning for the show, which would be called *The Ride*, and would feature six young filmmakers traveling throughout the United States, making films about the diversity of American youth.

The 17-year-old Patton sent in her application letter, and Garr selected her to participate in *The Ride.* Patton put her college plans on hold and eagerly joined the project. The crew of six young filmmakers traveled together for three months, making films about a wide range of issues of concern to young people, such as eating disorders, school, ethnic identity, and gangs. The films were aired on PBS in eight 30-minute episodes in 1996.

Began Career in Production

Patton's experience in filming *The Ride* inspired her to consider filmmaking as her career. Though she entered the University of California at Berkeley as she had planned, she soon transferred back to the University of Southern California School of Cinematic Arts, where she earned her bachelor's degree in critical studies in 1997. She sought employment in the entertainment industry and became a production assistant, working on several television documentaries and the *Howie Mandel Show,* a syndicated talk show that ran during the 1998-99 season.

Being a production assistant often meant little more than running errands and fetching coffee for the cast and crew, and Patton soon tired of the work though it would forever give her an appreciation for the role that low-level workers play on a production crew. Working as a production assistant also helped her to understand that a film is much more than the product of the actors and the director. Everyone working on the set contributes to the success of the final product. When she became an actor and was given star status on the set,

she would remember to be respectful and friendly to the assistants who took care of her needs.

Patton's next career move was into production itself, as she got a job producing segments for the documentary series *Medical Diaries* on the Discovery Health Channel. Though she found the work interesting, she gradually became convinced that production was not her dream job. Working on programs about life, death, and illness, she was impressed with the fragility of life and the importance of taking risks to create the life she wanted. She decided to stop working behind the camera and put her energies into fulfilling her dream of becoming an actor.

Insecure about her abilities, and worried that she might be humiliated in a class, she took private acting lessons for a year. At the end of that time, she began auditioning for film roles. Her success was almost immediate. In 2005, she landed a leading role in a pilot for a television program called *Murder Book,* which gave her acting experience, even though the pilot was never aired. This was followed by small roles in a little-seen film about drug use and relationships called *London*, and a warm-hearted Will Smith romantic comedy called *Hitch.*

On June 11, 2005, Patton married her longtime boyfriend Robin Thicke, a musician and singer. She has appeared in her husband's music videos and modeled for the cover of his album, *A Beautiful World.*

Turned to Acting

In 2006, Patton auditioned for a vintage musical film called *Idlewild* and was stunned to be given one of the leading roles. The film, directed by Bryan Baker, was a showcase for the hip-hop duo OutKast, the stage name of singers Antwan A. Patton (no relation to Paula) and Andre Benjamin. It was set in prohibition-era Idlewild, Georgia, and told the story of gangsters, juke joints, and the love affair between a mortician and a jazz singer. Patton played the singer, Angel Davenport. Even though she did not have a strong singing voice (her songs were dubbed by another singer), Patton's easy glamour and sultry sweetness contributed to the film's stylish glitter. While *Idlewild* received mixed reviews, many critics praised Patton's stage presence.

Soon after the release of *Idlewild*, Patton was cast in another leading role, this time opposite Academy-award winning actor Denzel Washington. The film, *Deja Vu*, directed by Tony Scott, was a science fiction thriller about an FBI agent who falls in love with one of the victims of a crime he is investigating, then gets a chance to travel back in time and save her life. As the beautiful victim, Claire Kuchever, Patton captivated both the agent, played by Washington, and film audiences. For the role, she was given the Nova Award of the Multicultural Motion Picture Association and nominated for the Black Reel Award for Best Breakthrough Performance. As of April 2007, Patton was scheduled to star in another major film, *Mirrors*, a ghost story directed by Alexandre Aja and co-starring Kiefer Sutherland.

Though Patton's acting career began in a dramatically successful way, she understood well the difficulties faced by aspiring actors, especially women and people of color, and she hoped to challenge the many barriers placed before anyone who does not fit the Hollywood image of beauty. In an interview with Lynn Hirschberg in the Spring 2007 *New York Times Magazine,* she said, "In this business, there are just too many boundaries and boxes. You have to not listen."

Selected works

Films

London, 2005.
Hitch, 2005.
Idlewild, 2006.
Deja Vu, 2006.

Television

The Ride, 1996.

Sources

Periodicals

Back Stage West, November 2, 2006, p. 2.
Ebony, February 2007, p. 36.
Essence, March 2007, p. 46.
Entertainment Weekly, November 24, 2006, p. 29.
Esquire, December 2006, p. 49.
Interview, December 2005, p. 60.
Los Angeles Times, November 5, 2006, p. E20.
Marie Claire. October 2006, pp. 128-131.
New York Times Magazine. Spring 2007, pp. 70-4.
Oakland Post (Oakland, California), September 6-12, pp. 8-10.
Sentinel (Los Angeles, California), November 16, 1994, p. B7; November 9-15, 2006 pp. B5-B7.

On-line

"*Idlewild:* An Interview With Paula Patton," *Black-film.com,* www.blackfilm.com/20060818/features-/paulapatton.shtml (July 18, 2007).
"Paula Patton," *Ask Men.com,* www.askmen.com/women/celeb_profiles_actress/49_paula_patton.html (July 18, 2007).
"Paula Patton," *Internet Movie Database,* www.imdb.com/name/nm1745736/bio (July 18, 2007).

—Tina Gianoulis

Rosemary Sadlier

19??—

Historian, author

The president of the Ontario Black History Society, Rosemary Sadlier has been at the forefront of a host of initiatives aimed at educating the public on the history of blacks in Canada. She has given lectures on black history around the country and participated in conferences everywhere from Toronto to Trinidad and Tobago. Sadlier played a central role in the successful effort to lobby Canada's provincial and federal governments to officially declare February as Black History Month. She has collaborated with the Historica Foundation of Canada to create a black history portal on the Internet. And she is the author of several books on topics ranging from the Underground Railroad to Mary Ann Shadd, the first female newspaper editor in North America. Her most recent book is the award-winning *The Kids Book of Black Canadian History.*

Sadlier was born and raised in Toronto. She earned an Honors Bachelor of Arts degree in sociology from York University and a Bachelor's degree in education and a Masters of Social Work from the University of Toronto.

Much of her life's work has been aimed at raising the national awareness of black Canadian history. She has made most of her contributions through her writing and through her leadership of the Ontario Black History Society (OBHS). The president of the OBHS since 1993, she was at the head of a campaign that led to the 1996 official declaration of February as Black History Month in Canada. She told the *Toronto Sun* that part of the impetus for the effort was the dearth of black history courses in Canadian higher education: "I know someone who wanted to pursue doctoral studies in black Canadian history, who was told that there were insufficient resources here; they should conduct research in the United States." As she wrote in an essay published on the OBHS's Web site, the annual observation of black history is important for young African Canadians, who need to "feel affirmed, be aware of the contributions made by other Blacks in Canada, have role models, and understand the social forces that have shaped and influenced their community." In the same essay she argued that Black History Month is also important for helping the wider community get a clearer perception of their culture. "One needs traditional history to engender a common culture," she wrote. "One needs black history to engender a clearer and more complete culture."

Sadlier has led the OBHS in the development of a wide array of educational projects and presentations. The society offers "African Canadian History and Heritage Talks," produces oral history tapes and collections of historic photographs, organizes conferences and seminars, and runs a black history bus tour. The society recently collaborated with the Historica Foundation of Canada and the Canadian Encyclopedia to create the *Black History Canada* Web site. The site is organized by themes, such as "Black Settlement in Early Canada," "Black Contributions," and "Caribbean and African Immigration." Each section includes an essay written by Sadlier along with links to recommended information sources. Currently Sadlier is leading the society's effort to develop the Centre of African-Canadian History and Culture, a Toronto complex that

At a Glance . . .

Born Rosemary Sadlier in Toronto, Ontario, Canada; married Jay; children: Jenne, Raia, Alexander. *Education:* York University, Hon. BA, sociology; University of Toronto, BEd, MSW; pursuing doctorate at the Ontario Institute for Studies in Education/ University of Toronto.

Career: Women's Bureau of the Office of the Deputy Premier; Ontario Black History Society, president, 1993–.

Memberships: The Black Ice Hockey and Sports Hall of Fame, board of directors.

Awards: Ministry of Citizenship, Ten-Year Volunteer Service Award, 1994; Toronto Eaton Centre, Salute to the City Award, 1997; City of Toronto, City Council, William P. Hubbard Race Relations Award, 1999; Inter-City Multicultural School, Appreciation Award of Excellence, 2000; United Achievers of Brampton, Black History Makers Award, 2001; Planet Africa Television Marcus Garvey Award, 2005.

Addresses: *Office*—Ontario Black History Society, 10 Adelaide Street East, Suite 202, Toronto, Ontario M5C 1J3 Canada.

will incorporate a museum as well as a cultural center for conferences and concerts.

Sadlier's second main arena for her advocacy is her writing. She has authored four books: *Leading the Way: Black Women in Canada, Mary Ann Shadd: Publisher, Editor, Teacher, Lawyer, Suffragette; Tubman: Harriet Tubman and the Underground Railroad, Her Life in the United States and Canada*; and her most recent, *The Kids Book of Black Canadian History.* Sadlier told *Contemporary Black Biography* that she wrote the book "to create a resource on African-Canadian history that would resonate with young people even should they not have the opportunity to have an OBHS black history talk at their school. I wanted to do my part to ensure that my own children, as well as the diverse range of young people that my children will grow up to share this place with, would have something to understand and appreciate the long-term and ongoing nature of the black experience,

our challenges and triumphs in Canada." The book introduces readers to such people as Harriet Tubman, who helped black slaves from the United States reach freedom in Canada via the Underground Railroad, and the Colored Corps, an all-black unit that fought in the war of 1812. Writing in the Canadian education magazine *Resource Links,* reviewer Victoria Pennel called the book "Good, even great at times." She proclaimed it "a welcome addition to Canadian social studies programs at the elementary and junior high levels." In *CM: Canadian Review of Materials,* Grace Sheppard wrote, "teachers and librarians looking to fill a gap in their collections of Canadian history books will do a dance of joy when they read through this thorough treatment." In 2004 the book won the White Raven Award from Munich, Germany's International Youth Library.

Sadlier has also had an active career outside of her history crusade, particularly in the fields of education and social work. She has worked as a school teacher and a hospital social worker and done volunteer work with developmentally delayed adults, emotionally disturbed children, and recent immigrants. She sat on Toronto's Ministry of Education Advisory Panel and vetted the black history curriculum produced by Toronto's District School Board. She was employed in the Women's Bureau of the Office of the Deputy Premier, where she developed a series of programs to encourage women to pursue training and employment in science fields. In the mid-2000s she completed her doctoral coursework at the Ontario Institute for Studies in Education/University of Toronto in the Department of Sociology and Equity Studies in Education.

Selected writings

Books

Leading the Way: Black Women in Canada, Umbrella Press, 1994.
Mary Ann Shadd: Publisher, Editor, Teacher, Lawyer, Suffragette, Umbrella Press, 1995.
Tubman: Harriet Tubman and the Underground Railroad, Her Life in the United States and Canada, Umbrella Press, 1997.
The Kids Book of Black Canadian History, Kids Can Press, 2003.

Sources

Books

Directory of American Scholars, 10th ed. Gale Group, 2002.

Periodicals

CM: Canadian Review of Materials, Vol. X, No. 2, September 19, 2003.
Resource Links, December 2003, p. 29.

On-line

"Dr. Rosemary Sadlier (abd)," *Irie Music Festival,* www.iriemusicfestival.com/lit_tent/rosemary_sadlier.html (June 25, 2007).
"Everything Old Is New Again," *Toronto Sun Career Connection,* www.canoe.ca/CareerConnection-News/040218_blackhistory.html (June 25, 2007).
"First Canadian Black History Portal Launches," *Histori.ca,* www.histori.ca/release.do?id=15416 (June 24, 2007).
"Rosemary Sadlier," *Black History Society,* www.blackhistorysociety.ca/BLKCNDHistory.pdf (June 24, 2007).
"Rosemary Sadlier," *Wordfest,* www.wordfest.com/2003/festival_authors/Rosemary+Sadlier (June 24, 2007).
"Sadlier Named to Board of Directors of the Black Ice Hockey and Sports Hall of Fame," *Society of North American Hockey Historians and Researchers,* www.sonahhr.com/sonahhr/index.cfm?fuseaction=home.newsDetail&NEWS_ID=232 (June 25, 2007).
"Why a Black History Month," Ontario Black History Society, www.blackhistorysociety.ca/BH_Month.htm (June 20, 2007).

Other

Additional information for this profile was obtained through an interview with Rosemary Sadlier via e-mail on June 21, 2007.

—Robert Genovesi

Ousmane Sembène

1923-2007

Filmmaker, writer

Ousmane Sembène was often referred to as "the father of African cinema." Yet even such a grandiose title fails to capture the full impact of Sembène's accomplishments as an author, filmmaker, and social critic. Taken together, his work represents an ongoing literary battle against corruption, colonialism, and hypocrisy in all its forms. Despite the international attention his films and novels received, Sembène ignored the lure of commercial moviemaking, preferring instead to remain in his homeland of Senegal, where he was revered as a champion of working people and other victims of exploitation. Sembène died in 2007 after a long illness. Upon his passing, Manthia Diawara, professor of comparative literature and Africana studies at New York University, told the *New York Times* that "He really is the most important African filmmaker. The one that all subsequent filmmakers have to be measured against."

Raised in French-ruled Senegal

Sembène was born into a family of fishermen on January 1, 1923, in the village of Ziguinchor, Senegal, which was then a French colony. His parents divorced when he was a child, and the young Sembène was sent to live for varying periods of time with different relatives. Of all the family members he spent time with, the most influential was his mother's oldest brother, Abdou Rahmane Diop. Diop, a teacher, intellectual, and devout Muslim, instilled in Sembène a sense of pride in his African heritage. At the age of eight, Sembène was sent to Islamic school. When Diop died in 1935,

however, Sembène moved to Dakar to live with another uncle. In Dakar, he began attending French schools. His formal education ended at the age of 14, when he quit school after a physical fight with a teacher.

During the next few years, Sembène worked at a series of odd jobs to support himself, including stints as a mechanic, a carpenter, and a mason. It was during this period that he became mesmerized by the cinema, where he and his friends would spend as much of their free time as possible. He also absorbed a great deal of Senegalese culture from traditional storytellers (griots) and musicians. In 1938 Sembène had what he described as a mystical experience, resulting in a renewed commitment to Islam. Although his religious fervor was short-lived, it sparked in Sembène a sense of justice and commitment that he carried into his subsequent secular life.

When he was 19, Sembène joined the French colonial forces in their battle against Nazi Germany. After four years in the military, during which he fought in Europe and Africa, Sembène returned to Dakar, where he helped organize the Dakar-Niger railroad strike of 1947 and 1948. His experience in the railroad strike provided the material for his 1960 epic novel *God's Bits of Wood*, widely considered to be his literary masterpiece. When the strike was over, and with job opportunities in Senegal scarce, Sembène made his way to France as a stowaway on a ship. Arriving in Paris, he worked at a series of factory jobs. He then moved to Marseilles, where he became a longshoreman; he also resumed his activities as a labor organizer

At a Glance . . .

Born Ousmane Sembène on January 1, 1923, in Ziguinchor, Senegal; died on June 10, 2007, in Dakar, Senegal; son of a fisherman; married Carrie Moore, 1974; one other marriage; children: Alain and Moussa, both sons. *Education*: Attended Gorki Film Studios, Moscow, 1962. *Politics*: Leftist.

Career: Worked as a laborer in a variety of occupations, including fisherman, plumber, mechanic, and bricklayer, 1938-42; served in the Free French Forces, 1942-46; dockworker, 1948-60; novelist, 1956-92; filmmaker, 1963-2004; *Kaadu* newspaper, founding editor, 1972.

Memberships: Senegalese Association of Film Makers, co-founder; Pan African Federation of Film Makers (Fepaci), co-founder; African Association of Culture; Pen Club International.

Awards: First Film Award, Tours (France) Film Festival, 1963; Dakar Festival of Negro Arts prize, 1966; Cannes Film Festival prize, 1967; International Critics' prize, Venice Bienale, 1968; Venice Film Festival prize, 1969; Atlanta Film Festival prize, 1970; Silver Medal, Moscow Film Festival, 1971; Paul Robeson Prize, 1978; Nahouri Bronze Medal from the government of Burkina Faso, 1987; Grand Prix, Venice Film Festival, 1988; Gold Medal, Venice Film Festival, 1992; Akira Kurosawa Award for Lifetime Achievement, San Francisco International Film Festival, 1993; Prix un Certain Regard, Cannes Film Festival, 2004; Best Foreign Film, American Association of Film Critics, 2004, for *Moolaadé*; Lifetime Achievement Award, Chicago International Film Festival, 2005.

and became affiliated with the French communist party.

Took Up Writing in France

By the early 1950s, Sembène had begun writing on a regular basis, mostly as an outlet for his political and philosophical thoughts. His poetry and short fiction began appearing in such magazines as *Presence Africaine* and *Action poetique*. In 1956 Sembène's first novel, *Le Docker noir* (*The Black Docker*), was published. *Le Docker noir* incorporated Sembène's expe-

riences as a Senegalese dockworker laboring in Marseilles. Although the novel did not gain widespread attention, it set the tone for much of his later writing in dealing with the difficulties of an African trying to adapt to Western life. Sembène's second novel, *O Pays, mon beau peuple!* (*Oh My Country, My Beautiful People!*), was published the following year.

Meanwhile, Sembène traveled the world to connect with writers from different regions. In 1956 he attended the First International Congress of Black Writers and Artists in Paris. Two years later, Sembène went to the Soviet republic of Uzbekistan to attend the First Congress of African and Asiatic Writers, where he met and was strongly influenced by American writer and social critic W. E. B. DuBois. He also met with other writers and artists in China and North Vietnam during the last part of the 1950s.

Sembène's biggest career breakthrough came with the 1960 publication of *Les Bouts de bois de Dieu* (*God's Bits of Wood*). The novel received international acclaim, and after its publication Sembène was finally able to devote himself to writing full-time. It also made him a visible figure among France's leftist and intellectual communities, both black and white.

Told His Tales on Film

Sembène's filmmaking career began in the early 1960s. Traveling in West Africa, he became increasingly aware of the difficulties of reaching out to a population that was largely illiterate. In 1962 he went to Moscow for a crash course in filmmaking technique. Upon his return to Africa, Sembène was commissioned by the government of Mali to make a short documentary, *L'Empire Sonhria*, which was completed in 1963. He then formed his own production company and made his first important film, *Borom Sarret*, which won the First Film Award at the 1963 Tours Film Festival in France. His next film, *Niaye*, won an award at Tours, as well as an Honorable Mention at the Locarno Film Festival in Switzerland. All of these films were shot on a shoestring budget using nonprofessional actors.

In 1966 Sembène cemented his international reputation as a gifted filmmaker with his first feature-length film, *La Noire de...* (*Black Girl*). The film, about a Senegalese nanny who accompanies her white employers back to France, won a number of awards, and was the first film by a black African to premiere at the Cannes Film Festival. It is generally considered a milestone in the history of African cinema.

Over the next two decades, Sembène worked steadily in both literature and film, often adapting his fiction for the screen. *Le Mandat* (*The Money Order*) published in 1965, became Sembène's second feature film, *Mandabi*, in 1968. Another example was his 1973 novel *Xala*, which was filmed a year after its print publication. Those two works reveal the lighter side of Sembène. Unlike the socio-realism (picked up in Russia) of some of his earlier writing, they are farcical, poking fun at the bourgeoisie and their bureaucratic allies. The Senegalese government was not always pleased with the point of view expressed in Sembène's work; while the films were applauded all over the world, they were often heavily censored at home.

Xala was Sembène's only novel of the 1970s, but he made a few other important films. *Emitai* (1971) involves the attempt by French troops to draft the young men of a Senegal village into service during World War II. *Ceddo* (1977) describes the forced conversion of an African village to Islam. It was banned by the Senegalese government in order to avoid offending the country's 80-percent Muslim majority. Sembène also kept busy during the decade helping establish *Kaddu*, a magazine in his native Wolof language. Sembène's only film of the 1980s was *Camp de Thiaroye* (1987), which deals with the problems faced by Senegalese veterans of World War II upon their return to Africa. His literary work of the decade includes a novel, *Le Dernier de l'Empire* (*The Last Days of the Empire*, 1980), and two novellas.

Reemerged as the Master of African Filmmaking

In 1992 Sembène reemerged on the scene, to the delight of the international film community, with *Guelwaar*, which incorporates many of the themes of his earlier work, such as religious tensions, government corruption, the evils of colonialism. *Guelwaar* was received with worldwide enthusiasm, and its release was accompanied by African film festivals and Sembène retrospectives in many cities. Sembène followed this triumph with the first film in what would become his final trilogy of films examining the role of women in African culture as they respond to colonialism, modernism, and tradition. The short film *L'heroisme du Quotidien* (1999) examined the ways that women in a small Senegalese village make their first contact with European culture in the early twentieth century. Set in contemporary Dakar, *Faat-Kiné* (2000) tells the story of a single mother who tries to navigate the demands of her two ex-husbands, traditional expectations of women, and her own desires to establish an independent identity. Though the film was light hearted, it also offered a "penetrating analysis of the interplay of gender, economics and power in today's Africa," according to the *California Newsreel* Web site.

Sembène's last film—and perhaps his greatest triumph—was *Moolaadé* (2004), a stirring polemic against the practice of female genital mutilation in traditional African cultures. Told with what *New York Times* film critic Elvis Mitchell called his "trademark empathy," *Moolaadé* manages to stir viewer outrage while also telling a warm story of human interest. The

film was greeted with adulation, winning a variety of awards, including a prestigious award at the Cannes Film Festival, and earning showings at film festivals around the world.

Throughout his career, Ousmane Sembène took the idea of the "independent" filmmaker to its extreme. He never relinquished control of any part of the process. He preferred to work with nonprofessional actors, and the amount of money he typically spent on a film would have barely paid the catering bill for a Hollywood production. Because Sembène remained fiercely loyal to the principles that got him started as a writer, he never had to worry about such mundane matters as funding, censorship, or box office receipts. Diawara noted in the *New York Times* that Sembène "could criticize Africa, he could criticize racism and he could criticize colonialism. He never spared anybody."

Sembène died at his home in Dakar on June 10, 2007, following a long illness. Sembène will not only be remembered as the "father of African cinema," but, as was once noted in *Film Comment*, perhaps he was also the "only filmmaker…in the world who cannot be bought and sold."

Selected works

Fiction

Le docker noir, Debresse, 1956 (published in English as The *Black Docker*, Heinemann, 1987.) *O pays, mon beau people!*, Le Livre Contemporain, 1957.
Les bouts de bois de Dieu, Le Livre Contemporain, 1960 (published in English as *God's Bits of Wood*, Anchor Books, 1970.)
Voltaique, Presence Africaine, 1962.
L'Harmattan, Presence Africaine, 1964.
Le mandat, Presence Africaine, 1966 (published in English as *The Money Order*, Heinemann, 1972.)
Xala, Presence Africaine, 1973 (published in English as *Xala*, L. Hill and Co., 1976.)
Le dernier de l'Empire, L'Harmattan, 1981 (published in English as *The Last Days of the Empire*, Heinemann, 1983.)
Niiwam, Presence Africaine, 1987 (published in English as *Niiwam and Taaw: Two Novellas*, Heinemann, 1992.

Films

L'Empire Sonhrai, 1963.
Borom Sarret, 1963.
Niaye, 1964.
La Noire de…, 1966.
Mandabi, 1968.
Taaw, 1970.
Emitai, 1971.
Xala, 1974.
Ceddo, 1976.
Camp de Thiaroye, 1989.

Guelwaar, 1992.
L'heroisme du Quotidien (short), 1999.
Faat-Kiné, 2000.
Moolaadé, 2004.

Sources

Books

Gadjigo, Samba, Ralph Faulkingham, Thomas Cassirer, and Sander Reinhard, editors, *Ousmane Sembène: Dialogues with Critics and Writers*, University of Massachusetts Press, 1993.
The Cinema of Ousmane Sembéne, A Pioneer of African Film, Greenwood, 1984.
Ousmane Sembéne: Dialogues with Critics and Writers, ed. by Samba Gadjigo and Ralph Faulkingham, 1993.

Periodicals

Film Comment, July/August, 1993, pp. 63-69.
Guardian Unlimited, June 5, 2005; June 12, 2007.

Houston Chronicle, February 18, 1996, p. 11.
Los Angeles Times, January 1, 1995, p. 30.
New York Times, December 28, 1972; October 13, 2004; June 11, 2007; June 12, 2007.
Time, June 25, 2007.
UNESCO Courier, January 1990, pp. 4-7.

On-line

"*Faat Kiné*," *California Newsreel,* www.newsreel.org/nav/title.asp?tc=CN0125 (July 24, 2007).
Gadjigo, Samba, "Ousmane Sembène: The Life of a Revolutionary Artist," *California Newsreel,* www.newsreel.org/articles/OusmaneSembene.htm (July 24, 2007).
Ousmane Sembène: "Senegal's Most Admired Film Maker of the Century," www.mtholyoke.edu/courses/sgadjigo/ (July 24, 2007).
Ousmane Sembène, www.english.emory.edu/Bahri/Sembene.html (July 24, 2007).

—Robert R. Jacobson and Tom Pendergast

Portia Simpson Miller

1945—

Politician

In 2006, Portia Simpson Miller became the first woman to lead a government in the West Indian island nation of Jamaica. She had campaigned on pledges to reduce crime, poverty, and unemployment, and during her first few months in office she scored record-high approval ratings in public-opinion polls. A writer for the *Economist* magazine described the career politician as "something of a breath of fresh air for a country whose politics has long been dominated by elderly men," adding that Simpson Miller, often referred to by Jamaicans as Sista P, had celebrated her 60th birthday by the time she took office yet "looks younger and has an easy, magnetic charm."

Simpson Miller was born on December 12, 1945, in Wood Hall in the parish of St. Catherine on Jamaica, and attended Marlie Hill Primary School. She studied at St. Martin's High School for Girls, and was first elected to office in her late 20s when she ran for a local councilor's seat in the Trench Town West constituency of the Kingston & St. Andrew Corporation (KSAC), as the combined parish governments are known. Trench Town West was a notoriously poor district and had been a Jamaican Labour Party (JLP) stronghold for many years. Simpson Miller's victory in the 1974 local election marked the first time a member of the country's other leading political organization, the People's National Party of Jamaica, or PNP, had won there.

Two years later, Simpson Miller went on to achieve another PNP first when she stood in parliamentary elections as the party's candidate for the Constituency of South West St. Andrew and won. Party officials made the new legislator its parliamentary secretary in the Ministry of Local Government, but in 1980 her party was trounced in elections by the Jamaican Labour Party. She was one of the few PNP candidates to hold her seat after that race, however, and became the opposition spokesperson on women's affairs, pension, social security and consumer affairs from 1983 to 1989.

The PNP returned to power in 1989, and longtime party leader Michael Manley became prime minister once again. He named Simpson Miller to serve as his Minister of Labour, Social Security and Sport, a trio of portfolios she kept for most of the 1990s. In 1992, however, she challenged another PNP cabinet minister, P.J. Patterson, for the party leadership when Manley's health declined, but was soundly defeated at the PNP congress. Patterson was a decade older than her, educated at the London School of Economics, and won his first election back in 1969 with the campaign slogan, "Young, gifted, and black." During her political career Simpson Miller was sometimes criticized for her own lack of educational credentials, and decided to remedy that by enrolling in distance courses at the Union Institute & University in Florida. She flew into Miami for Saturday classes in between her job duties and earned her undergraduate degree in public administration. She also completed a course in advanced management at the University of California at Berkeley and also attended the Executive Program for Leaders in Development at Harvard University's John F. Kennedy School of Government.

Patterson succeeded Manley as prime minister and in 2000 named Simpson Miller to head what is consid-

At a Glance . . .

Born on December 12, 1945, in Wood Hall, St. Catherine, Jamaica; married Errald Miller. *Education:* Union Institute & University, FL, BA, public administration; University of California Berkeley, Advanced Management certificate; attended John F. Kennedy School of Government, Harvard University, Executive Program for Leaders in Development. *Politics:* People's National Party of Jamaica.

Career: Kingston & St. Andrew Corporation (KSAC) local government, councilor representing Trench Town West, 1974; Jamaica's parliament, Constituency of South West St. Andrew, representative, 1976; Ministry of Local Government, parliamentary secretary, 1977-?; PNP spokesperson on women's affairs, pension, social security and consumer affairs, 1983-89; Minister of Labour, Social Security and Sport, 1989-2000; Minister of Tourism (also kept Sport portfolio), 2000-02; Minister of Local Government, Community Development and Sport, 2002-06; Minister for Sport, 2006–; PNP, chair, February 2006; Jamaica, prime minister, March 30, 2006–.

Memberships: People's National Party of Jamaica (PNP), member.

Addresses: *Office*—Office of the Prime Minister, 1 Devon Rd., Kingston 10, Jamaica, West Indies.

ered the country's most important cabinet department, the Ministry of Tourism. After 2002 elections, Patterson made a cabinet shuffle and named Simpson Miller to head the Ministry of Local Government, Community Development and Sport. In early 2006, she made another bid for the PNP leadership, this time facing Peter Phillips, Jamaica's Minister for National Security. In the build-up to the February 25 party balloting, she campaigned with the unofficial slogan, "It's woman time now," and loudspeakers at her political rallies pumped out pro-feminist classic reggae songs like "The Strength of a Woman" and "Thank You Momma."

Simpson Miller won the election at the party conference and became prime minister-elect. She took office in late March at the start of a new legislative session, a jubilant day in the country for her supporters who had affectionately dubbed her "Auntie Portia" and "Sista P." Her first months in office were marked by an outpouring of national goodwill, and in public-opinion polls she reached approval ratings as high as 70 percent. Many Jamaicans saw her rise to power as signaling the start of a new era for the country. "Even skeptics felt that it was hard to do worse than what the men had achieved for the mass of Jamaicans in abysmal poverty," noted Orlando Patterson in the *New York Times*, "after four decades of modernization that had benefited only the middle and upper classes."

Jamaican electoral law required Simpson Miller to schedule new elections before October of 2007, and though some thought she and the PNP would capitalize on the groundswell of support that followed her installation as prime minister, they did not, and the opportunity passed. In September of 2006, her government was rocked by a revelation that a Dutch commodities firm had donated nearly $470,000 to her campaign. The contribution was off the books, as is common in Jamaican politics, but raised questions over a potential conflict of interest because the firm, Trafigura Beheer BV, had a lucrative government contract for shipping and selling Jamaica's crude oil on the export market. Jamaican law does not prohibit such donations, but for a two-week period Simpson Miller refused to comment on the scandal, and her political opponents attacked her for it. Her silence was said to have damaged her government's credibility, and some believed that if parliamentary elections were called, the PNP might lose and Simpson Miller would become one of the briefest-serving prime ministers in Jamaican history.

Despite her professional and educational achievements, Simpson Miller remained the target of criticism for her humble background, lack of prestigious college credentials, Creole speech, and habit of kissing supporters at political rallies. After the Trafigura Beheer debacle, she began avoiding the press altogether, telling Patterson—the *New York Times* contributor whom she had known for 30-plus years—that she had been "beaten, banged and bashed by the media...every time they see me they are looking at the majority of Jamaicans who are poor and they can only think, 'How dare this uppity woman.'"

Sources

Periodicals

Christian Science Monitor, March 13, 2006, p. 6.
Cincinnati Post, December 14, 2006, p. A15.
Economist, March 25, 2006, p. 43.
Financial Times, March 29, 2006, p. 6.
International Herald Tribune, April 3, 2007, p. 2.
Jamaica Gleaner, February 26, 2006.
Miami Herald, May 7, 2007.
New York Times, January 9, 2007.
Times (London, England), March 25, 2006, p. 46.

—Carol Brennan

Ian Smith

1970(?)—

Diet and fitness expert, author

Dr. Ian Smith combined his medical training with his interests in journalism and sports to become a television celebrity and bestselling author. As he told Tony Felton of the *New York Beacon* in 1999: "There is so much to do, and so much that I want to do. I want to taste all the 'flavors' of life. I want to smell all the aromas." By 2006 "Dr. Ian" was hosting television's most popular diet show and had published bestselling diet books as well as a detective novel. As a TV reporter and medical columnist Smith addressed healthcare disparities and medical issues that were of particular concern to the black community.

Studied Medicine

Ian Keith Smith and his twin brother Dana were raised in Danbury, Connecticut, by their divorced mother, Rena Cherry Bustion, a human resources manager for an alternative energy company. In a 2004 *Men's Health* feature Smith wrote about the peculiarities of growing up as an identical twin. His earliest memory was of his grandfather telling them on the way to nursery school: "There are only the two of you. Learn how to protect each other from the rest of the world." Smith wrote: "My identical twin is a physical duplicate and a portal into my mind. But most of all, he's the competitor I can't shake." In the fifth grade the boys decided to forge individual identities. They stopped dressing alike and chose different friends. Ian would be the scholar and Dana the athlete. However their competitiveness reached new heights when they were both

starters on their high-school basketball team. By their senior year, they had learned to work together and led the team to the conference finals. The Smith brothers continued to play basketball as undergraduates at Harvard. When Dana took a year off from college, Ian did too because he couldn't imagine graduating ahead of his brother.

Smith's vocation was evident early on. He told Felton: "When I was nine years old, I read in *Ebony* magazine that there was a paucity of neurosurgeons in this country. After reading that article, I decided I wanted to be a doctor. Soon I began dissecting insects." Smith was also a self-described "news junkie."

After graduating from Harvard Smith earned his master's in science education at Columbia University. At Dartmouth Medical School he established a mentoring program for minority students. He told Felton: "It started as a challenge for me at first, the challenge of accepting the leadership role of trying to get Afro-American students interested in medicine...I want to engineer and facilitate programs for the disadvantaged. To encourage and educate young people about the endless opportunities that are out there, and not just in medicine." Smith graduated from the University of Chicago's Pritzker School of Medicine. He told Felton: "The worst of times for me was the geographic separation from my family.... No one really understood the demands.... But I can tell you this, after you've completed medical school, you get the feeling that you can do...almost anything."

At a Glance . . .

Born Ian Keith Smith in 1970(?) in Danbury, CT; married Triste Noelle Lieteau, 2005; children: one. *Education:* Harvard College, AB, 1992; Teacher's College of Columbia University, MS, science education, 1993; Dartmouth Medical School; University of Chicago Pritzker School of Medicine, MD, 1997(?).

Career: Albert Einstein College of Medicine Hospitals, New York City, surgical intern, orthopedics, 1997-99(?); *Time* magazine, medical columnist, 1999-2001; WNBC-TV News, New York City, medical reporter, 1999(?)-2002, news anchor, 1999; NBC News, *Nightly News, Today Show,* medical correspondent, 2001(?)-03; *New York Daily News,* weekly health columnist, 2001-04(?); *Men's Health,* columnist and contributing editor, 2003–; VH1, *Celebrity Fit Club,* diet/medical expert, 2004–; ABC, *The View,* medical contributor; American Urban Radio Networks, *HealthWatch,* host, 2006(?)–; BET, *Meet the Faith,* host, 2006–; 50 Million Pound Challenge, organizer, 2007–.

Selected memberships: American Council on Exercise, board member; Cancer Research Foundation of America, board member; Henry H. Kessler Foundation, trustee; New York City Mission Society, board member; New York Council for the Humanities, board member.

Selected awards: National Academy of Television Arts and Sciences, 2001; Support Network, Inc., Excellence in Education Award, 2001; Black Caucus of the American Library Association (BCALA) Honor Book Award for Fiction, 2005; African American Literary Awards Show, Inc., for *The Fat Smash Diet* (self-help), 2006; Alpha Kappa Alpha Sorority, Maxine W. Smith Literary Award, 2006.

Addresses: *Office*—P.O. Box 765, FDR Station, New York, NY 10150.

Turned to Journalism

Smith had interned in a newsroom while still in medical school. After completing a surgical internship in orthopedics at the Albert Einstein Medical School Hospitals, he became a medical reporter for WNBC-TV News in New York City and a medical columnist for *Time* magazine. His stories began appearing on NBC's *Nightly News.* At a party Smith approached the vice president of WNBC-News with his dream of becoming an anchorman. She decided to give him a chance and Smith began co-anchoring the weekend news broadcasts.

Within a couple of years Smith had become medical correspondent for NBC's *Today Show* and was penning a weekly health column in the *New York Daily News.* He told Ayana Jones of the *Philadelphia Tribune* in 2002 that "journalism allows me to get important health messages to a wide array of people."

Recognizing that the Internet had become an invaluable medical resource for the public, but that it was also awash with misleading and contradictory information and outright misinformation, Smith published his *Guide to Medical Websites* in 2001. He ranked sites on a scale of one to three according to the legitimacy of their sources, ease of navigation, ability to answer individual questions, and overall quality.

Smith took a break from television to concentrate on writing. His detective novel, *The Blackbird Papers,* is set at Dartmouth. When a Nobel-Prize-winning black scientist is murdered, his estranged brother, Sterling Bledsoe, a hardboiled New York City FBI agent, takes over the case. The bodies pile up. Michael Agger wrote in the *New York Times Book Review:* "The investigation advances smoothly until it becomes clear Sterling has a problem: he's being mercilessly pursued by cliché." Other reviewers were much more enthusiastic and *Essence* magazine picked it as a "best beach book" of 2004.

Became a Diet Expert

Smith's 2001 *The Take-Control Diet* was a straightforward guide to gradual weight loss and long-term weight control through sound nutrition, portion control, and exercise. Readers designed their own eating and exercise plans to fit their lifestyles and preferences. On the NBC *Nightly News* Smith covered four individuals who were following his diet.

When first asked to appear on VH1's *Celebrity Fit Club* in 2004, Smith declined, not wanting to hurt his credibility as a medical journalist. The show's producer talked him into it. He told Bobbi Booker of the *Philadelphia Tribune* in 2006: "It was one of the best random decision/gambles that I've ever taken.... I have a much bigger practice because I have millions of people whom I dispense advice and information to and in some way I impact them, I hope, in a positive manner." One of the most-watched shows in the history of cable television, the *Fit Club* was a reality series in which eight minor celebrities competed to lose weight and get in shape over a 100-day period. Smith told Booker: "to see celebrities put on a pedestal battle the same kind of issues that we battle and to suffer the same types of failures that we suffer is very interesting to us and we like to see it for all kinds of reasons.... I want African Americans to look in the mirror and realize that we are a beautiful, strong, powerful and capable people, but that there are things that we can change to make ourselves even more beautiful, more powerful, healthier and happier."

Smith developed his "fat smash" diet for *Celebrity Fit Club*. His book quickly topped the *New York Times* bestseller list. In April of 2007 VH1, Rodale, Inc., and St. Martin's Press launched an on-line subscription weight-loss and fitness program based on the fat smash diet.

Although *The Fat Smash Diet* was subtitled *The Last Diet You'll Ever Need,* the following year Smith published his *Extreme Fat Smash Diet.* In contrast to his other diets, which emphasized gradual weight loss, the extreme fat smash was a radical plan for losing 12 pounds in three weeks. Unlike the original fat smash, the extreme fat smash was a very specific diet that had to be strictly adhered to. Smith explained that "extreme fat smash is for people who are determined to reach what they might've considered unthinkable success in a weight-loss journey. The idea is simple: if you want big results, then you'll have to push yourself beyond the normal limits to attain them."

Attained Celebrity Status

In 2001 *Ebony* named Smith one of the "29 most eligible super bachelors." He told the magazine: "I want someone who knows what [she wants] and then goes for it. I like the idea of a woman being strong." In May of 2005 Smith married his college sweetheart, Triste Noelle Lieteau. With a law degree from the University of Chicago and a medical degree from Harvard, Lieteau was director of government relations and associate general counsel at Northwestern Memorial Hospital in Chicago.

By 2007 Smith had embarked on a hectic schedule of lectures and television appearances. He was a commentator on National Public Radio's *The Tavis Smiley Show* and a contributor to ABC's *The View.* He hosted the nationally syndicated *HealthWatch* on American Urban Radio Networks and the weekly talk show *Meet the Faith* on BET. As a columnist and contributing editor for *Men's Health,* Smith gave advice on sports injuries. His second novel was due out in 2008.

Smith was evangelical on the issue of obesity. "Our very existence is in jeopardy; our futures are ominous," he wrote in *Ebony* in 2006. "We are dying too fast and too painfully, and in many respects the power to turn the tide resides within our control. But will we summon our epoch courage, wisdom, and strength to defeat an enemy that, in many ways, we have created? The answer to this question is the answer to our very future." Smith worked hard to help people tackle the problem of obesity. On April 7, 2007, Smith launched one of the largest black health initiatives in history. His "50 Million Pound Challenge" was a nationwide crusade to fight obesity in the black community. Smith calculated that if one-quarter of the 20 million overweight black Americans lost ten pounds each, it would equal 50 million pounds. He kicked off his star-studded 14 city tour at the Mall in Washington with a one-mile walk and health screenings. Within the first week more than 20,000 people had signed on.

Selected writings

Books

Dr. Ian Smith's Guide to Medical Websites, Random House, 2001.
The Take-Control Diet: A Life Plan for Thinking People, Ballantine, 2001.
The Blackbird Papers, Doubleday, 2004.
The Fat Smash Diet, St. Martin's Griffin, 2006.
Extreme Fat Smash Diet, St. Martin's Griffin, 2007.

Periodicals

"Black Women Are Dying from Neglect," *Savoy,* May 2001, pp. 33-34.
"Death by 100 Degrees," *Time,* Vol. 158, No. 6, August 13, 2001, p. 66.
"This Has Never Happened Before!" *Savoy,* Vol. 2, No. 4, May 2002, p. 50.
"World of Hurt," *Men's Health,* Vol. 19, No. 2, March 2004, pp. 130-137.
"Being Double," *Men's Health,* Vol. 19, No. 6, July/August 2004, pp. 100, 102.
"Life or Death? It's Your Choice!" *Ebony,* Vol. 61, No. 12, October 2006, p. 50.

Sources

Periodicals

Black Book Review, January-February 2005, p. 35.
Ebony, June 2001, pp. 50-58.
In Style, October 4, 2005, p. 292.
New York Beacon, February 24, 1999, p. 12; December 16-22, 2004, p. 16.
New York Times, January 15, 2002, p. F7; May 29, 2006, p. 12.
New York Times Book Review, July 4, 2004, p. 16.
Philadelphia Tribune, February 12, 2002, p. 4B; October 1, 2006, p. 1D.
Washington Post, April 12, 2007, p. T3.

On-line

Celebrity Fit Club, www.celebrityfitclub.com/www/xnt/cfc/pages/Splash.aspx (July 5, 2007).

"The Diet Channel Interviews VH1's Celebrity Fit Club Diet Expert Dr. Ian Smith, Author of 'The Fat Smash Diet,'" *The Diet Channel,* www.thedietchannel.com/VH1-Celebrity-Fit-Club-Diet-Expert-Dr-Ian-Smith-Fat-Smash-Diet-Interview.htm (July 5, 2007).

Dr. Ian Smith, www.doctoriansmith.com (July 5, 2007).

The 50 Million Pound Challenge, www.50million-pounds.com (July 5, 2007).

"Get Celebrity Fit with the Fat Smash Diet," *diet.ivillage,* http://diet.ivillage.com/celebprog/0,,962-g6pll,00.html (July 5, 2007).

—Margaret Alic

Dakota Staton

1930(?)-2007

Vocalist

"There's nothing I sing that doesn't have the blues in it somewhere," vocalist Dakota Staton told Patricia Smith of the *Boston Globe*. During her heyday in the late 1950s and early 1960s Staton was classified as a jazz singer, but her voice, tough and passionate, broke through genre barriers. Influenced by Dinah Washington, she in turn influenced a generation of African-American female singers who aimed toward success on pop and urban contemporary radio and recordings but had jazz sophistication in their vocal approaches. Never as famous as her talent would suggest, Staton nevertheless remained active as a singer for most of her long life.

Dakota Staton (pronounced STAY-ton) was born in Homewood, Pennsylvania, near Pittsburgh, on June 3 of either 1930 or 1931 (most sources indicate 1930). Her older brother Fred, who became a jazz saxophonist, told Jacki Lyden of National Public Radio that her career started as early as age seven, when "[s]he'd go around in the neighborhood, entertaining the neighbors from time to time." By her teens she was taking classical singing lessons at Pittsburgh's Filion School of Music and performing in small clubs. The emotional jazz-blues style of Dinah Washington, who was more closely connected to the jazz world than to pop in the late 1940s and early 1950s, was a major influence on the budding singer.

After a two-year stint with Pittsburgh's Joe Westray Orchestra in the early 1950s, Staton became a regional headliner at a number of prime Midwest jazz clubs, including Detroit's Flame Bar. By 1954 she had moved to New York, initially staying with her older brother. Her shows immediately began to gain attention from jazz fans, and she released a single, "What Do You Know About Love?" Bandleader Willie Bryant was an early backer of her career. The influential jazz magazine *Down Beat* chose her as its most promising jazz vocalist of the year for 1955. Capitol label executive Dave Cavanaugh took charge of her career after hearing her perform at the Baby Grand club in Harlem, and in 1957 Staton's debut LP recording, *The Late, Late Show,* was released.

The album gave Staton something that was already rare for a jazz musician in the era of rock and roll and rhythm-and-blues: a hit single in the form of the title track, a sweet song about the natural world coming alive late at night to witness the antics of a pair of kissing lovers. "The album's title track was a significant pop hit, but Staton revealed a swing-singer's talent for cruising freely over a jazz pulse," noted John Fordham of England's *Guardian* newspaper. The *Late, Late Show* album rose to the number-four spot on sales charts, and a follow-up, *Dynamic!,* cracked the top 25. The rough edge of Staton's voice drew rock and blues fans even on quiet pieces like "The Late, Late Show," and in the late 1950s Staton's name was mentioned along with those of Washington and Sarah Vaughan in lists of the top female jazz vocalists of the day.

Pure jazz fans also flocked to buy Staton's recordings, attracted by the presence of top sidemen such as trumpeter Jonah Jones (on *The Late, Late Show*) and Harry "Sweets" Edison of the Count Basie Orchestra (on *Dynamic!*). One of her most sympathetic collaborators was British-American pianist George Shearing,

At a Glance . . .

Born on June 3, 1930 (some sources say 1931) in Homewood, PA; died on April 10, 2007, in New York, NY; married Talib Ahmad Dawud, a jazz musician, late 1950s (divorced); used name Aliyah Rabia after conversion to Islam. *Education:* Attended Filion School of Music, Pittsburgh, PA, studied classical voice. *Religion:* Islam.

Career: Joe Westray Orchestra, Pittsburgh, PA, singer, early 1950s; Flame Bar, Detroit, and other Midwestern venues, singer, 1952-54; Capitol Records, singer, 1957-61; United Artists, singer, 1963-64; England, singer, 1965-71; Groove Merchant, singer, 1972-73; Simitar, Muse, and High Note labels.

Awards: *Down Beat* magazine, most promising newcomer award, 1955.

with whom she recorded the *In the Night* in the late 1950s. Her talents extended to recordings with string orchestras as well as small-group material, and top-rank Capitol arrangers Nelson Riddle and Sid Feller worked on her albums. Staton headlined a major jazz concert at New York's Town Hall in 1959 and toured with Benny Goodman's big band the following year. In 1963 she appeared at the Newport Jazz Festival.

By that time Staton's career was about to enter its second phase. In 1958 she had married jazz trumpeter Talib Ahmad Dawud and converted to the Islamic faith. She changed her name to Aliyah Rabia and performed under that name for a short time. Dawud, Staton, and pianist Ahmad Jamal, however, soon ran afoul of Nation of Islam leader Elijah Muhammad, who condemned their involvement in the world of secular entertainment; they in turn were among the founders of a splinter group called the Muslim Brotherhood. Staton moved to United Artists in 1963, recording *From Dakota with Love* and two more albums for the label, but jazz in the mid-1960s was in commercial decline. Disillusioned with both politics and the music business, Staton moved to England in 1965 and made a living as a live performer. "I didn't want to be limited to (the same) 12 tunes, and that's all anyone wanted to hear here. I wanted to go somewhere where it didn't matter and I could stretch out and sing the songs I wanted to sing," she explained to Michael J. Renner of the *St. Louis Post-Dispatch*. The marriage to Dawud ended in divorce.

In the early 1970s Staton returned to the United States and to a jazz scene commercially rejuvenated by soul-jazz and other fusion styles. Although her name had been largely forgotten, she was signed to the Groove Merchant label and recorded a pair of raw, soul-oriented albums, *Madame Foo Foo* (featuring organ work by Groove Holmes) and *I Want a Country Man*. Those albums, like most of Staton's earlier work on Capitol, were reissued on CD and remain highly valued by jazz collectors. Staton later recorded for the small Muse and Simitar labels, and her final album, 1999's *A Packet of Love Letters*, was released on the High Note label.

Staton remained notable as a live performer during her later years. Rob Mariani of the *All About Jazz* Web site heard Staton at Scullers jazz club in Boston in the late 1990s. "And the voice, the very same identical voice I'd heard over forty years ago in the Village Vanguard, emerges, unchanged, strong and full of beautiful, lyrical energy," he wrote. She sometimes returned to her hometown of Pittsburgh, performing with pianist Frank Cunimondo, who told Nate Guidry of the *Pittsburgh Post-Gazette* that "Dakota was very demanding musically. She was one of the innovators when it came to the jazz vocalists. As she matured, her voice got deeper and better." In poor health in the early 2000s, Staton died in New York City on April 10, 2007.

Selected discography

Albums

The Late, Late Show, Capitol, 1957.
Dynamic!, Capitol, 1958.
(With George Shearing) *In the Night,* Capitol, 1958.
Ballads and the Blues, Capitol, 1959.
Time to Swing, Capitol, 1959.
Dakota, Capitol, 1960.
Softly, Capitol, 1960.
Dakota at Storyville (live), Capitol, 1961.
Round Midnight, Capitol, 1961.
From Dakota with Love, United Artists, 1963.
Live and Swinging, United Artists, 1963.
Dakota Staton with Strings, United Artists, 1964.
Madame Foo Foo, Groove Merchant, 1972.
I Want a Country Man, Groove Merchant, 1973.
Dakota Staton, Muse, 1990.
Darling Please Save Your Love, Muse, 1991.
Ms. Soul, Simitar, 1997.
A Packet of Love Letters, High Note, 1999.
The Ultimate Dakota Staton, Capitol, 2005.

Sources

Periodicals

Boston Globe, January 18, 1991, p. 42.

Guardian (London, England), April 16, 2007, p. 37.
New York Times, April 13, 2007, p. A17.
Pittsburgh Post-Gazette, April 13, 2007, p. A13.
St. Louis Post-Dispatch, October 13, 1999, p. E3.

On-line

"Dakota Staton," *All Music Guide,* www.allmusic.com
(June 5, 2007).
"Dakota Staton," *Swingmusic.net,* www.swingmusic.
net/Dakota_Staton.html (June 5, 2007).

"The Great, Late Show with Dakota Staton," *All
About Jazz,* www.allaboutjazz.com/php/article.
php?id=23755 (June 5, 2007).

Other

Weekend Edition, National Public Radio, April 14,
2007 (transcription).

—James M. Manheim

Marshall W. Taylor

1878-1932

Cyclist

Bicycle racer Marshall Walter "Major" Taylor may merit designation as the first African-American sports hero. In the face of the racist resistance that plagued African Americans in all fields of endeavor in the years around 1900, Taylor became a celebrity athlete whose exploits, in America and abroad, filled newspaper sports sections. He was likely the first black athlete to be sponsored by a corporation, and he was among the first to be recognized as a champion in his field. Taylor had various nicknames, including the "Colored Cyclone" and the "Worcester Whirlwind," after the Massachusetts city where he was based for much of his career. Beyond the many races he won and the reputation he gained as an athlete, Taylor set a long-lasting example for African-American youngsters as a role model who worked patiently to overcome the effects of racism and gained widespread popularity.

A native of Indianapolis, Indiana, Marshall Walter Taylor was born on November 26, 1878. His grandparents had been slaves in Kentucky who had crossed into the free state of Indiana, and his father, Gilbert Taylor, put his skills with horses to work as a coach attendant for a well-off white Indianapolis family named Southard. Young Taylor and one of the Southard children, Daniel, became friends, and the family bought him his first bicycle. As Taylor began to mimic the ways of his upper-class benefactors, he grew more distant from his own family. When the Southards moved to Chicago, however, he was left to his own devices and had to fend for himself. At first he got a job delivering newspapers for five dollars a week.

He found that he was happier riding a bicycle, and he made extra money doing stunts on the street and passing the hat in front of a store called Hay and Willis. The store hired him as a custodian and bicycle demonstrator, giving him a new bicycle and a uniform that led to the nickname of Major. He was 13 at the time. Taylor soon began winning races. His success was impeded, however, because he was often barred from competing in heavily segregated Indiana. Fortunately, bicycle racing was at a peak of popularity, and a circuit of black-organized races allowed him to develop his skills. Taylor caught the eye of Louis "Birdie" Munger, a bicycle maker and former racer who saw in him a potential champion. Munger became his coach. By the mid-1890s, Taylor was winning races at both short and long distances, including a 75-mile race from Indianapolis to Matthews, Indiana.

He continued to experience frustrations at races. Taylor was sometimes banned from competition or, when allowed onto the track, was subjected to abuse from white riders—anything from being boxed in on a straightaway or having nails thrown in front of his wheels to direct physical attack. Frustrated by this state of affairs, Taylor and Munger move to the more liberal town of Worcester, Massachusetts (with a brief stop in Middletown, Connecticut) in 1895.

Taylor's performance continued to improve. He finished eighth in the first eastern competition he entered, a six-day endurance race at New York's Madison Square Garden in December of 1896. And, finding the doors of Worcester's YMCA open to him, he embarked on an all-around physical conditioning program. The

At a Glance . . .

Born on November 26, 1878, in Indianapolis, IN; died on June 21, 1932, in Chicago, IL; married Daisy Morris, 1902; children: Sydney. *Education:* Some private tutoring in home of Southard family, Indianapolis. *Religion:* Baptist.

Career: Employed as custodian, bicycle demonstrator, and bicycle riding teacher at Indianapolis department stores, 1892-95(?); moved to Worcester, MA, 1895; placed eighth in six-day endurance race, Madison Square Garden, New York, 1896; won world championship in one-mile race, lowered own world record in mile to 1:19, 1899; toured and competed in Europe, 1901-04; temporary retirement, 1905-06; returned to cycling but was injured in Bordeaux, France, 1907; retired from bicycle racing at age 32, 1910; unsuccessful manufacturing ventures, 1910s and 1920s; self-published autobiography, *The Fastest Bicycle Rider in the World,* 1928.

Memberships: League of American Wheelmen, National Cycling Association.

results were visible in Taylor's race performance over the next several years, although he was consistently harassed and threatened when touring in Southern states and sometimes elsewhere. By 1898 he had set several world records, including a time of one minute, 41.4 seconds in a one-mile sprint from a standing start. The Sager Gear Company backed his tours, in return for which Taylor used the company's new chainless bicycle in competition—perhaps the first commercial sponsorship arrangement entered into by an African-American sportsman. By the end of the next year, he had shaved his one-mile time to one minute, 19 seconds. The year 1899 marked another milestone in Taylor's career: in a one-mile race in Montreal, Canada, he beat fellow Massachusetts cyclist Tom Butler and won the world championship at that distance. He thus became the second generally recognized black world champion in any sport, after Canadian-born boxer George Dixon.

Taylor capitalized on his fame, traveling to Europe between 1901 and 1904 and taking on the continent's best in one-on-one races. A devout Baptist, he refused to race on Sundays for many years. Though he declined to enter several world championships, he won many of his direct contests, beating a slew of European champions in 1901. American newspapers gave Taylor's races heavy coverage, and his celebrity grew. In

1902 he married Daisy Morris in Worcester, and they raised one daughter, Sydney. Her name came from the Australian city where she was born in 1904. By that time, Taylor's fame was truly international.

But Taylor himself was exhausted, not only by his constant touring schedule but also by the strain of dealing with racist attitudes. Observers, he wrote in his autobiography (as quoted in *Notable Black American Men*), did not "seem to realize the great mental strain that beset me in those races, and the utter exhaustion which I felt on the many occasions after I had battled under bitter odds against the monster prejudice, both on and off the track." Taylor took the years 1905 and 1906 off, returning to the racetrack in 1907. That year he was injured in a crash in Bordeaux, and though he recovered, he had lost a step to younger riders. After a victory over French champion Victor Dupré in 1909 and a race in Utah the following summer, Taylor retired at age 32.

Taylor was a relatively wealthy man at that point, with thousands of dollars of winnings saved. But the post-cycling phase of his life was not happy. He embarked on various ventures, mostly connected with automobile manufacturing, that sapped his fortune. During the 1920s he worked on his autobiography, *The Fastest Bicycle Rider in the World,* but he had to publish it and attempt to market it himself. The book sold poorly and he sank into poverty; his marriage eventually broke up. He lived at the YMCA in Chicago in his final years, suffering from heart and kidney problems. After he died on June 21, 1932, no one claimed his body, and he was buried at public expense. In 1948 a group of cycling history enthusiasts that included Frank Schwinn of the Schwinn bicycle-manufacturing firm learned the story of his end. He was disinterred and reburied on May 23, 1948, after a memorial service attended by sprinters Ralph Metcalfe and Jesse Owens.

Sources

Books

Ritchie, Andrew, *Major Taylor: The Extraordinary Career of a Champion Bicycle Racer,* Bicycle Books, 1988.

Smith, Jessie Carney, ed., *Notable Black American Men,* Gale, 1998.

Taylor, Marshall W. "Major," *The Fastest Bicycle Rider in the World,* repr. ed., Books for Libraries Press, 1971.

Periodicals

Bicycling, June 2006.

On-line

Alston, Wilton D., "Who Is Major Taylor?," LewRockwell.com, www.lewrockwell.com/alston/alston16.html (June 7, 2007).

"Marshall Taylor, Cyclist and Sports Trail Blazer," *African American Registry,* www.aaregistry.com (June 7, 2007).

Major Taylor Society, www.majortaylor.com (June 7, 2007).

—James M. Manheim

Susan C. Taylor

1957—

Physician, author

Susan C. Taylor is a dermatologist and specialist in ethnic skin care and health in Philadelphia and New York City. Since 1999 she has served as director of the Skin of Color Center at St. Luke's Roosevelt Hospital Center, the first medical practice in the United States devoted to treating patients with pigmented skin, hair, and nails. She forecasted this focus to be a growing part of twenty-first century dermatology, she explained in an article that appeared in *Dermatology Times*. "The United States is becoming a country in which the majority of its citizens will no longer have white skin but will instead have skin of color," writer Karen Nash quoted her as saying. "They will be of diverse racial and ethnic backgrounds, and will include people of African-American, Hispanic, and Asian descent."

Susan Charlene Taylor was born on October 7, 1957, in Philadelphia, Pennsylvania, where she and her younger sister were raised by their single mother. During her high school years she attended Friends Select School, a private Quaker academy whose Philadelphia origins dated back to 1689. "I was the kid who wanted to grow up to be a doctor and take care of people and make them better," Taylor recalled on her Web site, *Brownskin.net*. "I was lucky that everyone along the way supported that goal."

In 1979 Taylor earned her undergraduate degree in biology, graduating magna cum laude from the University of Pennsylvania. She went on to Harvard Medical School, and graduated with her M.D. in 1983. While in medical school, Taylor had planned on specializing in an area with relevance to African-American health—cardiovascular diseases and diabetes both affect a dis-proportionate number of blacks in America—but during her fourth-year medical school rotation she was assigned to the hospital's dermatology department and found her calling. "It was a completely eye-opening experience," she wrote on *Brownskin.net*. "It was a specialty that really incorporated internal medicine in terms of the collagen vascular diseases and rheumatologic diseases, but beyond that there was a surgical component to it and an aesthetic component. I could also see patients of all ages."

Taylor spent her medical internship and first years as a resident at Pennsylvania Hospital in Philadelphia, then went on to Columbia-Presbyterian Medical Center, an affiliation between Columbia University and Presbyterian Hospital, in New York City for a three-year residency in dermatology. When she finished in 1989, she returned to Philadelphia and entered private practice with Society Hill Dermatology. Yet she returned to both of her alma maters, Penn and Columbia, to serve as assistant clinical professor of dermatology. In 1999, she and her Columbia University mentor, Dr. Vincent A. DeLeo, co-founded the Skin of Color Center at St. Luke's Roosevelt Hospital Center.

Affiliated with the Columbia University College of Physicians and Surgeons, the Skin of Color Center in New York City became the first facility of its kind in the United States in its focus on patient care and research into dermatology concerns of particular ethnic groups. Black men's skin, for example, is prone to pseudofolliculitis barbae (PFB), or shaving-razor bumps, and there are a range of other conditions that dermatologists know are particular to specific ethnic groups.

At a Glance . . .

Born on October 7, 1957, in Philadelphia, PA; daughter of Charles and Ethel Taylor; married Kemel W. Dawkins, 1983; children: Morgan Elizabeth, Madison Lauren. *Education:* University of Pennsylvania, BA (magna cum laude), 1979; Harvard Medical School, MD, 1983. *Religion:* African Episcopal.

Career: Pennsylvania Hospital, Philadelphia, PA, intern, 1983-84, and resident, 1984-86; Columbia-Presbyterian Medical Center, New York, NY, 1986-89; Society Hill Dermatology, physician, 1989–; University of Pennsylvania School of Medicine, assistant clinical professor of dermatology; College of Physicians and Surgeons at Columbia University, assistant clinical professor of dermatology; St. Luke's Roosevelt Hospital Center, Skin of Color Center, director, January 1999–.

Memberships: American Academy of Dermatology, chair, Women's Health Task Force; Skin of Color Society, board chair; United Way of Southeastern Pennsylvania, board member; Jack and Jill, Inc. of Montgomery County, PA; James Brister Society, co-chair.

Awards: University of Pennsylvania, Alumni Award of Merit, 2000.

Addresses: *Office*—Society Hill Dermatology, 932 Pine St., Philadelphia, PA 19107.

"With more than 35 [percent] of the United States population comprised of non-Caucasians, it's important for dermatologists to develop treatments which do not interfere or compete with the skin's color," a report in *Health & Medicine Week* quoted Taylor as saying.

The Skin of Color Center has received several grants to conduct research on various skin conditions, but carrying out those studies also presented certain issues. "In terms of African-Americans, according to the literature overall, African-Americans have a distrust of the healthcare system," Taylor explained in another article that appeared in *Dermatology Times.* "The Tuskegee experiment with syphilis is cited. It's my observation that many patients are averse to participating in clinical trials—they feel they're being experimented on and know that, in the past, those experiments weren't necessarily positive."

Beyond serving her own patients, Taylor reached out to the general population through media, offering advice and detailing her own skincare regimen. Taylor's book, *Brown Skin: Dr. Susan Taylor's Prescription for Flawless Skin, Hair, and Nails,* was published in 2003. Her skin-care advice and comments were regularly featured on the pages of *Essence* and *O, The Oprah Magazine.* She also involved herself in numerous professional, charitable, and civic organizations, several of them associated with the University of Pennsylvania. Married to Kemel W. Dawkins since 1983, she is the mother of two daughters. Asked by writer Jenny Bailly in *O, The Oprah Magazine* about her own cosmetic-dermatology regimen, she cited regular salicylic acid peels and injections of Botox, and advised readers to be wary of "anything that hasn't been around at least five years." She also scoffed at ads for some over-the-counter products, noting that "any that claim they can penetrate the muscles and have an effect comparable to Botox. That's just ridiculous."

Selected writings

Books

Brown Skin: Dr. Susan Taylor's Prescription for Flawless Skin, Hair, and Nails, Amistad Press, 2003.

Sources

Periodicals

Dermatology Times, February 2001, p. 33; August 2002, p. 38; June 2006, p. 1.
Health & Medicine Week, November 25, 2002, p. 5.
New York Times, November 3, 2005, p. G1.
O, The Oprah Magazine, November 2006, p. 151.

On-line

"Professional Background," *Dr. Susan Taylor's BrownSkin.net,* www.brownskin.net/people.html (July 4, 2007).
Society Hill Dermatology, www.societyhilldermatology.com (July 4, 2007).

—Carol Brennan

Augustine Tolton

1854-1897

Priest

Former slave Augustine Tolton overcame daunting obstacles to become the second African-American to be ordained a priest in the Roman Catholic Church. Trained in Rome and ordained in 1886, Tolton served in Quincy, Illinois, and later in Chicago until his premature death in 1897 at the age of 43. He was assigned to small, often desperately poor parishes of black Catholics during an era when this religion was viewed with great prejudice in America as the faith of immigrants. Accounts written by his contemporaries describe him as admirably pious as well as a warm, charismatic leader of his flock.

Tolton was born on the first day of April in 1854, in Ralls County, Missouri. Missouri was a slave state at the time, but its populace—a mix of settlers from both northern and southern states—was bitterly divided over the slavery question. Tolton's mother, Martha Jane Crisley, had come to Missouri with her owners, the Elliotts, a Catholic family from Kentucky. Crisley was a personal maid to Mrs. Elliott and had been baptized in the Roman Catholic Church, as had her husband, Peter Paul Tolton, another Elliott slave. Their two sons—Augustine and his older brother Charley—were baptized in the Church and given religious instruction by Mrs. Elliott, who served as Augustine's godmother.

Entered Parish School

When the U.S. Civil War (1861-65) broke out in 1861, Tolton was seven years old. His family either escaped in the uproar that ensued in Missouri as various militias from the Union and Confederate sides battled to control the state, or were freed by the Elliotts. In any event, they made their way to a Union Army encampment near Hannibal, where Peter Paul Tolton decided to enlist in the Union Army. His wife, two sons, and a year-old daughter fled across the Mississippi River to Illinois, a free state. Their father died of dysentery later in the war.

Martha Tolton settled in Quincy, the Illinois city located directly across from Hannibal on the banks of the Mississippi. She and her sons worked in a cigar factory which shut down during the winter months, and this hiatus allowed Tolton to begin his first formal schooling. He attended a local public school and then entered the parish school of St. Boniface, one of Quincy's Roman Catholic churches. Some parishioners objected to worshipping alongside the Toltons, however, and to the youngster's presence in the classroom with their children, so Martha switched allegiances to St. Lawrence's, a church run by a sympathetic but strong-willed Irish immigrant priest, Father Peter McGirr, who took sympathy on the family. McGirr installed Tolton in the parish school, ignoring the threats from white parents that they would leave the parish and school, and he became an important mentor to Tolton.

During his teen years, Tolton worked for a local saddle maker, as a custodian at St. Lawrence's (by then renamed St. Peter's), and in a factory. He was drawn to the priesthood but was hampered by his lack of formal schooling. At the time, Roman Catholic religious texts and services were written entirely in Latin, and so McGirr arranged for some local Franciscan priests—who had recently established a Catholic college in

At a Glance . . .

Born on April 1, 1854 in Ralls County, Missouri; son of Peter Paul Tolton and Martha Jane Crisley; died of heatstroke, July 9, 1897, in Chicago, IL. *Education:* Attended the College of the Propagation of the Faith, 1880-85. *Religion:* Roman Catholic.

Career: Worked in a cigar factory in Quincy, IL, as a child; also held jobs in a saddlery, as a church custodian, and factory worker; ordained Roman Catholic priest, 1886; St. Joseph's Catholic Church, Quincy, IL, priest, 1886-89, St. Monica's Roman Catholic Church, Chicago, IL, priest, 1889-97.

Father James Augustine Healy, but he was born to a slave mother and a white father, and was by then serving as Bishop of Portland, Maine.

Back in Quincy, Tolton took over the pastorship of St. Joseph's Catholic Church for Negroes, but the parish struggled financially and had but two dozen members. Still, Tolton emerged as a popular figure in Quincy, and his sermons grew particularly eloquent—enough so that they began attracting more African-American congregants from Protestant churches and even a few whites. His immediate superior in Quincy, however, decreed that integrated church services were forbidden, and some local black ministers reportedly also viewed Tolton as a threat. His fame continued to spread, however, and he was beloved by his parishioners, who called him "Good Father Gus." Contemporary accounts noted that he played the accordion and had an excellent singing voice.

Quincy—to begin tutoring him in the classical language. Tolton began his evening classes with the friars around 1873, when he was 19, while McGirr began writing letters to seminaries inquiring if they would accept a black candidate for the priesthood.

Mentors Pulled Strings

No seminary would permit Tolton to enroll, not even one specifically aimed at training missionaries for Africa, and so McGirr and one of the Franciscans, a Father Richard, pleaded with contacts they knew in Rome and the Vatican, the seat of the Roman Catholic Church. They assured their colleagues in the church hierarchy that the 26-year-old Tolton displayed an ardent commitment to his faith, attending Mass sometimes twice daily and often stating his intention to serve as a missionary priest in Africa. Their effort bore fruit, and Tolton was admitted to the College of the Propagation of the Faith, the seminary in Rome that trained missionary priests. Tolton's travel expenses were paid by a fundraising drive spearheaded by McGirr and the other priests in Quincy. The onetime slave arrived in Rome, Christendom's holiest city, in 1880, entered the seminary, and five years later was ordained at St. John Lateran Church in Rome, a structure whose origins as a church dated back to 314 CE.

Tolton's superiors debated over his first assignment as a priest. He hoped to be sent to Africa to work as a missionary, feeling certain that despite his new priest's collar he would still be subject to humiliating racism in the United States, but the decision of church hierarchy was binding, and Tolton complied with it and returned to Illinois. The first Mass he celebrated in the United States was at a church called St. Benedict the Moor in New York City, which served an African-American community of Roman Catholics there. Tolton was feted as a celebrity of sorts, for there was only one other black priest of the faith in the country at the time,

Took Over Chicago Flock

Tolton found it difficult to find potential Roman Catholic converts in Quincy, but his fame had reached other cities, including Chicago. A struggling congregation of black Catholics there petitioned their archbishop to transfer Tolton to their parish, and he moved there in 1889. He took over a small basement church attached to a larger white parish, but church authorities in the city had recently been given a generous donation of $10,000 from a woman named Anna O'Neil to establish a permanent, bricks-and-mortar Roman Catholic church for blacks in the city. Tolton's mother, sister, and several loyal Quincy parishioners eventually followed him to Chicago, and became part of St. Monica's Roman Catholic Church for Negroes, named for the mother of early church theologian St. Augustine, who was African. "These dear people feel proud that they have a priest to look after them," Tolton wrote in one letter to a benefactor, according to *Seattle Times* writer Martha Irvine, and he noted that some blacks of other faiths requested his prayers at their sickbed. "That makes me feel that there is great work for me here."

Tolton also made contact with Mother Katherine Drexel, one of the first American-born Catholics to be canonized a saint after death. Drexel had been born into great wealth but went on to found a religious order and become a generous benefactor to Native American and African-American causes. She provided some additional funds for Tolton's church, then under construction on the corner of 36th Street and Dearborn Avenue. By then Tolton was well-known among Roman Catholics in America and was an active participant in the Congresses of Black Catholics that took place during this era. In the summer of 1892 he spent a month in Boston at a conference of black Catholics, telling his audience at one event, "the Catholic Church considers [ours] a double slavery, that of the mind and that of the body," he said, according to a report that appeared in *Irish World and American Industrial Liberator* newspaper. "She endeavors to free us from both. I was a poor slave boy, but the priests of that Church did not disdain me…. It was the priests of the Church who taught me to pray and forgive my persecutors."

St. Monica's, which had some 600 parishioners at its peak, was still under construction when Tolton—already plagued by poor health—traveled to Kankakee, Illinois, in July of 1897, for a religious retreat. On the way home, he was sickened by the heat on a day when the temperature reached 105 degrees. He died on July 9, 1897, at Mercy Hospital in Chicago, at the age of 43. His funeral services took place in Quincy at St. Peter's, the church helmed by Father McGirr, who had died four years earlier. The Tolton grave in Quincy's cemetery became a pilgrimage site for black Catholics.

Tolton's congregation at St. Monica's was later folded into that of St. Elizabeth's, and construction on the church was never completed. The site is near Stateway Park, and across the Dan Ryan Expressway from US Cellular Field, now home of the Chicago White Sox baseball team. Though the number of black Catholics in America grew impressively in the years following his death, few Americans of any color know about Tolton's brief but committed service to the church. One of his contemporary followers is Archbishop Wilton D. Gregory of Atlanta, the first black president of the U.S.

Conference of Catholic Bishops. "When he was alive, his life would probably not have been considered that newsworthy," Wilton told Irvine in the *Seattle Times.* "He lived at a time when to be a person of color automatically meant that you were not a person of significance. So the very fact that he was able to accomplish what he accomplished under severe limitations was to his credit."

Sources

Periodicals

Atchison Daily Globe (Atchison, KS), December 28, 1893.
Irish World and American Industrial Liberator, (New York, NY), June 11, 1892, p. 8.
St. Louis Globe-Democrat, February 16, 1887.
St. Louis Post-Dispatch, November 4, 2002, p. B1.
Seattle Times, January 13, 2007, p. B5.

On-line

Bauer, Roy, "They Called Him Father Gus," http://shamino.quincy.edu/tolton/tolton2.html (May 18, 2007).
"Father Augustine Tolton First Black Priest," *Roots Web,* www.rootsweb.com/~momonroe/tolton.htm (July 4, 2007).

—Carol Brennan

Lance Tooks

1962—

Graphic novelist, cartoonist

Lance Tooks was born into a family where art was as essential as brushing your teeth before bed. "[My father] saw all the arts as being completely interconnected," Tooks recalled in an interview with Denise Sudell for the on-line comics magazine *Sequential Tart*. From almost the time he could speak, Tooks was given creative assignments to complete—plays, paintings, poetry. It gave him a wide range of artistic talent, but one driving desire. "I always knew I wanted to be a storyteller," Tooks revealed to *Contemporary Black Biography* (*CBB*). To do that he chose a single art form—comics—since the age of 16, he has worked diligently on his craft, filling hundreds of sketchbooks with his ideas, self-publishing critically acclaimed comics, and making a name for himself in the emerging genre of graphic novels with his award-winning *Narcissa*. By 2007, with half a dozen projects on the horizon, Tooks was poised to reach success as a major talent in comics. However, committed to further pushing his own creative boundaries, he told *CBB*, "I'm proud of the work I've done but humbled by how much I've still ahead of me to learn."

Groomed to be an Artist from Childhood

Lance Tooks was born on September 15, 1962, in Brooklyn, New York, and raised, along with siblings Eric and Kim, in a home simmering with creativity. "My father, Ed Tooks was a painter, photographer, musician, singer, playwright, and theater producer," Tooks told *CBB*. "He would give my sister, brother, and I weekly creative assignments. We loved him for it and never imagined that other kids might be raised in a different fashion." While his mother Hazel held down the practical side of the household—Tooks told *Sequential Tart*, "She was the civilian, so basically she kept reminding my father that the bills had to be paid"—his father employed the children as back up singers in his basement recording studio, taught them to write plays and stories, and encouraged them to explore creativity in all its forms. "I learned from my father that all of the arts are one," Tooks told *CBB*. "Storytelling is the basis from which they all spring, and the differences between media are superficial at best. An artist can tell the same story of a love affair through song, a painting, a photo, or a movie."

His father had taught him to read before he was two, and Tooks developed an enormous appetite for books at a very young age. However, he happened onto comic books almost by chance. "I think the first ones I saw were in a recording studio where my father was doing a session," he told *Sequential Tart*. "And I think just the fact that they were stories that were told with pictures was something that interested me." By the time he entered New York's High School of Art and Design, he had decided to focus his talent on comics, partly in reaction to his father's refusal to stick with just one art form. He explained to *Sequential Tart* that his father's interest in so many mediums was both a strength and a liability. "You know, he would be interested in photography for many years, and then painting would take his attention away from that, and so I figured I wanted to choose the one that I felt the most connection to. Which turned out to be comics—I thought that all the interests that I had, I could funnel through comics."

At the age of 16, Tooks landed an internship at Marvel Comics. Two years later, after graduating from high school, Marvel hired him as an assistant editor. Tooks has since referred to his time there as Marvel University. Though he never worked as an artist for Marvel, he told *Sequential Tart*, "I was drawing all the time. And by far, the best thing about being there was having access to the brilliant artists who worked there, who had been doing it for years, and who I could show my art work [to], and they would tell me to work on my anatomy, or tell me why something works better in a panel, design-wise." One of the best pieces of advice he received while working there was to draw every day. Tooks committed himself to doing just that and since 1982 he has filled two hard-bound sketch books per year with drawings, sketches, and ideas.

Found Success in Graphic Novels

At the age of 21, Tooks was fired from Marvel and for a few years toyed with the idea of getting into film. "I thought a good way to get into filmmaking would be to—well, first, watch a lot of movies," he told *Sequen-*

tial Tart. He did this by working a series of jobs in video rental stores and movie theaters and building up a personal video library that he has estimated at over 10,000 films. However, after a disappointing run at the Director's Guild Trainee test, he decided to return to art. He got his foot back in the door by becoming a messenger at Broadcast Arts, an animation studio most famous for *Pee-Wee's Playhouse*. When he found out they were also working on the animated opening credits for the Madonna film, *Who's That Girl*, Tooks brought his sketchbooks to the production office. "And so within about two weeks, I stopped being a messenger, and was an inker on this animated film," he told *Sequential Tart*. This led to 15 years of working in animation at dozens of production companies including MTV and Nickelodeon, including collaborations with such names as George Lucas, Bill Cosby, Spike Lee, and the Red Hot Chili Peppers. He has estimated that his work has appeared in over 100 projects from commercials to music videos.

As his career in animation evolved, Tooks also kept his creativity peaked with other projects. He designed album covers for the reggae record label PowWow, did set design for theater, briefly worked as a movie stuntman, and sat for two years as a juror on the Queens Council of the Arts, a seat vacated when his father died. Throughout all of this, Tooks never stopped drawing. He not only continued to fill his sketchbooks, but also started publishing original comics such as *Danger Funnies* and *Divided by Infinity*. His comic work regularly appeared in national magazines and comic anthologies. He also illustrated books such as *The Black Panthers for Beginners* by Herb Boyd. Though his name was not unknown in comic circles, he jokingly recalled to *Sequential Tart*, "I thought only me and my mother knew [my comic books] existed." He was wrong. In 2000, Deborah Cowell, an editor at Random House/Doubleday tracked him down and asked him to contribute a book to their new line of graphic novels—novels told in comic form with drawings and text.

Given complete artistic freedom, Tooks created *Narcissa*, the story of a young, black filmmaker who flees to Spain after being given only a week to live. Published in 2002, it won an award as Best Graphic Novel from *Publishers Weekly* and opened the door for Tooks to develop more works in this genre. Tooks particularly enjoyed the genre. He told Karen Juanita Carrillo of the *New York Amsterdam News* "I love storytelling in general, and this the best way I've found to tell stories." From 2005 to 2007, he published *Lucifer's Garden of Verses*, an award-winning four-part series that features the Devil himself as a protagonist in stories involving love, art, and Miles Davis. By mid-2007, Tooks was busy with several more projects including graphic adaptations of works by Nathaniel Hawthorne, Mark Twain, and Oscar Wilde. He was also hard at work on another original work, *Anansi's Dreambook*, the story of a skateboard messenger who gets lost in his daydreams. On reflecting on his success, Tooks who moved to Spain fulltime in 2004 told *CBB*, "I've come nowhere near the kind of success I'd like to achieve, however. I hope to someday create a work that communicates to all people equally."

Selected works

Books

Narcissa, Random House/Doubleday, 2002.
Lucifer's Garden of Verses, The Devil on Fever Street, ComicsLit, 2005.
Lucifer's Garden of Verses, Darlin' Niki, ComicsLit, 2005.
Lucifer's Garden of Verses, The Student, NBM Publishing, 2006.
Lucifer's Garden of Verses, Between the Devil And Miles Davis, ComicsLit, 2007.

Sources

Periodicals

New York Amsterdam News, February 6, 2003, p. 33.
Publishers Weekly, September 23, 2002, p. 52.

On-line

"Following His Own Beat: Lance Tooks," *Newsarama,* http://forum.newsarama.com/showthread.php?s=0d9124a14a1f45d6b5dec2bb144e1365&threadid=11805&highlight=narcissa (June 29, 2007).
"Getting Graphic," *New York Public Radio,* www.wnyc.org/shows/bl/episodes/2003/05/23 (June 29, 2007).
"Giant Dog, Single Mothers, and Groucho Bronte: Lance Tooks Draws Like Himself," *Sequential Tart,* www.sequentialtart.com/archive/mar03/ltooks.shtml (June 29, 2007).
Lance Tooks, www.LanceTooks.com (June 29, 2007).

Other

Additional information was obtained through an interview with Lance Tooks on April 25, 2007.

—Candace LaBalle

Chris Tucker

1972—

Comedian, actor

Tucker, Chris, photograph. Fitzroy Barrett/Landov.

Chris Tucker launched himself from stand-up comic to top-billed actor in short order. From his introduction to television audiences in 1993's *Def Comedy Jam* to his first starring role in 1995's *Friday,* which became "one of the biggest video rentals in history," according to Lynn Hirschberg of *New York Times Magazine,* to his star-making performance in 1998's *Rush Hour,* Tucker quickly became a celebrity, able to command more than $20 million per film. Tucker, however, took his newfound fame in stride: he refused to amass an entourage of bodyguards and managers, took long hiatuses between filming new features, and kept his stand-up skills honed with appearances in clubs throughout the country. The executives in Hollywood "all think Chris is crazy," President of New Line Cinema Michael DeLuca explained to Hirschberg. "He won't jump at an open checkbook, and people out here get frustrated. Chris is picky. They get impatient when they can't get him in their lousy scripts. But Chris is not just another actor for hire. He wants to have a long career."

Honed Humble Roots into Stand-Up Routine

Born on August 31, 1972, in Atlanta, Georgia, Tucker had to create quite a ruckus to make himself heard; he's the youngest of six children. He started trying to make people laugh as a teenager. "My older brother would have a friend over, and I would act a fool just so I could hang with them," he related to Veronica Rowe in *Venice Magazine.* Clowning around at home led to the more of the same at school. Tucker was given the Most Humorous Award by his classmates.

While in school, Tucker also began participating in talent shows. "When I was growing up," he explained in *The Real State!,* "I watched a lot of comedians on television: Robin Harris, Eddie Murphy, Richard Pryor. I was fascinated with the whole art of comedy and watched all their movies. I decided I could do comedy. I just felt like being funny! I love to perform." Apparently he *needed* to perform, so much so that he snuck into a small, popular comedy club in Atlanta, talked his way on to the stage, and eventually received a standing

At a Glance . . .

Born August 31, 1972, in Atlanta, GA.

Career: Stand up-comic, late 1980s–; actor, 1994–; Comedy Café, Atlanta, GA, owner; Chris Tucker Foundation, founder.

Addresses: *Agent*—Samantha Mast, Rogers & Cowan, 8687 Melrose Ave, 7th Floor, Los Angeles, CA 90069. *Web*—www.christucker.com.

ovation, "which was quite something at the time considering I was too young to even get into a club," he remarked to *The Real State!*. Tucker became such a local icon that complete strangers would stop to give him a high five on the street.

Tucker decided to try his hand in Los Angeles, moving there at age 19. He slept on a friend's living room floor in a Sunset Boulevard apartment that had a leaky icebox. "I just kept hustling for work as a comic and started getting fixed up for shows," he mentioned in *The Real State!*. After making a name for himself around town, Tucker earned himself a spot on *Russell Simmons' Def Comedy Jam*, a Home Box Office (HBO) cable television showcase for African-American comics. Unlike many of the other comedians on the program, who used explicit language about drugs, sex, and violence, Tucker highlighted his everyday life, without swear words or talk of sex or race. His performance made him "instantly accessible to a wide audience," HBO President of Original Programming Chris Albrecht told Hirschberg.

Tucker held a unique niche in comedy. Todd Williams of the *Source* described it with Tucker himself making parenthetical comments as "a little bit Richard Pryor ('he used so many facial expressions'); a smidgen of Robin Harris ('his quick punchlines'); and some Eddie Murphy to top it off ('nobody can control an audience like him')." Williams continued singularly, saying of Tucker, "Whether he knows it or not, he's probably more Jim Carrey than anything." The combination was hilarious. Omoronke Idowu wrote in *Vibe* "If you haven't heard a joke delivered in Chris Tucker's high-pitched rhythmic drawl, then you've used only part of your laugh muscle." In the same article, Tucker explained, "I don't try to speak that way, but when I'm hyper and on the mike, that's how it comes out." He also told Williams, "Whenever I would have to deal with bill collectors my voice would go up, but I didn't notice. I started doing it on stage, not really for laughs though, and people would love it. They would say, 'talk in that voice,' and I would always be like, 'What voice? What are you talking about?'"

Tucker continued to hone his skills on the comedy circuit until the rapping/acting duo Kid 'N Play caught Tucker's show one night in Los Angeles. They had already made their successful films *House Party I* and *II*, and offered Tucker a role in their upcoming *House Party III*. Tucker had just 90 seconds of onscreen time in the 1994 movie, but in that minute-and-a-half he managed to make a huge impression as the outrageous party promoter "Johnny Booze." "His skill for milking something-from-nothing…turned a brief 90-second appearance into the film's brightest moment," wrote *BAM*'s Victor Everett, just one of the many critics in consensus. Tucker actually received standing ovations at press screenings and was featured in the film's promotional billing.

Breakthrough Performance in Friday

Not long after, rapper and filmmaker Ice Cube happened to be at a club where Tucker was headlining. Cube remembered his performance from *House Party* and was impressed by Tucker's skills. He decided to take a chance on Tucker and cast him in the comedy motion picture he was making with DJ Pooh about a day in the life of a South Central LA "homeboy." In *Friday*, Tucker played a guy named Smokey—so named for his constant marijuana use—but he was a bit worried about the potentially stereotypical nature of the character. "[Smokey] isn't a drug addict," Tucker cautioned Rowe in *Venice*. "I didn't want to portray him as strung out and unable to talk. He acted the same, high or not, smokin' was just a part of him."

According to *BAM*'s Everett, "The critics all agreed: Tucker's on screen performance as the weeded out 'Smokey' seemed so natural, it was uncanny. He has had no formal training as an actor, so what filmgoers saw was an honest portrayal from a guy who's still much too green to brown nose." The film was attacked by some critics who suggested *Friday* was a warmed-over *Boyz N the Hood* that inappropriately poked fun at the issue of violence. Others, like Lisa Schwarzbaum of *Entertainment Weekly*, felt that "at least *Friday* has energy, and sass, and the nerve to suggest that the line between tragedy and comedy may be in the bloodshot eye of the beholder."

Tucker next landed the role of Skip in *Dead Presidents*. As directed by twin brothers Albert and Allen Hughes—the two men behind the hit *Menace II Society*—1995's *Dead Presidents* tells the story of lower-middle-class kids in the South Bronx during the late 1960s and early 1970s. It follows them to Vietnam and back, detailing their trouble on the return home. Tucker was confident in his turn to a dramatic role. "It felt natural to play Skip," he told Idowu in *Vibe*, "because of the seriousness that's in my comedy. I was glad I got the part, because it will prove to directors I can go in any direction." Although not a huge hit, the movie was well received by audiences and critics. *Entertainment Weekly*'s Ken Tucker, who gave the film an "A-," remarked that "The Hughes brothers get [a] subtle [performance] from…the stand-up comic Chris Tucker, whose heroin-addicted Skip speaks in a nonstop Richard Pryoresque patter." That comparison surely came as a complement to Tucker, who has cited Pryor as one of his influences.

In 1997, Tucker teamed with Bruce Willis in the science fiction adventure *The Fifth Element*. As a cross-dressing talk show hostess named Ruby Rhod, Tucker made his presence known on screen. In his big yellow wig and flowing gown, *Entertainment Weekly* described Tucker as a "kind of interstellar descendant of RuPaul." *The Fifth Element* was a highly successful film, and exposed Tucker's comedic talents to an even wider audience.

Following his outstanding performance in *The Fifth Element*, Tucker played a street hustler named Franklin Hatchett in the 1997 film *Money Talks*. However, the film suffered from a muddled plot and a lack of chemistry between Tucker and co-star Charlie Sheen. *Money Talks* was panned by critics and moviegoers alike. Tucker finished 1997 with a cameo role as Beaumont Livingston, a small-time drug dealer, in Quentin Tarantino's successful film *Jackie Brown*.

Fueled Rush Hour Franchise

Tucker scored a box office smash in 1998 with the film *Rush Hour*. The film featured Tucker as Detective James Carter, a cocky Los Angeles police officer who is given the assignment of hosting a visiting Hong Kong police officer, played by martial artist Jackie Chan. The two men form an unlikely duo as they try to capture a Chinese crime lord and rescue the kidnapped daughter of a Chinese diplomat. *Rush Hour* grossed more than $240 million worldwide and was a number one hit for several weeks. The comic thrust of *Rush Hour* and its sequels came from the hilarious coupling of Tucker and Chan, who struggle to understand each other as they pursue criminals. *Rush Hour 2* became "the highest grossing comedy of all time," according to *Speakin' Out News* in 2006. The box office success enabled Tucker to sign a deal with New Line Cinema worth $45 million for two sequels to *Rush Hour,* putting Tucker among Hollywood's highest paid actors.

Aside from *Rush Hour 2* in 2001 and *Rush Hour 3* in 2007, however, Tucker limited his film work. He rejected a part in *Shaft,* dropped out of *Black Knight,* and began work on his own project, a film about the first black president of the United States. He took time off from all work to travel the world and spent a great deal of time involving himself in humanitarian work in Africa and setting up the Chris Tucker Foundation to provide further help with youth education, HIV/AIDS efforts, and provisions of safe water in African nations.

Tucker credited his time off as providing him with creative fuel. "I observe, I'm curious, I like to learn, and I take that to my stand-up—being educated," Tucker explained to Kimberly C. Roberts of the *Philadelphia Tribune.* "I think that's part of stand-up comedy, because most stand-up comics are very smart, and they need to be educated to what's going on…." Tucker began touring on the comedy circuit in 2005, prepping for a live concert film he planned to release in 2007, after *Rush Hour 3.* In the comedy concert film, "I'm back to my roots," Tucker told Roberts. "I started out doing stand-up, and it helped me get to the movies. It's a new show. It talks about what I've been going through the last six years…." Tucker's desire to remain true to his roots despite his enormous box office earnings has endeared him to his fans and kept him in touch with what brought him such success in the first place. Tucker's value as a comedian was aptly noted by DeLuca, who told Hirschberg: "It's great when you find a personality that can break out in a movie…. When you find someone like Chris Tucker, they are worth their weight in gold." While studios pegged Tucker as a box-office winner for comedies, Tucker planned to broaden his roles beyond comedy to "roles that people have never seen me play in movies," he told Roberts. Given his track record for selecting films, Tucker may eventually reveal all aspects of his talent to audiences…in his own good time.

Selected works

Films

House Party III, 1994.
Friday, 1995.
Dead Presidents, 1995.
The Fifth Element, 1997.
Money Talks, 1997.
Jackie Brown, 1997.
Rush Hour, 1998.
Rush Hour 2, 2001.
Rush Hour 3, 2007.

Television

Russell Simmons' Def Comedy Jam, 1993.

Sources

Periodicals

BAM, August 11, 1995, p. 11.
Entertainment Weekly, May 12, 1995, p. 43; October 20, 1995, pp. 45-46; November 6, 1998, pp. 52-53; January 22, 1999, pp. 107-108.
Jet, August 6, 2001, p. 58.
Los Angeles Times, July 29, 2001, p. 1.
New York Times Magazine, September 3, 2000, p. 34.
People, May 8, 1995, p. 24.
Philadelphia Tribune, October 1, 2006, p. 19.
The Real State!, Issue Nine, pp.17-20.

Savoy, September 2001, p. 58; May 2002, p. 31.
The Source, January 1996, p. 38.
Speakin' Out News (Huntsville, AL), May 17-23, 2006, p. B2.
Venice (CA), May 1995, pp. 36-38.
Vibe, August 1995, p. 114.

On-line

Chris Tucker Official Site, www.christucker.com (July 31, 2007).

—David G. Oblender, Shirelle Phelps, Joanna Rubiner, and Sara Pendergast

Charles Wesley Turnbull

1935—

Governor, educator

Dr. Charles Wesley Turnbull served two terms as governor of the U.S. Virgin Islands (USVI). Prior to his election Turnbull was Commissioner of Education and a history professor. As governor of the Caribbean territory—populated by approximately 110,000 people of diverse ethnic backgrounds—Turnbull faced perpetual financial crises. He repeatedly proposed tax increases in an attempt to stabilize the islands' faltering economy and rebuild its dilapidated schools and infrastructure

Attended Hampton University

Charles Wesley Turnbull was born on February 5, 1935, in the USVI capital of Charlotte Amalie on St. Thomas Island. His parents, Ruth Ann Eliza Skelton and John Wesley Turnbull, were poor immigrants from Tortola in the British Virgin Islands. Turnbull attended public schools, graduating from Charlotte Amalie High School in 1952.

Turnbull won a Ford Foundation Scholarship to attend Hampton University, a historically black school in Hampton, Virginia. There he served as vice president of his freshman class and president of both his sophomore and senior classes. He was also chief justice of the student court. Turnbull earned a bachelor's degree in history with honors in 1958 and a master's degree in secondary education in 1959.

Returning home to St. Thomas, Turnbull taught elementary school and high school, eventually becoming principal of Charlotte Amalie High School. In 1967 he

was named Assistant Commissioner of Education. He returned to the mainland to earn his doctorate in educational administration from the University of Minnesota in 1976.

Appointed Education Commissioner

Turnbull served as Commissioner of Education from 1979 until 1987. He was responsible for the construction of new schools, eliminating the double sessions that had plagued the system. He instituted vocational and technical programs, as well as alternative education, and encouraged the involvement of volunteers. Notably, Turnbull established the Cultural Education Division to promote awareness of the history and culture of the Virgin Islands and the greater Caribbean region.

In 1987 with the advent of a new administration, Turnbull lost his position. He joined the faculty of the University of the Virgin Islands as a history professor. Over the decades Turnbull had stayed politically involved. He was a longtime member of the Territorial Committee of the Virgin Islands Democratic Party and, beginning in 1964, he served as a delegate to each of the Islands' first four Constitutional Conventions. He also served on the Board of Elections.

Elected Governor

In 1998 Turnbull defeated the incumbent Republican Governor Roy Schneider, garnering 59% of the vote.

At a Glance . . .

Born Charles Wesley Turnbull on February 5, 1935, in Charlotte Amalie, St. Thomas, U.S. Virgin Islands. *Education:* Hampton University, BA, history, 1958, MA, secondary education, 1959; University of Minnesota, PhD, educational administration, 1976. *Religion:* Methodist. *Politics:* Democrat.

Career: Virgin Islands Department of Education, St. Thomas, USVI, social-studies teacher, 1959-61, Charlotte Amalie High School, assistant principal, 1961-65, principal, 1965-67, assistant commissioner of education, 1967-79, commissioner of education, 1979-87; University of the Virgin Islands, St. Thomas, USVI, professor of history, 1988-99, professor emeritus, 1999–; Governor of the U.S. Virgin Islands, 1999-2007.

Selected memberships: Roy Lester Schneider Hospital, board member; University of the Virgin Islands, trustee; Virgin Islands Board of Education, chair; Virgin Islands Historical Society, president; West Indian Company, Ltd., director.

Selected awards: Iota Phi Lambda Sorority, Citation for Excellence, Leadership and Service in the Field of Education, 1989; Alpha Phi Alpha Fraternity, Theta Epsilon Lambda Chapter, Citation for Excellence in the Service of Humanity, 1992; Turner Broadcasting System, Trumpet Award for outstanding contributions to public service and education, 2001; Virgin Islands Humanities Council, Humanist Award, 2005; All Saints Cathedral, Diakonia Award for Community Service, 2006.

Addresses: *Home*—PO Box 2265, Charlotte Amalie, St. Thomas, VI 00803.

He was the sixth elected USVI governor, since prior to 1970 the governor had been appointed by the U.S. president. During his campaign Turnbull promised to boost the islands' deficit-ridden economy by promoting tourism through advertising and air travel improvements and by encouraging businesses to relocate to the USVI. He told *Success* magazine: "Under my administration, we will not only do our best to make people aware of the opportunities in the Virgin Islands, but we'll also make it easier for them to do business once they get here."

However the problems confronting the new governor were immense. He faced a budget deficit of $100 million. In November of 1999 the Virgin Islands sustained nearly $32 million in damage from Hurricane Lenny. By the end of 1999 Turnbull's government was an estimated $1 billion in debt. Turnbull managed to shrink the government workforce, which had previously accounted for one-third of the territory's employees. However he was criticized for putting his friends and relatives on the government payroll and for giving them substantial raises.

Turnbull's tourism campaign got off to a rocky start. Between January of 1999 and March of 2000 he hired and fired four tourism directors. The terrorist attacks of September 11, 2001, further hurt tourism, the mainstay of the USVI economy. In 2002 Carnival Cruise Line and others pulled out of St. Croix, USVI, because of crimes against passengers and crew. However by 2004 most of the cruise ships had returned, due in part to Turnbull's aggressive advertising campaign that promoted the USVI as a safe American territory, in contrast to foreign Caribbean destinations. Major new tourism projects were initiated including a $75-million expansion of the Ritz-Carlton on St. Thomas, a theme park, and a mega-resort with casino and golf course on St. Croix.

Defeated Seven Challengers for Reelection

With the territory in crisis and increasing concerns about Turnbull's managerial skills, he faced seven challengers in the 2002 election, including his lieutenant governor and former running mate. Nevertheless Turnbull was reelected with 50.5% of the vote.

In 2003 a week-long storm caused more than $5 million in damage and Turnbull declared a state of emergency. The public works department had no money to repair damaged sewers, roads, and culverts. By 2004 failure to upgrade sewer systems had cost the territory more than $25 million in fines. However Turnbull was successful in getting the federal government to forgive hurricane-related loans.

The USVI's fiscal crisis continued unabated. As chairman of the Public Finance Authority, Turnbull was criticized for chronic fiscal mismanagement. He responded by commissioning new software to streamline government operations. In 2003 the federal government took over the territory's Housing Authority because of poor accounting and failure to repay federal loans. Turnbull's administration sometimes had difficulty meeting its payroll, paying vendors, and refunding taxes. In 2004 Turnbull vetoed raises and spending increases passed by the senate. His repeated proposals to raise hotel and rental-car taxes met with vehement opposition from both the tourism industry and the senate. Increasingly Turnbull was seen as anti-business.

Threatened with Financial Oversight

The USVI's nonvoting U.S. congressional representative repeatedly called for the appointment of a chief financial officer (CFO) with veto power over all government spending, a proposal that enraged Turnbull. The *Virgin Islands Daily News* of February 1, 2005, quoted from his State of the Territory address: "Our success in 2004 in growing our revenues, holding the line on spending, reducing the size of the government and eliminating 20 percent of our total debt simply tells truth to the lie that Virgin Islanders are incapable of governing themselves, especially in the area of financial management. It would be a good thing if our delegate to Congress withdraws her recently re-introduced bill to impose a CFO on the Virgin Islands. We really do not need it!" Turnbull testified against the bill before the U.S. Senate.

By the end of 2005 private-sector investment had led the USVI into a period of economic expansion. In his 2006 State of the Territory address Turnbull promised to establish a stock exchange in the territory, to develop new resorts and casinos, and to lobby the U.S. Congress for more help. However some senators credited the improved economy to the threat of a CFO.

Turnbull did not push for statehood for the USVI but did advocate for more local authority. In 2004 he signed a bill creating a supreme court, a significant step toward self-governance. He also signed a bill convening the territory's fifth convention to draft a constitution that would give the islands greater self-governance.

Faced Crime Wave and Crumbling Schools

Many senators were critical of Turnbull's failure to address education and crime. Under the self-declared "education governor" three public schools lost their accreditation. Schools were closing because of severe mold and lack of maintenance. In 2005 Turnbull declared a public exigency to supply millions of dollars to keep the buildings from collapsing. The territory was also experiencing a large increase in gun-related crime, while allegations of police brutality and corruption abounded.

Turnbull's administration was also tainted by scandal. In 2006 his former special assistant pleaded guilty to conspiracy to commit theft and bribery, wire fraud, and conflict of interest in a case involving a multimillion-dollar sewer-repair contract to Global Resources Management, a company that Turnbull had served as president of for one month. Turnbull was accused of improperly declaring a state of emergency to award the contract without competitive bidding. He later canceled the contract and cooperated with prosecutors.

Turnbull left office in January of 2007, having served his allowable two terms. He had spent much of the past eight years at odds with the senate, even though Democrats held the majority. His vetoes were frequently overridden by the legislators. In one of his last acts as governor Turnbull pardoned or commuted the sentences of four murderers, six sex offenders, and three armed robbers.

Sources

Periodicals

Success, November 1998, p. 37.
Virgin Islands Daily News, February 1, 2005; August 8, 2005; January 31, 2006; February 4, 2006; May 8, 2006; October 3, 2006; October 21, 2006.

On-line

"Charles Wesley Turnbull," *Biography Resource Center,* www.galenet. com/servlet/BioRC (February 24, 2007).
"Governor's Information," *National Governors Association,* www.nga.org/portal/site/nga/menuitem. 29fab9fb4add37305ddcbeeb501010a0/?vgnex-toid= 7ca6ae3effb81010VgnVCM1000001a01010aRCRD (March 6, 2007).
"Turnbull's State Address Receives Lukewarm Senate Response," *St. Thomas Source,* www.onepaper. com/stthomasvi/?v=d&i=&s=News:Local&p= 1138080033 (March 6, 2007).
"US Virgin Islands State of the Territory," *Council of State Governments-Eastern Regional Conference,* www.csgeast.org/page.asp?id=weeklynewsbulletin84 (March 6, 2007).
"USVI in a Campaign Mode," *Revista INTERFORUM,* www.revistainterforum.com/english/articles/072202collins_usvi.html (March 7, 2007).

—Margaret Alic

Bobby Valentino

1980—

Singer

Rhythm and blues crooner Bobby Valentino has said that he aims to "bring R&B back to its roots," according to an interview on the *Hi5* Web site. After a promising but short-lived start as part of the vocal group Mista in 1996, Valentino returned as a solo artist in 2005. His two albums of smooth neo-soul—2005's *Disturbing tha Peace Presents...Bobby Valentino* and the 2007 release *Special Occasion*—both hit Number 1 on *Billboard*'s R&B/Hip-Hop Albums chart. And his two most popular songs, "Slow Down" from 2005 and

Valentino, Bobby, photograph. Robert Pitts/Landov.

"Anonymous" from 2007 rose to Number 1 and Number 21, respectively, on *Billboard*'s R&B/Hip-Hop Songs chart. Valentino was signed by rapper Ludacris's Disturbing tha Peace production company in 2003. Described by Ludacris as "a singer trapped in a rapper's body," Valentino is the only R&B singer on the company's roster of rap and hip-hop talent.

Valentino was born Bobby Wilson on February 27, 1980, in Jackson, Mississippi, and raised in Atlanta, Georgia. He earned the "Valentino" nickname because his parents had expected him to be born on Valentine's Day. He was drawn to music at an early age, inspired by artists such as Marvin Gaye, Boyz II Men, Anita

Baker, Prince, and Stevie Wonder. Despite his parents' skepticism about the music business, he was determined to pursue a musical career. By his early teens he was on his way: he joined with three other teens—Darryl Allen, Brandon Brown, and Byron Reeder—in the vocal group Mista, which was put together by producer Eric Johnston and former TLC manager Ian Burke. The group's first single, 1996's "Blackberry Molasses," was produced by Organized Noize Productions, a top outfit in the Atlanta R&B and rap scene that had produced records for TLC, En Vogue, and OutKast. A song with smooth, Boyz II Men-style harmonizing, "Blackberry Molasses" rose to Number 13 on the *Billboard* R&B/Hip-Hop Songs chart and Number 53 on the *Billboard* Hot 100 (the magazine's general pop chart). The group's debut album, *Mista*, also released in 1996, did not do as well, however. It reached Number 37 on the R&B/Hip-Hop Albums chart but only made it to Number 183 on the Hot 200 Albums chart. A second album, recorded with famed producers Tim & Bob, was never released. The group disbanded largely as a result of what Valentino referred to as "management issues" on his Web site. On his MySpace page, Valentino called the group's travails "a learning expe-

At a Glance . . .

Born Bobby Wilson on February 27, 1980, in Jackson, MS. *Education:* Clark Atlanta University, BA, mass communications, 2003.

Career: Mista, vocal group, singer, 1996; Disturbing tha Peace label, solo R&B artist, 2005–.

Addresses: *Label*—Disturbing tha Peace Recording, Atlanta GA 30318 . *Web*—www.bobbyvalentino.com.

rience, as it shows how you can be here today and gone tomorrow." He told the *All Hip Hop* Web site that the experience influenced his decision to enter college: "I felt like this music business is so competitive, so I felt like if it's something you want to do, you definitely have to have something to fall back on." Valentino entered Clark Atlanta University, where he played football and baseball and earned a bachelor's degree in mass communications in 2003. "This was a rough time in my life," Valentino remembered in his MySpace biography. "One day you're on TV, living the life, and the next day you are back to reality. But I didn't give up; my dream was to do music and that's what I did. Every day was the same routine: school in the morning, baseball practice in the evening, and the studio at night."

Valentino recorded a series of demos, and after he left college one of these caught the ear of Ludacris (Chris Bridges), who, with his business partner Chaka Zulu, signed Valentino to their Disturbing tha Peace production company. Valentino's Tim & Bob-produced debut, *Disturbing tha Peace Presents...Bobby Valentino*, was released in 2005 on the DTP label (distributed by Def Jam Recordings). The album went to Number 1 on *Billboard's* R&B/Hip-Hop Albums chart and reached Number 3 on the Hot 200 Albums chart, and it included the hit singles "Slow Down" and "Tell Me," which reached Numbers 1 and 13, respectively, on the R&B/Hip-Hop Songs chart. The album eventually sold more than 800,000 copies, winning a gold record award. It also garnered nominations from the annual National Association for the Advancement of Colored People (NAACP) Image Awards for Outstanding New Artist and from the Soul Train Awards for Best Male R&B/Soul Single and Best R&B/Soul or Rap New Artist. *Rolling Stone* magazine contributor Bill Werde rated the album 4.5 out of 5 stars and wrote: "Valentino portrays the lovable lothario, an R&B singer you can take home to the family. Just hope your sister isn't his type."

Valentino followed his solo debut success in 2007 with the release of his album entitled *Special Occasion*. The singer co-wrote most of the tracks and collaborated with a bevy of top producers—Tim & Bob, Timbaland,

Dre & Vidal, Delite, Sean Garrett, Brian Cox, and Rodney Jenkins. Valentino described the recording as "a classic R&B album with a Valentino twist," according to his DefJam Web site. It shot to Number 1 on *Billboard's* R&B/Hip-Hop Albums chart, but the reviews were mixed. *Entertainment Weekly* critic Simon Vozick-Levinson complained that "his self-assured attitude isn't always enough to sell these songs" and concluded that "The songs...will provide agreeable mood music for a candlelit dinner in a pinch, if nothing else." *Billboard* reviewer Mariel Concepcion proclaimed, however, that "the crooning on 'Where You Belong' and 'Over and Over'...remind us why we fell in love with Valentino's sound in the first place."

Valentino possessed a deep drive to develop skills that would enable him to enjoy a long life in the music business. Despite his early success as a solo artist, Valentino wrote: "I feel that I haven't done nothing yet. I have just scratched the surface," according to his MySpace page. "I'm going to continue to work hard and grow as an artist and to make music that people will love not only today but twenty years from now." He credited Ludacris as a mentor in the art of sustaining a career, taking note of how the rapper has branched into the business side of music—through Disturbing tha Peace—as well as into acting. Valentino has taken his own tentative steps into "brand extension" by introducing his Bobby V line of jeans for women. As he told National Public Radio's Ed Gordon, "I just watch everything [Ludacris] does, as far as his interviewing skills, as far as him being an actor, as well as his business skills. Those are three great things a black man needs in today's society to really make it. It's not just doing music."

Selected works

Albums

Mista, Elektra, 1996.
Disturbing tha Peace Presents...Bobby Valentino, DTP, 2005.
Special Occasion, DTP, 2007.

Sources

Periodicals

Billboard March 26, 2005, p. 30; May 12, 2007, p. 37.
Entertainment Weekly, May 11, 2007, p. 75.
Rolling Stone, June 2, 2005

On-line

"About Bobby," *MySpace,* www.myspace.com/bobbyvalentino (June 20, 2007).
"Artist Chart History: Bobby Valentino,"*Billboard,* www.billboard.com/bbcom/retrieve_chart_history.

do?model.vnuArtistId=653540&model.vnuAlbu-mId=790050 (June 19, 2007).

"Bobby Valentino," *All Music Guide,* www.allmusic.com/cg/amg.dll?p=amg&sql=11:hjfixq8aldhe (June 19, 2007).

Bobby Valentino, www.justbobby.com/home.html (June 19, 2007).

"Bobby Valentino: A Class of His Own," *VIBE,* www.vibe.com/news/online_exclusives/2006/08/bobby_valentino_a_class_of_his_own (June 19, 2007).

"Bobby Valentino: Behind the V," *Yo! Raps,* www.yoraps.com/interviews1.php?subaction=showfull&id=1178832572&archive=&start_from=&ucat=3& (June 19, 2007).

"Bobby Valentino Biography," *BobbyValentino.com*, www.bobbyvalentino.com/biography/ (June 19, 2007).

"Bobby Valentino Exclusive Interview," *Female First,* www.femalefirst.co.uk/celebrity_interviews/Bobby+Valentino+Exclusive+Interview-6384.html (June 19, 2007).

"Bobby Valentino: No Slowing Down," *Soundslam,* www.soundslam.com/articles/interviews/interviews.php?interviews=in050222bobbyv (June 19, 2007).

Bobby Valentino Official Website @ defjam.com, www.defjam.com/site/artist_bio.php?artist_id=580 (June 19, 2007).

"Bobby Valentino: Raising the Bar," *All Hip Hop.com,* www.allhiphop.com/blogs/alternatives/archive/2005/03/11/18135422.aspx (June 19, 2007).

"Bobby Valentino "Slows Down" for AC," *Associated Content,* www.associatedcontent.com/article/186694/bobby_valentino_slows_down_for_ac.html (June 19, 2007).

"Conversation with Bobby Valentino," *Honey Soul,* www.honeysoul.com/wp/?p=608 (June 19, 2007).

"Exclusive Interview: Bobby Valentino," *Concrete Loop,* http://concreteloop.com/interviews-bobbyv (June 19, 2007).

"Interview with Bobby Valentino by the Rap Hype/Hi5," *Hi5,* www.hi5.com/friend/profile/displayProfile.do?userid=100825457 (June 20, 2007).

"Mista,"*All Music Guide,* www.allmusic.com/cg/amg.dll?p=amg&token=&sql=11:dnfixqqgld0e (June 19, 2007).

"No 'Slow Down' for R&B Fave Bobby Valentino," *National Public Radio,* www.npr.org/templates/story/story.php?storyId=4693956 (June 19, 2007).

"Organized Noize," *All Music Guide,* http://www.allmusic.com/cg/amg.dll?p=amg&sql=11:k9fixqlgldkeze). (June 19, 2007).

"Valentino's Day," *Cleveland Free Times,* www.freetimes.com/stories/15/1/valentinos-day (June 19, 2007).

—Bob Genovesi

Andre Ward

1984—

Boxer

Riding a winning streak that stretched back to 1998, Andre Ward entered the 2004 Olympics and pummeled his way to a gold medal. He followed that achievement by entering the professional arena where his rocket-powered fists downed bigger boxers and dazzled fans. By mid-2007, he had racked up an impressive 12 straight wins and was touted as the next big thing in boxing. "We feel he has the abilities to be a great world champion," promoter Dan Goossen told the *Fresno Bee*. Ward, a deeply religious man who goes by the nickname S.O.G. (Son of God) and has the name of his father and two children tattooed along his chiseled arms, wanted more. "As long as I am in this game I want to be the best that I can be," he said, according to the *Goossen Tutor Promotions* Web site. "I have a hunger, a desire to win that I believe is second to none. And I want to touch as many people as I possibly can touch, be it on the airwaves, on the TV, or just coming to my fights."

Followed Father's Footsteps into Ring

Andre Ward was born on February 23, 1984, in San Francisco, California, and raised in the Bay Area by his parents Frank and Madeline. In school, he excelled at all sports and his skills on the football field drew the interest of college recruiters. However, Ward dropped out of school before reaching his senior year. He was too busy earning an education in the boxing ring. His father had been a top amateur heavyweight with an impressive 15-0 record, and the elder Ward could see the fighting spirit of a boxer in his son. "My father just

loved to fight," Ward told *USA Today*. "It's the same reason why I got into it, because I love to fight. But you've got to do it in an organized way. It's too dangerous in the streets."

Frank Ward took his son to King's Gym in Oakland, California, and put him under the training of Virgil Hunter, a top local boxing coach, family friend, and young Ward's godfather. Not only did Ward prove to have the raw talent for the sport, he had a single-minded desire that was unusual for someone so young. While other kids slept in, he would rise a full three hours before school to hit the gym. His hard work paid off, and he was soon holding his own against some of King's teenaged boxers. However, it wasn't enough to give him a victory during his first amateur fight at the age of ten. The loss pushed Ward to work even harder and when a rematch was scheduled, Ward trounced his opponent thoroughly. By the age of 14, Ward had started a winning streak that continued to hold in 2007. His relationship with Hunter also held. The trainer and his wife became like family to Ward.

As a teenager, Ward gained a reputation for the lightening speed of his punches and his ability to hit with both his right and left fists. He also impressed with his capacity to take down bigger boxers. Though his natural weight falls easily in the middleweight classification (155 to 160 pounds), he chose to fight in the light heavyweight division (161 to 175 pounds). This decision was not based on a boastful display of prowess, but rather a simple commitment to family. His cousin, DonYil Livingston was a middleweight boxer. "We made a pact we wouldn't fight each other," Ward

At a Glance . . .

Born on February 23, 1984, in San Francisco, CA; married, Tiffiney; children: Andre Jr., Malachi. *Religion:* Christian.

Career: Amateur boxer, 1998-2004; professional boxer, 2004–.

Awards: California Silver Gloves Champion, 1998, 1999, 2000; U.S. Championship, light heavyweight, 2001, 2003; Under-19 National Championship, light heavyweight, 2002; Gold Medal, light heavyweight, Olympic Games, 2004; Key to the City of Oakland, CA, Oakland City Hall, 2004; Athlete of the Year, USA Boxing, 2004.

Addresses: *Promoter*—Goossen Tutor Promotions, 15300 Ventura Blvd., Suite 400, Sherman Oaks, CA 91403. *Web*—www.goossentutor.com.

recalled to *USA Today*. The weight difference never affected Ward's success in the ring. "A lot of guys, they see my physique and they misread me and they think I'm weak," Ward told the *Knight Ridder/Tribune News Service* following a 2004 bout. He added, "I've been fighting bigger guys my whole life."

Fulfilled Dream of Olympic Gold and Found God

From 1998 on, Ward steadily climbed up the amateur boxing ranks as a light heavyweight. As he won bout after bout, he started racking up awards including the U.S. National Championship in 2001 and 2003 and the Under-19 National Championship in 2002. At every match, Ward's father Frank was ringside, cheering him on. Together, the two dreamed of bigger things. Frank wanted his son to go as far as he could as an amateur—the Olympics, a dream that was not always easy for the financially struggling Ward to follow. "There were times I got frustrated and wanted to turn pro and make some quick money," he told *USA Today*. Instead, Ward followed his father's dream and by 2004 was the top-ranked amateur light heavyweight in the country and headed to the Summer Olympics in Athens, Greece.

Unfortunately, the elder Ward was not there to see his son's success. He had died suddenly from a heart attack in 2002. His father's death was a major blow to Ward. "My father was here today and gone tomorrow," Ward told the *Tampa Tribune*. "I needed some answers. The furthest thing from my mind was boxing." He found his answers in God, and Christianity became such a strong

part of his life that he toyed with the idea of becoming a minister after the end of his boxing career. Until then, he reserved the ring for his preaching. "I believe this is my ministry," Ward told the *Tampa Tribune*. "This is a platform to give God the glory." He practices what he preaches out of the ring as well. Rather than going out on the town after a win, Ward heads home to his wife Tiffiney and their sons Andre Jr. and Malachi. "Whatever I'm doing with my family," Ward told the *San Francisco Chronicle*, "whether we're camping, bowling, going to the park, sitting at home doing nothing, that's my party."

In Athens, with a picture of his father taped to his boot, Ward stunned audiences by solidly defeating bigger, more accomplished fighters including the six-foot-six Russian World Champion Evgeny Makarenko. After earning the American team its only boxing gold medal of the games, Ward returned to the States a champion and to the ring a professional. Fighting as a middleweight, he won his first pro match in 2004. Over the next three years, he added another 11 straight wins to his record. Along with his run of amateur wins, his streak has been estimated at over 60 fights. He has taken this impressive record in stride. "If I win a tournament or a big fight, I put it behind me the next day and just keep moving on," Ward told *USA Today*. "If you're worried that, 'Oh, I've got 60 straight wins,' to me that kind of takes your focus away." Ward's focus was not going anywhere. He told the *San Francisco Chronicle*, "I'm looking at 12 years. I'll be 32. If everything goes well, get in, get out, make a lot of money and touch a lot of lives." He added, "It depends on how long God wants for me."

Sources

Periodicals

Fresno Bee (Fresno, CA), February 9, 2005, p. D1.
Knight Ridder/Tribune News Service, August 30, 2004, p. K2027.
San Francisco Chronicle, November 12, 2003, p. C1; August 30, 2004, p. B1; November 23, 2004, p. F2; November 14, 2006, p. E1; March 27, 2007, p. D6.
Tampa Tribune (Tampa, FL), September 30, 2005, p. 12.

On-line

"Andre Ward, 2004 US Olympic Gold Medalist," Goossen Tutor Promotions, www.goossentutor.com/pages/athelets/ward.htm (July 3, 2007).
United States Olympic Committee, www.usoc.org (July 3, 2007).
"Ward Can Return Luster to USA Boxing," *USA Today,* www.usatoday.com/sports/olympics/athens/fight/2004-08-10-portrait-ward-boxing_x.htm (July 3, 2007).

—Candace LaBalle

Isaiah Washington

1963—

Actor

Isaiah Washington has enjoyed a distinguished acting career that includes a wide variety of stage, television, and film roles. He has played gangsters and hustlers, cops and hardworking average Joes, a gay Republican man, and a coolheaded and talented surgeon at a major city hospital. For his costarring role as Dr. Preston Burke on the ABC hit series *Grey's Anatomy* Washington was honored with the 2007 NAACP Image Award.

Born on August 3, 1963, and raised in Houston, Texas, Washington had boyhood dreams of playing professional football. By his later teens, though, he had shifted his focus to a military career, and after graduating from high school he joined the U.S. Air Force. He completed a four-year hitch but decided not to reenlist, moving instead to Washington, D.C., to study drama at Howard University. Washington fell in love with acting and moved to New York City after finishing college to pursue a career on the stage.

Washington soon began to get roles in major plays, including August Wilson's *Fences* and Lorraine Hansberry's *Raisin in the Sun*. In 1990 he was cast as Reed, a teenaged drug addict, in Michael Henry Brown's *Generations of the Dead in the Abyss of Coney Island Madness*. Hailing the play as a "threatening portrait of urban insanity," *New York Times* critic Mel Gussow observed that Washington's performance was "permeated with authenticity." Washington again attracted notice as the character Foos in the debut production of Kevin Heelan's *Distant Fires* at the Atlantic Theater in New York in 1991. Gussow, reviewing the play in the *New York Times*, praised it as

a "perceptive group portrait of men at work" that was enhanced by the acting of its ensemble cast. The following year Washington landed the part of Henry in the Goodman Theatre of Chicago's production of Thornton Wilder's *The Skin of Our Teeth*.

By the early 1990s Washington had begun to busy himself with film roles as well as stage plays. He began with small parts in such films as *The Color of Love* and *Strictly Business*, but soon caught the attention of director Spike Lee, who cast him in a supporting role in his 1994 comedy, *Crooklyn*. Washington went on to appear in Lee's acclaimed cop thriller *Clockers* in 1995, playing Victor, the uptight and hardworking brother of the drug-pushing main character, Strike. Level-headed and law-abiding, Victor shocks the cops by confessing to a murder that they suspect Strike of having committed. Though the role was relatively small, Washington's performance was considered powerful. Washington worked with Lee again in 1996 when played the shoplifter in Lee's comedy, *Girl 6*. Also in 1996, Washington was cast in *Get on the Bus*, Lee's ensemble film about a group of black men who take a bus to Washington, D.C. to join a rally roughly based on the Million Man March. Washington played Kyle, a gay Republican who is traveling with his lover.

Through the 1990s Washington continued to add to his film roles and to work with other major directors. He was cast as Darnell in Warren Beatty's comedy 1998 *Bulworth*, and played the role of Frank Beechum, a death-row inmate, in Clint Eastwood's *True Crime* in 1999, a performance that New York Times

At a Glance . . .

Born on August 3, 1963, in Houston, TX; married Jenisa Marie, February 14, 1999; children: three. *Education:* Howard University.

Career: Actor, 1991–.

Awards: NAACP Image Award, Best Actor in a Drama Series, 2007.

Addresses: *Agent*—Innovative Artists, 1505 Tenth Street, Santa Monica, CA 90401.

contributor Anita Gates described as "breathtaking." At the same time, Washington was doing a substantial amount of television work. He had begun working on the small screen in the early 1990s with small guest parts on *Law and Order, Homicide: Life on the Street, NYPD Blue,* and *New York Undercover.* In 1996 he appeared in several episodes of *Living Single,* and in 1998 appeared in two episodes of *Ally McBeal.*

Joining the cast of *Grey's Anatomy* in 2005, Washington quickly achieved star status. He was attracted to the show, he told *Jet* writer Melody K. Hoffman, because he found it "the best-written script, probably since *Love Jones,* that I've ever been a part of. All I have to do is open my mouth and act." The series, set in fictional Seattle Grace Hospital, follows the experiences of a group of young doctors who deal with typical patient crises as well as off-hours romance. As Matthew Fogel described it in *New York Times,* Seattle Grace is a "frenetic, multicultural hub where racial issues take a back seat to the more pressing problems of hospital life: surgery, competition, exhaustion and—no surprise—sex." The series has been widely admired for its no-nonsense casting of African Americans, Asian Americans, and women in roles of authority and power. As *New York Times* reviewer Alessandra Stanley put it, "There are no token blacks on *Grey's Anatomy.* The three top surgeons who rule the interns with princely authority are all African Americans, and that sign of social advancement is presented as a given, without fanfare or comment."

Washington's Dr. Burke is a brilliant, ambitious, and compassionate cardio-thoracic surgeon who is strongly attracted to a Korean-American intern, Cristina Yang. As the actor explained to Hoffman in *Jet,* he finds it "revolutionary" to be able to portray a character who is a complex individual—attractive, intelligent, articulate,

and talented, but also flawed—without having to clash with the director about giving life to such a role. Critics have been consistently impressed with Washington's work on the show, for which he won the NAACP Image Award for Outstanding Actor in a Drama Series in 2007.

Some less flattering publicity haunted the actor that year, however, after he was heard using anti-gay epithets on the *Grey's Anatomy* set and at the Golden Globe Awards, in reference to his co-star, T.R. Knight. At first Washington denied using the word, but later apologized and announced that he was checking into a psychological treatment facility to learn about why he had behaved in such a way and how he could make sure it would not happen again. The actor also filmed a public service announcement for the Gay & Lesbian Alliance Against Defamation and the Gay, Lesbian & Straight Education Network after the incident. The story set off a storm of controversy, including rumors that Washington would be fired from the show. The program's season finale in 2007 featured a plotline that left Dr. Burke's fate undecided.

Washington, who lives in California with his wife and three children, has established a charity to benefit the people of Sierra Leone, the West African nation that, according to DNA tests, was the home of his maternal ancestors. In addition to providing public health materials, such as mosquito netting, the charity is constructing a school scheduled to open in 2007.

Selected works

Films

Strictly Business, 1991.
The Color of Love, 1991.
Crooklyn, 1994.
Clockers, 1995.
Stonewall, 1995.
Girl 6, 1996.
Get on the Bus, 1996.
Love Jones, 1997.
Dancing in September, 2000.
Romeo Must Die, 2000.
Exit Wounds, 2001.
Ghost Ship, 2002.
Hollywood Homicide, 2003.
Wild Things 2, 2004.
Dead Birds, 2004.

Television

Living Single, 1996.
Ally McBeal, 1998.
Soul Food, 2000.
Grey's Anatomy, 2005—.

Sources

Periodicals

Boston Globe, January 25, 2007.
Jet, February 19, 2001, p. 59; April 24, 2006, p. 58.
New York Times, December 9, 1990; October 17, 1991, January 4, 2004; March 25, 2005; May 8, 2005; January 22, 2007.
Newsweek, September 25, 1995, p. 92.
People, October 25, 2006.

On-line

Grey's Anatomy, http://abc.go.com/primetime/greysanatomy/ (May 22, 2007).
"Rep: Isaiah Washington Remaining on 'Grey's Anatomy,'" *Fox News,* www.foxnews.com/story/0,2933,274196,00.html (May 22, 2007).

—E. M. Shostak

Joyce Wein

1928-2005

Music promoter, biochemist, philanthropist

Joyce Wein and her husband and business partner, jazz impresario George Wein, were a major force in the acceptance of jazz as a serious art form. Together they organized and promoted music festivals in the United States and abroad. They were also noted collectors of African American art. Joyce Wein was a founder of the New York Coalition of 100 Black Women, an organization devoted to empowering women of color and helping disadvantaged youth. It spawned similar coalitions across the country. Wein's promotion of music and art, and her concern for others will be long remembered.

Married George Wein

Joyce Wein was born Joyce Alexander on October 21, 1928, in Boston, Massachusetts, the sixth of Columbia and Hayes Alexander's seven children. Two of Joyce Alexander's mother's 12 siblings had been born into slavery, so the family had a deep understanding of the racial divide in the United States. From an early age, Joyce Wein made the most of her opportunities, graduating from Boston's Girls Latin School to enter Simmons College in Boston at age 15. Four years later, she graduated with a chemistry degree in 1948 and pursued a career as a biochemist, first at Massachusetts General Hospital in Boston and later at Columbia University Medical School in New York City.

Her academic accomplishments did not deter her from enjoying herself. Wein grew up listening to the music of Duke Ellington, Count Basie, Billie Holiday, and Art Tatum, among others. As an adult she would come to know many of these musicians well. It was her love of music that first brought her in contact with her future husband. Joyce Alexander first met George Wein, backstage at the Boston Opera House after a 1947 concert featuring Sidney Bechet, the New Orleans clarinetist, and pianist James P. Johnson. At the time, she was the jazz columnist for the Simmons student newspaper, and George Wein, a jazz pianist and pre-med student, was working his way through Boston University as the leader of a nightclub band. George Wein remembered their meeting to Tom Long of the *Boston Globe* in 2005, saying "I offered her a ride home, but she wouldn't take it." Soon George Wein and Joyce Alexander were helping to integrate Boston jazz clubs.

Interracial dating was unusual in the 1940s, and both families objected. However Joyce Alexander's mother was more disturbed by the young man's jazz aspirations than by the fact that he was white. George Wein's father told him: "Live together, but don't get married." In his memoir George Wein recalled Joyce saying when she was 27, "I'll give you until I'm 30."

During the 1950s George Wein operated the legendary Boston jazz club Storyville. In 1954 he founded the Newport Jazz Festival in Newport, Rhode Island, the world's first annual jazz event. The Weins were secretly married in a small town in New York in 1959. George Wein told Long: "We could have been put in jail in 25 states when we got married, but in Boston we never had a problem." However Wein's father vowed to never speak to his son again and didn't for about seven months.

At a Glance . . .

Born Joyce Alexander on October 21, 1928, in Boston, MA; died on August 15, 2005, in New York City; married George Wein, 1959. *Education:* Simmons College, BS, chemistry, 1948.

Career: Massachusetts General Hospital, Boston, MA, and Columbia University Medical School, New York City, biochemist, 1948-59; Festival Productions, vice president, 1962-late 1990s.

Memberships: The Jazz Community of Saint Peter's Church; Studio Museum, Harlem, vice president of the board of directors.

Awards: Studio Museum, Patrons of the Arts Award (with George Wien), 1995; New School University's Jazz and Contemporary Music Program, Beacons in Jazz Award (with George Wien), 1999.

Founded the Newport Folk Festival

By the time of their marriage the Newport Jazz Festival had brought George Wein fame and large debts. Joyce abandoned her career as a biochemist and became George's business partner. In 1962 they founded Festival Productions with George as chief executive officer and Joyce Wein as vice president, a position she held until the late 1990s. Joyce Wein remained involved with company operations until her death in 2005.

Together with the folk singer Pete Seeger and his wife, Toshi, the Weins founded the Newport Folk Festival in 1963. It became a focal point of the folk music revival of the 1960s. Joyce Wein worked tirelessly behind the scenes, even cooking for the performers during the festival's early years.

In addition to the Newport Jazz and Folk Festivals, the Weins organized the Newport Opera Festival and the Grande Parade du Jazz in Nice, France. Joyce Wein imported chefs from New Orleans for the Nice festival. She also pioneered the concept of festival food booths selling local cuisine. The Hampton Jazz Festival at historically black Hampton University in Virginia came about when the Hampton president, a longtime friend, told Joyce about plans for the school's centennial in 1968. The festival was so popular that it became an annual event. Initially the Weins's interracial marriage prevented them from staging the Jazz and Heritage Festival in New Orleans. However in 1970 Joyce Wein won over the support of the police and local community and the festival was established.

George Wein led pianist Thelonious Monk on numerous European tours. In his memoir Wein recalled an incident when Joyce went to pick up Monk for the airport and found the temperamental genius in bed complaining that his hands hurt. "Joyce held his large hands in hers like a caring mother. 'I'll kiss it and make it better,' she said in a soothing voice, kissing both hands. Then, more firmly: 'I think you can go to Europe now, Thelonious.'" Monk caught his plane.

The Weins began producing festivals sponsored by JVC in 1984. Each year they hosted the kick-off media receptions for the JVC Jazz Festival-New York at the Supper Club and on the lawn of the mayoral residence, Gracie Mansion. In 2001 Festival Productions produced 35 festivals around the world with nearly one million attendees.

Collected African-American Art

In the 1980s Kool cigarettes, which had taken over sponsorship of the Newport Jazz Festival, paid the Weins a large sum of money to remove the name Newport from their festival, since it was the name of a competing cigarette brand. For the first time the Weins had extra money and they began collecting art. Although they bought a painting by Pierre-Auguste Renoir to please George Wein's parents, their collection became known for its reflections of black American culture, in a variety of artistic styles from the late 1920s through the 1990s, and for its many jazz-influenced works. Their collection included paintings, drawings, sculpture, and fabric art by artists such as Jacob Lawrence, Elizabeth Catlett, and Faith Ringgold. There were paintings by jazz trumpeter Miles Davis and collages by Romare Bearden. When John Leland of the *New York Times* visited the Weins in their Upper-East-Side Manhattan apartment in 2001, he asked Joyce Wein whether the couple had children. She "shook her head, then gestured to the paintings. 'You're looking at them.'" In 2005 Boston University launched the exhibition *Syncopated Rhythms: 20th-Century African American Art from the George and Joyce Wein Collection* and published the catalog in book form. It was the first public viewing of the Wein collection.

George Wein told Leland: "Joyce is my greatest teacher. She reads more than I do and pays attention to things I don't. Our marriage has everything to do with where we are now and everything we've done." They often presented a joint lecture entitled "Love and Jazz across the Color Line."

Joyce Wein was known as the consummate hostess as well as an expert cook. For the last decade of her life, the Weins joined Kenneth and Kathryn Chenault in hosting an annual dinner for Geoffrey Canada and the Harlem Children's Zone, raising more than $500,000. In 2003 the Weins announced their $1-million endowment of the George and Joyce Wein Chair in African American Studies at Boston University and the Alexander Family Endowed Scholarship Fund at Simmons College.

Joyce Wein died on August 15, 2005, in New York Presbyterian Hospital, after an extended battle with cancer. Jazz pianist Dave Brubeck told Long of the *Boston Globe*: "I met her before they were married, when she was trying to be with George and he was trying to be with her…. She was a brilliant woman who was cultured in every way." George Wein told Long: "She was my most important critic. She was involved in everything I did." In a paid notice in the August 19, 2005, *New York Times,* Erwin Frankel Productions wrote that Joyce Wein was "instrumental in bringing American Jazz to the world."

Sources

Books

Hills, Patricia, and Melissa Renn, *Syncopated Rhythms: 20th-Century African American Art from the George and Joyce Wein Collection,* Boston University Art Gallery, 2005.
Wein, George, and Nate Chinen, *Myself Among Others: A Memoir,* De Capo, 2003.

Periodicals

Boston Globe, August 17, 2005, p. E13.
Christian Science Monitor, November 30, 2005, p. 19.
International Review of African American Art, 1999, pp. 18-26.
Los Angeles Times, August 18, 2005, p. B10.
New York Beacon, June 16, 1999, p. 33; August 25-31, 2005, p. 27.
New York Times, August 2, 2001, p. F1; August 18, 2005, p. A23; August 19, 2005, p. 14.
Providence Journal, August 17, 2005, p. G7.

On-line

"Joyce Wein: Wife, Business Partner of George Wein," *All About Jazz,* www.allaboutjazz.com/php/news. php?id=6915 (April 23, 2007).
"The Last Post: Joyce Wein," *JazzHouse.org,* www. jazzhouse.org/gone/lastpost.php3?edit= 1124223601 (July 3, 2007).

—Margaret Alic

Kehinde Wiley

1977—

Artist

Kehinde Wiley became one of the most talked-about new figures of the modern art scene in the early 2000s with his paintings of young African-American men whom he met on New York City's streets—in poses modeled on classic paintings from the European artistic tradition. "It's art that's both brainy and ballsy, earning nods of approval from fans of Tupac [Shakur] and [Italian painter Giovanni Battista] Tiepolo alike," explained *Interview* magazine. Wiley's paintings were enjoyable for viewers who tried to pick out references to both urban African-American culture and European art history, but his intentions were serious. He tried both to challenge an art world that had long excluded African Americans and to ask questions about the nature of African-American male roles in the inner city.

Museum Trip Sparked Lifelong Interest in Art

Wiley was born in Los Angeles, California, in 1977 and grew up in the city's South Central district. His first exposure to art came at age 11 when his mother sent him to a free city-funded arts program class. The class involved museum visits, and Wiley was fascinated by the lush portraits by British painters Thomas Gainsborough and Joshua Reynolds that he saw at the Huntington Library in suburban San Marino. "They were so artificial and opulent," he recalled to Mia Fineman of the *New York Times*. "There was this strange other-worldliness that, as a black kid from Los Angeles, I had no manageable way of digesting. But at the same time,

there was this desire to somehow possess that or belong to that."

Enrolling at the Los Angeles County High School for the Arts, Wiley decided that art was going to be a permanent part of his life. "I always felt like this would be something I would do—whether I was a professional artist full-time or an artist who had a day job supporting my art habit," he told Andre Banks of *Colorlines Magazine*. He entered the art competition in the National Association for the Advancement of Colored People's ACT-SO (Academic, Cultural, Technological Scientific Olympics) program repeatedly, advancing from a bronze medal in his first year to a gold in his third. Wiley earned a bachelor of fine arts degree at the San Francisco Art Institute in 1999 and moved on for a master's at Yale University, a stronghold of both classical European technique and sophisticated art theory.

At first Wiley was unhappy at Yale, feeling that he was being pigeonholed as an African-American artist. "There was this overwhelming sense of, 'O.K., Kehinde, where's your Negro statement?'" he told Fineman. Frustrated, Wiley painted watermelons in the styles of 20th-century European artists René Magritte and Giorgio de Chirico. He kept those paintings for himself even after he became well known and his canvases began to fetch prices in five figures. "While they're not some of the most sophisticated or beautiful paintings I've made," he told Fineman, "they're some of my favorites because they remind me of a point in

At a Glance . . .

Born 1977 in Los Angeles, CA. *Education:* San Francisco Art Institute, BFA, 1999; Yale University School of Art, MFA, 2001.

Career: Artist; Studio Museum of Harlem, New York, artist-in-residence, 2001-02.

Awards: NAACP ACT-SO academic olympics, gold medal; Studio Museum of Harlem, residency, 2001-02.

Addresses: *Gallery representation*—Deitch Projects, 76 Grand St, New York, NY 10013. *Web*—www. kehindewiley.com.

my life that felt absolutely desperate and lost and powerless."

Found Inspiration in New York

After receiving his M.F.A. from Yale in 2001, Wiley became an artist-in-residence at the Studio Museum of Harlem, a major center for African-American art. At the time he was unaware of the institution's prestige and was just happy to have a place to create art free of obligations. He lived on a shoestring for several years, sometimes sleeping on the floor in one of the museum's studio spaces, but he was fascinated by the rich street life of the Harlem neighborhood. It was similar in some ways to what he had experienced growing up in South Central Los Angeles, but there were some major differences as well: California was a car culture, but New Yorkers tended to display their styles on foot. "In the space of five blocks you get the chance to shop, eat, peacock, parade, and be seen," Wiley told Banks. "It's violent in the shocking immediacy of people's presence. For me, it's incredibly engaging…something I wanted to somehow grapple with in my work."

Wiley began to reflect that in some ways, the ideas of power that young men in hip-hop culture tried to convey were not so different from those in the classic European portraits he had studied—the men who commissioned those portraits did so as a way of displaying their wealth and influence. Inspired to try to put his surroundings and training together, he began to approach total strangers on the streets of Harlem and ask whether they would pose for portraits. He looked, he told Banks, for "alpha-male types. People who had this sort of energy surrounding them." The answer at the beginning was usually a more or less polite no, but Wiley found ways of breaking down his subjects' resistance. Having an attractive woman friend come along helped, he found.

But what was most helpful was getting a conversation going with the subject about what he was trying to do. Sometimes he would be able to convince the subject to come to the Studio Museum and look at art history books—and then he would leave it to the young man involved to choose a classical portrait on which he wanted his own to be modeled. "I've seen people choose small figures in large paintings, not even the stars of the show," Wiley told Fineman, "and I've seen people who directly want to see themselves as Christ in heaven." The subject, still in street clothes, would then strike the pose in the painting, and Wiley would photograph him and paint from the photograph. The subjects remained anonymous; many of Wiley's paintings bore the name of the European works on which they were based (such as 2004's "St. Clement of Padua"), while others had abstract titles such as "Easter Realness No. 5."

Used Techniques of Old Masters

Well trained at Yale in the same techniques that the Old Masters themselves used (such as painting an underlying layer of red in order to heighten the color intensity of the whole canvas), Wiley was able to create portraits that had much of the impact of the originals. "Wiley can do a credible likeness, though his work is a trifle flat," observed Dan Bischoff of the Newark, New Jersey *Star-Ledger*. But his subjects were not European kings, churchmen, and merchants, but young men from Harlem, and their signs of influence were not crowns and Bibles but the corporate logos emblazoned on clothing and shoes. For Wiley those logos had an ambiguous function: he likened them to slave brands, but he also recognized that they represented empowering free choice for those who wore them. Wiley's paintings had the same kind of ambiguity: he was paying tribute to European art and at the same time deeply questioning it, and he was carving out a place for hip-hop culture in studios and museums while at the same time questioning its consumerist aspects.

The backgrounds added another layer of meaning to Wiley's paintings. They showed neither European interiors nor New York City street scenes. Instead they consisted of abstract or semi-abstract patterns, drawn on anything from Irish calligraphy to repeated representation of biological sperm cells. In "Investiture of Bishop Harold as the Duke of Franconia No. 1" a fleur-de-lis pattern seemed to bleed into the image of a man in a Los Angeles Dodgers shirt and a blue baseball cap. The effect was to make the three-dimensional subjects jump out unexpectedly from a flat background. Richly colorful and slightly larger than life, Wiley's canvases instantly grabbed the attention of those who saw them.

The results, Fineman noted in the *New York Times*, brought Wiley "the kind of meteoric success that most young artists only dream about." Top galleries, not only in New York but also in other art centers like Chicago and Los Angeles, signed on to represent him. A steady stream of articles, both in mainstream publications like *Essence* and specialist art magazines such as the brainy *Artforum International,* kept readers up to date with his career. Wiley did not have to go through the round of group shows that most young artists use as a springboard to more prominent solo exhibitions; his first solo show was in 2003, at New York's Deitch Projects gallery, and by the next year his paintings were the subject of a major show called *Passing/Posing* at the Brooklyn Museum of Art.

Cultivated Interesting Public Persona

Key to Wiley's continuing success was his knack for presenting himself publicly in colorful ways. He acquired a pair of Italian greyhounds of the kind that sometimes appeared in paintings of the houses of the aristocracy in the golden age of the great Italian cities. His parties got talked-about among the New York art elite thanks to boundary-crossing that paralleled the devices found in his paintings, with a tuxedo-clad string quartet playing the Kelis hit "Milkshake" on one occasion. By 2006 Wiley's paintings were commanding prices in the $20,000 range—and customers had to enter their names on a waiting list in order to get one.

Wiley's art continued to develop in new directions in the mid-2000. He expanded into sculpture in 2006, creating busts of young men in hooded sweatshirts that were influenced by Italian models of the Baroque era (1600s and early 1700s); writers began to use the terms Urban Baroque and neo-Baroque to describe his style. His fame began to spread beyond New York with museum exhibitions in many other cities (and at a show in Belgium called Sorrywereclosed); in the fall of 2006, for the first time, he traveled to the Columbus (Ohio) Museum of Art to create portraits based on paintings in a specific museum's collection. He got the invitation, curator Joe Houston explained to the *Columbus Dispatch,* because "I felt he is one of the most interesting emerging artists," and few observers of the art scene would have disagreed with that assessment.

Selected works

Exhibitions

Faux/Real, Deitch Projects, New York, 2003.
Pictures at an Exhibition, Roberts & Tilton, Los Angeles, 2003.
Easter Realness, Rhona Hoffman, Chicago, 2004.
Passing/Posing: The Paintings of Kehinde Wiley, Brooklyn Museum of Art, 2004.
Rumors of War, Deitch Projects, New York, 2005.
WHITE, Conner Contemporary, Washington, DC, 2005.
BOUND: Kehinde Wiley Paintings, Franklin Art Works, Minneapolis, MN, 2005.
Sorrywereclosed, various locations, including Brussels, Belgium, 2006.
Infinite Mobility, Columbus Museum of Art, 2006-07.

Sources

Periodicals

Artforum International, November 2002, p. 189.
Art in America, April 2005, p. 120.
Colorlines Magazine, Winter 2005, p. 57.
Columbus Dispatch, September 3, 2006.
Interview, October 2005, p. 158.
New York Times, December 19, 2004, p. AR39; December 9, 2005, p. E41.
Star-Ledger (Newark, NJ), January 9, 2005, p. 5.
Star Tribune (Minneapolis, MN), February 18, 2005, p. E20.

On-line

"Biography," *Kehinde Wiley Official Website,* www.kehindewiley.com (June 26, 2007).
"Kehinde Wiley: Urban Baroque," *Culture Kiosque,* www.culturekiosque.com/art/artmrkt/kehinde_wiley.html (June 6, 2007).

—James M. Manheim

Venus Williams

1980—

Tennis player

When Venus Williams made her debut in professional women's tennis in 1994, *New York Times* contributor Robin Finn called her "the most unorthodox tennis prodigy her sport has ever seen." Three years later, the 17-year-old, six-foot-two-inch athlete was an international celebrity: photographs of Williams with the beads in her cornrowed hair clicking through the air, her face a study in determination as her racket smacked the ball to her opponent, were some of the most memorable of the 1997 tennis season. By 2007, when she claimed her fourth Wimbledon title, Williams was acclaimed as "the best athlete in the history of women's tennis" by *Sports Illustrated.* In the years between her promising debut and her astonishing Wimbledon comeback, Williams dominated her sport at the same time that she designed clothes, gobbled up endorsement deals, and even appeared in the swimsuit issue of *Sports Illustrated.* Williams is more than a great tennis player: she is a true tennis celebrity.

Unlikely Prodigy

Williams was born in the Watts area of Los Angeles, California, in June of 1980, the fourth of Richard and Oracene Williams's five daughters. Richard Williams was part-owner of a security business, and Oracene was a nurse. In the early 1980s the family moved from Watts to nearby Compton. All five Williams daughters played tennis as youngsters, but the two youngest, Venus and Serena, were outstanding players from an early age. Compton was infamous for its troubles with gang-related activity, and the girls practiced the game

at a court in a park frequented by gang members. Williams, in fact, lost a sister, Yetunde Price, in 2003 following a dispute with local residents. Venus Williams began entering competitions, went unbeaten in 63 games, and at age ten had won the Southern California title for girls in the under-12 division.

Both *Sports Illustrated* and *Tennis* magazine noticed Williams's talent, and ran stories on her in the summer of 1991 calling her "tennis's newest pixie" and "a prodigy." Her father contacted Rick Macci, a tennis coach in Florida, and asked him to come to Compton to meet his daughter and judge her potential. "I hear it all the time: 'I've got the next Jennifer [Capriati],'" Macci told *Tennis* magazine's David Higdon. "Richard said he'd like to meet me but the only thing he could promise me was that I wouldn't get shot. All I could think of was: 'Who is this guy?'" he recalled. Early one morning Richard drove the visiting Macci to the park. "There must have been 30 guys there already playing basketball and another 20 lying on the grass passed out," Macci recollected in *Tennis* magazine. He played a few games with Venus, and was unimpressed. Then, he remembered, she "asks to go to the bathroom and as she walks out the gate, she walks at least 10 yards on her hands. Then she went into these backward cartwheels for another 10 yards. I'm watching this and the first thing I thought was: 'I've got a female Michael Jordan on my hands.'"

The Williams family moved to Florida when Venus enrolled in Macci's tennis academy there. She also withdrew from junior tennis that year at the age of 11. Instead of mixing practice with the competition circuit,

At a Glance . . .

Born Venus Ebone Starr Williams on June 17, 1980, in Los Angeles, CA; daughter of Richard (a security-business owner and daughters' coach) and Oracene (a nurse) Williams. *Education*: Studied fashion design at the Art Institute of Florida.

Career: Professional tennis player, 1994–; winner of 14 Grand Slam titles, including six singles titles, six women's doubles titles, and two mixed doubles titles.

Memberships: Women's Tennis Association.

Awards: 2000 Olympic Games, Gold Medals in women's singles and women's doubles.

Addresses: *Office*—c/o Women's Tennis Association, One Progress Plaza, Suite 1500, St. Petersburg, FL 33701.

Williams stayed put, was schooled at home, and practiced six hours a day, six times a week. She did this for four years—a decision, Macci said, that Williams and her family had made based on her unique temperament. "Putting her in a traditional development system would be like putting her in prison," the coach told Finn in the *New York Times*. When she was 13, companies were already contacting Williams and her family to offer endorsement contracts if she did turn pro.

Tennis-watchers wondered when Williams would succumb to the lure—some young women in tennis entered professional competition at the age of 14, dropping out of school and playing the tournament circuit, and earning large sums of money either by winning prize purses or signing lucrative product endorsement contracts. It was a potentially disastrous situation for many young players. Richard Williams appeared on the ABC news program *Nightline* in the summer of 1994 after former preteen tennis prodigy Jennifer Capriati was arrested and faced drug charges, and declared he'd never allow Venus to turn pro at such a young age. He was criticized, however for wearing a hat and vest bearing the logo of a sports-energy food product during the television interview.

Turned Pro at 14

Surprisingly, Williams turned pro just a few months later. Her debut came in October of 1994 at the Bank of the West Classic in Oakland, California. There, the 14-year-old beat the woman ranked number 59 in the world, Shaun Stafford, then went on to give Arantxa Sanchez Vicario—women tennis's Number 2 player—a good game before losing. "She's going to be great for women's tennis," Stafford told the *New York Times*'s Finn. Some wondered, however, why Williams had suddenly entered the professional circuit, but new rules adopted by the Women's Tennis Council of the World Tennis Association at the time may have provided just cause. After the close of 1994, 14-year-olds were barred from turning pro, and young women under 18 who entered the competition level from 1995 onward were limited in the number of tournaments in which they could participate.

Though she had skated into the professional level exempt from these rules, Williams restricted her schedule anyway. She stayed in school and did not appear again on the pro circuit until an August 1995 event, the Acura Classic in Manhattan Beach, California; she lost in the first round. Some tennis analysts noted that because she lacked the junior-tournament experience, Williams had not learned to inject a competitive edge to her game. Her father has tried to rectify this, sometimes by rooting against her in public matches. Conversely, he told *New York Times Magazine* writer Pat Jordan, "Every time she loses, I pay her $50."

As the *New York Times Magazine* profile pointed out, however, the dedicated fathers of women's tennis are sometimes problematic: Steffi Graf's father was charged with tax evasion, and she herself was nearly arrested for complicity; an American teenage player, Mary Pierce, had to obtain a court restraining order against her father. Richard Williams was well aware of the dangers of the sport on young women, though, and controlled his daughter's career in order to avoid problems. He saw the lesson in Capriati, who turned pro at 14. "At 15, she lost her smile," he told Jordan in the *New York Times Magazine*. "At 16, there were problems. What happened? I want to make sure that doesn't happen to my kids," he added.

Venus's younger sister, Serena, also showed great promise as a player. Richard Williams predicted that some day the pair would have to play against one another for the women's world title, but he often received more press than either of them. "Richard Williams has been called a 'liar' and 'genius' and everything in between," wrote Higdon in *Tennis* magazine. The senior Williams asserted that his family did not receive any endorsement money from wearing the logo-emblazoned clothing of one sportswear maker at public appearances, but a spokesperson for the company said they had indeed paid him a consultant's fee. Yet Williams has also been lauded for shepherding his daughter's career down a non-traditional path that kept the focus on her education and allowed her to mature outside of the competitive pressures of the pro circuit. Newspaper reportage about Venus often remarks on her self-assuredness and impressive vocabulary. Her father and Macci, Finn wrote in the *New York Times*, "have produced a player who appears to possess wit and wisdom beyond her years—with a serve, volley, and vocabulary to match."

Adjusted to Competition

Again Williams stayed out of the limelight for much of 1996, and in the spring of 1997 made her debut at the French Open. A month later, as she turned seventeen, she traveled to England for Wimbledon, perhaps the sport's most famous tournament. Serena and Oracene Williams came with her to lend support, but her father stayed home. She received a great deal of attention, but had a poor showing and lost to Magdalena Grzybowska. "By the time it was over…Williams stood revealed as a huge talent with little idea of how to adjust to an opponent or adversity," wrote S. L. Price in *Sports Illustrated*. She remained imperturbable, though. "It's my first Wimbledon," she told reporters. "There will be many more."

Her father asserted that his daughter's "only weakness is she's overconfident," he said in the *New York Times Magazine*. Williams's U.S. Open performance in the late summer of 1997 went somewhat better: she advanced from 66th to 25th in the rankings in one day. "Williams's progress as a player was undeniable; almost overnight she had become a force every player but one fears," wrote Price in *Sports Illustrated*, referring to Martina Hingis, who would take home the title. Both young women were the same age, but Hingis had far more professional competition experience. Still, insiders predicted future greatness for Williams. Pam Shriver, a former U.S. Open titleholder, once played in a training match against Serena and Venus, and she told Higdon in *Tennis* magazine that Venus "didn't know tactically how to play points yet, but she had weapons and has this natural way of intimidating."

Unfortunately, Williams's U.S. Open showing was clouded by charges of racism. Her father, in a telephone interview, told journalists that some of the other players had directed racial epithets toward his daughter. Gracefully, the teenager tried to deflect attention from the potential furor at a press conference, but her father's comments caused some watchers of the sport to note this may limit her chances of obtaining endorsement contracts. Other African-American players have hinted that subtle discrimination does indeed occur in what has been called a "country-club" sport, and some of Williams's white competitors on the diva-rife circuit have accused her of not smiling, or of not being friendly enough. "Why don't you guys tell me what they want me to do?" she queried reporters at one press conference, according to *Sports Illustrated*. "They should come up to me and say, 'Venus, I want you to smile so I can feel better.'"

While the hints of racism continued to plague Williams, she nevertheless proved to be a fearless opponent. Over the next few years, Williams improved her game, and lost weight and the hair beads—she'd been fined when they spilled on the court. In 2000 Williams won Wimbledon by defeating Number 2-ranked Lindsay Davenport; Williams became the first African-American female since Althea Gibson to win at Wimbledon. Venus and Serena also won the doubles' title, becoming the first set of sisters to do so. When the two faced off in the Wimbledon singles' semifinals, it had been over 100 years since a sibling showdown. In the same year, Williams also won two Olympic gold medals in singles and doubles with her sister, Serena, as her partner. She continued the success of her first Grand Slam by winning the U.S. Open in 2000.

Rose to the Top

After a stellar 2000 season, Williams needed to prove to the tennis world that she was going to continue to win championships. The first step on that road was to defend her Wimbledon title. To the amazement of most, she did, defeating Justine Henin in three sets. Next in line was to defend her U.S. Open title. She battled it out through the semi-finals, until she met her opponent for the final: her sister, Serena. Both sisters made history once again by being the first set of sisters to play against each other in U.S. Open history. Venus defeated Serena, winning her second back-to-back grand slam tournament game.

Williams would come out on top in December of 2001 when Reebok re-signed her to a $40 million contract that was believed to be the most lucrative and comprehensive endorsement deal ever created for a female athlete. Of Williams, Reebok said in *Footwear News*, "Venus Williams is arguably the most admired female athlete and among the most recognizable and exciting young women in the world." Williams has also won numerous honors and awards in 2001, including: being named Ms. Women of the Year (along with Serena), by *Ms.* magazine. She was also named Female Player of the Year by *Tennis* magazine. She expanded outside of tennis by designing a clothing line for clothing company Wilsons. She has inked deals with not only Reebok, but also Wrigley gum, makeup giant Avon, and Nortel Networks. Many have criticized Williams for not being focused on tennis, including tennis legend Martina Navritolova, who was quoted in *Time* as saying her outside interests shows "arrogance and lack of commitment to tennis." Even her father felt that Williams should choose between tennis or the distractions, telling the *Florida Times Union*, "If it was up to me, I told Venus two or three years ago that she should retire. I think she should."

Despite the distractions, Williams rose to the top of women's tennis. In March of 2002, Williams reached her ultimate goal, earning the top ranking from the Women's Tennis Association. In an interview with *Jet* she said, "I'm very excited about this achievement and look forward to building on it. I have worked hard for it. I hope I can keep it." Keeping that ranking was not so easy, however, and some of the most intense competition she faced was from her sister. In both 2002 and 2003, for example, the Williams sisters faced off in the finals at Wimbledon; both times, Serena emerged triumphant and seized the top ranking from her sister.

Struggled to Maintain Dominance

Though 2002 was the year in which Venus Williams dominated tennis, she has been in contention for many titles in every year since. Williams, who missed the 2003 U.S. Open because of an injured stomach muscle, won two tournaments in 2004; her furthest penetration into a Grand Slam event that year was the French Open, where she reached the quarterfinals.

In many ways, Williams seemed to have things other than tennis on her mind. In 2005, Williams and her sister Serena starred in a six-episode reality show on ABC Family. They also published a book, *Serving from the Hip: 10 Rules for Living, Loving and Winning*, with Houghton Mifflin. Serena Williams told Yanick Rice Lamb in *Black Issues Book Review* that the book "talks about a lot of stuff—every issue that preteens and teens might have to deal with. We consider ourselves role models, and we wanted to do something positive for kids." Venus Williams added, "It was something that we had to do to pass on our knowledge, what we've gone through."

In the summer of 2005, Williams, who had slipped to the No. 16 spot in world rankings, perhaps because of the distractions of the book and television show, was knocked out of the French Open in the third round by 52nd-ranked Bulgarian player Sesil Karatantcheva. However, Williams fought hard and came back to win a third Wimbledon championship later in the summer. Her opponent, No. 1-ranked Lindsay Davenport, told S. L. Price in *Sports Illustrated*, "She just took it away from me. She just was...incredible." Williams said of her win, "I was just thinking, I've got to stay tougher. I've got to stay tougher than whoever's across the net." Later in the season, Williams defeated her sister, Serena, in the fourth round at the U.S. Open in New York; it evened their record in head-to-head matches at seven victories apiece. To top off a wonderful year, Williams was even featured in the swimsuit edition of *Sports Illustrated*.

The year 2006 was a down year for Williams, who spent the first third of the year recovering from injuries before getting knocked out of every tournament she entered without reaching the finals. Again, Williams's critics claimed that distractions kept her from playing great tennis. She began 2007 ranked 39th in the world, and promptly withdrew from the Australian Open because of a wrist injury. After some lackluster play in early tournaments, Williams came into the annual Wimbledon Championships ranked 31st. Williams started off slowly in a rain-interrupted tournament, but built pace and confidence with every match. By the time she reached the final against Marion Bartoli on July 7, 2007, Williams was back at the top of her game. Delivering blistering serves—one was clocked at 124 miles per hour—Williams destroyed Bartoli 6-4, 6-1 to take the title.

With her 2007 Wimbledon victory Williams laid claim to her sixth Grand Slam singles title and her Olympic gold medal, not to mention six Grand Slam victories each in women's and mixed doubles. Williams's meteoric return to the top of the tennis world pointed to her uncanny ability to rise above the distractions of superstardom to play great tennis. "I always believe in my game," she told *Sports Illustrated*. "Losing never really crosses my mind." With that attitude, it seems likely that more victories lie ahead.

Sources

Books

Edmondson, Jacqueline, *Venus and Serena Williams: A Biography*, Greenwood Press, 2005.
Rineberg, Dave, *Venus & Serena: My Seven Years as Hitting Coach for the Williams Sisters*, F. Fell, 2001.
Wertheim, L. Jon, *Venus Envy: Power Games, Teenage Vixens, and Million-Dollar Egos on the Women's Tennis Tour*, Perennial, 2002.
Williams, Venus, and Serena Williams, *Venus & Serena: Serving from the Hip, Ten Rules for Living, Loving, and Winning*, Houghton Mifflin, 2005.

Periodicals

Black Issues Book Review, September-October 2005, p. 22.
Footwear News, January 1, 2001.
Jet, July 23, 2001, p. 51; March 11, 2002, p. 48.
Ms.. Magazine, December 2001, p. 40.
Newsweek, July 17, 2000.
New York Times, November 1, 1994, p. B10; November 2, 1994, p. B9; March 10, 1997, p. C2; September 7, 1997; September 9, 1997.
New York Times Magazine, March 16, 1997.
PR Newswire, December 21, 2001; March 14, 2002.
Sport, February 1995, p. 14.
Sports Illustrated, June 13, 1994, p. 10; November 14, 1994, pp. 30-32; July 7, 1997, p. 26; September 15, 1997, pp. 32; September 17, 2001 pp. 40-43; July 11, 2005, p. 52 (swimsuit issue); June 25, 2007; July 16, 2007, p. 60.
Star-Tribune, August 31, 2001, p. 01D.
Tennis, July 1997, pp. 46-55; February 2001, p. 28.

On-line

"Venus on Top of Her Game," *Boston Herald.com*, http://sports.bostonherald.com/tennis/view.bg?articleid=1012186 (July 19, 2007).
"Venus Williams," *Sony Ericsson WTA Tour*, www.sonyericssonwtatour.com/2/players/playerprofiles/Playerbio.asp?PlayerID=230220 (July 23, 2007).
"Venus Williams Wins 4th Wimbledon Title," *Forbes.com*, www.forbes.com/feeds/ap/2007/07/07/ap-3891585.html (July 23, 2007).

—Carol Brennan, Ashyia N. Henderson, Ralph Zerbonia, and Tom Pendergast

Wendy Williams

1964—

Radio and television personality, author, businesswoman

"Shock jock diva," "radio gossip guru," and "the biggest mouth in New York" are among the monikers that have been applied to radio host Wendy Williams. As she branched out into television and publishing Williams proclaimed herself "queen of all media." Her tell-all memoirs made the *New York Times* bestsellers list. As of 2007 her syndicated SupeRadio program *The Wendy Williams Experience* was reaching 12 million listeners daily.

Throughout her 20-year radio career Wendy Williams courted controversy. Her brash blend of celebrity gossip, fashion, social commentary, and romantic advice earned her a broad base of devoted fans. She was famous for grilling celebrities on their drug use and sexual proclivities and her on-air interviews sometimes escalated into major blowups. Williams preached morality, family values, nutrition, fitness, and financial responsibility, while talking about her own ten-year cocaine addiction, her date-rape by an R&B singer, her abortion, miscarriages, and multiple plastic surgeries.

Grew Up a Suburban Misfit

Born on July 18, 1964, and raised in the upper-middle-class Wayside area of Ocean Township, New Jersey, Wendy Williams was an unlikely candidate for celebrity. Her father, Thomas Williams, was a junior high school principal and college English teacher. Her mother Shirley also taught school. One of only four black children in her class, by the sixth grade Wendy weighed 149 pounds. Almost six feet tall, she never attended a prom. She told Steve Fishman of *New York*

magazine in 2005: "I was the thing that did not fit in my family." Alone in her room Wendy read the *National Enquirer* and "Dear Abby" and watched *Divorce Court* on television. She graduated at the bottom of her high school class just as her sister Wanda was graduating from law school.

But Wendy Williams could talk. During high school she announced for her younger brother Tommy's Little League games. She told Fishman: "The best thing that could have happened to me was I found that microphone." Williams talked her way into Northeastern University in Boston, Massachusetts, planning to become a television newscaster. She began her career by reading the news on the college radio station. One day the disc jockey didn't show up. Williams took over and soon she had a regular on-air shift. Some afternoons she took the train to New York City just to hear her favorite disc jockeys. Williams interned at WXKS in Boston, where she plotted how to get the morning DJ's attention. She told *Billboard Radio Monitor* in 2005: "I didn't want to be like all the other interns; I wanted to be the queen of all interns. So, I'd get up at 3 a.m. so I could make it to the station before Matt [Siegel]'s show got started at 5:30 a.m." Soon Siegel had her on the air reviewing the evening's television programming. She told Fishman: "Virtually everything in my life I have plotted on to get it. Nothing has happened by fluke."

Williams graduated with a degree in communications and a minor in journalism. Her first job was at a tiny radio station in St. Croix, U.S. Virgin Islands. Friends and family were horrified that she would take such a

At a Glance . . .

Born Wendy Williams on July 18, 1964, in New Jersey; married Kevin Hunter, 1999; children: Kevin Samuel. *Education:* Northeastern University, BA, communications, 1986.

Career: *Matt Siegel Morning Show,* WXKS, Boston, MA, intern; WVIS, St. Croix, U.S. Virgin Islands, disc jockey, 1986-87; WOL-AM, Washington, DC, disc jockey, 1987; WQHT-FM, New York City, disc jockey, 1987-89(?), radio personality, 1995-98; WPLJ-FM, New York City, disc jockey, 1989-90(?); WRKS-FM, New York City, radio personality, 1990-95; WUSL-FM, Philadelphia, PA, radio personality, 1998-2001; WBLS-FM, New York City, radio personality, 2001-03; *The Wendy Williams Experience,* host, 2003–; American Urban Radio Networks, *On the Down Lo,* host, 2003–; author of fiction and nonfiction, 2003–; VH1, *Wendy Williams Is on Fire,* host, 2003, *The Wendy Williams Experience,* host, 2006–.

Awards: *Billboard* Magazine, Best On-Air Radio Personality, 1993; *Black Radio Exclusive,* Radio Personality of the Year; *Radio and Records* Magazine, Urban Personality of the Year, 2000.

Addresses: *Office*—WBLS-FM, 3 Park Ave #41, New York, NY, 10016.

low-paying job in such a far-off place and Williams was miserable, but she saw it as the first step in her career. After less than a year she moved to an "oldies" station in Washington, D.C.

Fired by "Hot 97"

After stints at WQHT and WPLJ in New York City, Williams was hired as a fill-in at WRKS-FM, KISS 98.7. When rival station WBLS began hiring staff away from KISS, Williams was given the morning show with a non-compete-clause. Although it was her first job playing the music that she liked, Williams soon morphed into a radio personality, telling stories and gossiping about the intimate lives of rap stars. The following year her evening show hit number one in the ratings and her career took off. In 1993 Williams was accused of making inflammatory remarks that transformed a private dispute between rap groups into a public feud that threatened to turn violent. Concerned for her safety, Williams stopped going to hip-hop events, but she

cultivated a system of moles—friends, listeners, hotel and airport workers—to keep her informed.

In 1995, after Emmis Broadcasting bought KISS and switched its format to classic soul, Williams moved back to WQHT, which had become the Emmis hip-hop station Hot 97. That year Williams repeated rumors that rapper Tupac Shakur had been raped in prison. In his song "Why U Wanna Turn On Me?" released after his death in 1996, Shakur hurled obscenities at Williams.

The circumstances of Williams's 1998 firing were disputed. The station claimed she was fired for fighting with a coworker and "outing" gay rap musicians on her Web site. Williams blamed hip-hop mogul Sean Combs, "Puffy," for her firing. Her fans staged protests and Williams took the station to court.

Contractually prevented from working in New York, Williams moved to the Philadelphia hip-hop station WUSL-FM. A motorcade brought her to the city's "Love Statue" and publicly "married" her to her co-hosts. She took the station from the bottom to the top of the ratings among 18-34-year-olds. Williams married her manager, Kevin Hunter, in 1999. The following year, bedridden with a difficult pregnancy, Williams broadcast her show from her home.

Launched The Wendy Williams Experience

In 2001 WBLS lured Williams back to New York. *The Wendy Williams Experience* debuted in 2003 and went into syndication. Williams also began hosting *On the Down Lo,* a daily entertainment and gossip feature that was nationally syndicated on American Urban Radio Networks. In her book *The Wendy Williams Experience* she wrote: "Scandals, gossip, innuendos, rumors—we love it all! We love it because it takes us out of our own reality. It gives us an opportunity to look at somebody else's problems and know that we are not alone." Her 2003 interview with Blu Cantrell, in which she questioned the R&B singer about her sex life and drug abuse, became a bonus DVD on Cantrell's *Bittersweet* album. After a 2003 interview with Judge Greg Mathis of the *Judge Mathis* show, Williams was hit with a gag order preventing her from ever rebroadcasting or discussing the interview.

It was Williams's 2003 telephone interview with pop star Whitney Houston that first brought her national attention. Confronted about her alleged drug use and marriage to Bobby Brown, Houston accused Williams of "going too deep." Williams told Houston that her breast implants looked like "two baseballs on a stick." The women got into a shouting match. Williams told the *New York Times:* "That interview was number 19 on the E! Network's 100 most shocking moments. I beat out Richard Pryor setting himself on fire."

Williams never let herself off the hook. She bragged about her breast implants, liposuctions, and tummy tucks. She talked about her husband's infidelity. Williams told the *Philadelphia Weekly:* "When you're so judgmental, and I am, people say, 'Well, nobody's perfect. What the hell is going on in your damn life?' So I chose to share some very intimate things."

Moved into Other Media

Simon & Schuster employees contacted Williams after hearing her say on the radio that she wanted to do a book. In *Wendy's Got the Heat* Williams wrote about her struggles with her weight and with drugs and her experiences with racism and sexism. Her second book featured celebrity interviews, anecdotes, and "scandalocity." Williams coined the term "Negroidian" to describe the flagrant spending of hip-hop artists. One particularly cynical chapter entitled "BMs (Baby's Mamas)" advised women who wanted a celebrity's baby: "Get pregnant by someone who has a future. Get the goodies in your name!"

Williams began appearing on television and had a small part in the 2004 Queen Latifah film *The Cookout.* Williams and her husband produced *Wendy Williams Brings the Heat,* a compilation of rap and hip-hop recording artists. Following a series of specials, *Wendy Williams Is On Fire,* on the cable network VH1, her late-night reality TV series, *The Wendy Williams Experience,* debuted on October 20, 2006.

That year Williams published the first in a series of novels featuring her alter-ego, DJ Ritz Harper. Williams told *Essence* in 2006: "Ritz and I have a lot in common. That competitive do-anything-to-succeed kind of hunger that drives her? I totally identify with that." Readers were left hanging until the sequel appeared in 2007.

In 2007 a limited edition of 1,000 "Wendy Williams Contribution Smart T" tee shirts was launched, in Williams's favorite color—hot pink. Sales benefited the "What Smart Girls Know" campaign promoting positive change and healthy choices. However Williams, WBLS, and its owner, Inner City Broadcasting, remained the focus of protests by groups who considered Williams's programming to be inappropriate and offensive.

Entered Business

Williams told *Essence* in 2004: "Half of me believes that I have a great deal of power and that I wield it well. The other half knows that it's all an illusion because this is a male-dominated industry and I'm a little girl trying to make my way...For a long time I've been faking the confidence that I finally own. That confidence comes from being able to walk out tomorrow and leave it all and know that I'll get hired somewhere else. I'm fearless, not because I have a million dollars to sit back on, but because I finally believe in my own power and worth."

Williams incorporated as Question Mark Entertainment and in 2006 became part owner and spokesperson for The House of Georges Vesselle champagne. Williams told the *AllHipHop* Web site: "This is for our son. This is that ride out to the sunset.... I thought my books were going to be my ride out...or maybe if I ever got a television show where I'm amassing a fortune.... I never in my wildest dreams thought that my ride out—our ride out, as a family, would be liquor, much less a fine champagne." That same year Williams signed an endorsement deal with Alizé liqueurs for a national advertising campaign and launched a promotional tour.

In 2006 Williams told *Essence:* "I'm a Black woman in a man's world, and the financial validation is only just now starting to catch up to my popularity. No matter what, a woman has got to fight. We make 75 cents for every dollar a man rakes in. It's not fair!"

Selected works

Albums

Wendy Williams Brings the Heat, Vol 1, Virgin, 2005.

Books (with Karen Hunter)

Wendy's Got the Heat: The Queen of Radio Bares All, Atria, 2003.
The Wendy Williams Experience, Dutton, 2004.
Drama Is Her Middle Name: The Ritz Harper Chronicles Book 1, Harlem Moon, 2006.
Is the B–tch Dead or What?: The Ritz Harper Chronicles Book 2, Harlem Moon, 2007.

On-line

"The Wendy Williams Experience," *VH1,* www.vh1.com/shows/dyn/the_wendy_williams_experience/series.jhtml (April 23, 2007).

Radio and television

Wendy Williams Is On Fire, VH1, 2003.
On the Down Lo, American Urban Radio Networks, 2003–.
The Wendy Williams Experience, WBLS-FM, 2003–, VH1, 2006–.

Sources

Periodicals

Billboard, June 18, 2005, p. 69.

Billboard Radio Monitor, July 8, 2005, p. 16.
Essence, October 2004, p. 266; June 2006, pp. 178-181, 226-227.
Network Journal, February 28, 2002, p. 14.
New York, October 24, 2005, pp. 36, 38-41.
New York Beacon, September 3, 2003, p. 30; June 16-22, 2005, p. 24.
New York Times, September 28, 2003, p. NJ1.
Philadelphia Tribune, April 3, 1998, p. 6E; September 10, 2004, p. 1D; October 20, 2006, p. 8E.
Philadelphia Weekly, September 15-21, 2004, p. 86.
Savoy, April 2003, pp. 26-28.
Village Voice, December 9, 1997, p. 53.

On-line

"On the Down Lo with Wendy Williams," *American Urban Radio Networks,* www.aurn.com/networks/renaissance/down_lo.asp (June 26, 2007).
The Wendy Williams Experience, www.thewendywilliamsexperience.com (June 14, 2007).
"Wendy Williams Invests in High-End Champagne Company," *AllHipHop,* http://allhiphop.com/hiphopnews/?ID=5387 (June 26, 2007).
"Wendy Williams' Raw Radio Style," *News & Notes,* www.npr.org/templates/story/story.php?storyId=9473350 (June 26, 2007).

—Margaret Alic

Kristal Brent Zook

1966(?)—

Journalist, scholar

A respected investigative journalist, scholar, and journalism professor, Dr. Kristal Brent Zook has written widely on issues of race and gender. Her writings on popular American culture, politics, education, empowerment, environmental and social-justice issues, and health and health disparities have been published in a wide range of newspapers and magazines. Zook's doctoral dissertation on black television programming led to her first book, *Color by Fox,* published in 1999. With her next book, *Black Women's Lives,* in 2006, Zook established herself among the leading writers giving voice to black feminist issues.

Earned Her Doctorate in Cultural Studies

In the mid-1960s Kristal Brent Zook was born and raised in Los Angeles, California, in an all-female household that included her mother, Beverly Guenin, her grandmother, Christine Brent, and her cousin Lisa Brent. Kristal's father, Phillip Zook, who was white, was a gardener and landscaper in the San Fernando Valley. Although her mother and grandmother at times earned below a living wage and were forced onto welfare, they encouraged young Zook to aim high. She did, earning acceptance into the University of California at Santa Barbara after high school.

As an undergraduate at the University of California (UC) at Santa Barbara, Zook studied African-American women writers and theories of race, class, and gender. Her mentor, Professor Elliott Butler-Evans, prodded

her to go on to graduate school. In 1987 Zook did field work in politics and Central American history in Managua, Nicaragua, and entered the History of Consciousness Program at UC Santa Cruz.

There were few precedents for Zook's doctoral research on black television. In her introduction to *Color by Fox* Zook described the genesis of her dissertation: "I was a twenty-two-year-old, self-consciously light-skinned graduate student, and I too wanted to be 'really black' (as opposed to, as one dreadlocked professor referred to me, 'not really black')." She eventually came to view her early interviews with rappers and black filmmakers as "attempts to come to terms with my own ambiguous racial positionality." Zook was mentored by the sociologist and television theorist Herman Gray. The film theorist Teresa de Lauretis chaired her dissertation committee, which included activist/scholar Angela Davis.

Analyzed Black Television

In 1996 Zook was a visiting professor in cultural studies and a lecturer in communication and media studies at Murdoch University in Perth, Western Australia. She wrote in *Essence* in 2002: "From the moment I arrived in Australia, it was as though the world had been turned upside down: Australia was forcing me to look at lifelong assumptions about 'blackness' from a new angle. Like doing a headstand in yoga, my worldview was being oxygenated, and I loved it."

During the 1990s Zook had established herself as a journalist and cultural reporter, writing regularly about

At a Glance . . .

Born Kristal Brent Zook in 1966(?), in Los Angeles, CA. *Education:* University of California, Santa Barbara, BA, English, 1987; University of Madrid, Spain, 1986-87; University of California, Santa Cruz, PhD, History of Consciousnesses, 1994.

Career: Author, journalist, editor, public speaker, 1990–; Humanities Research Institute, University of California, Irvine, resident scholar, 1993; University of California, Los Angeles, visiting assistant professor, African-American Studies, 1995-96; University of Nevada, Reno, visiting Hilliard Scholar, 1996; Murdoch University, Perth, Western Australia, visiting lecturer and fellow, 1996; editor and producer for television and radio, including National Public Radio's *The Tavis Smiley Show*, 2000–; Center for an Urban Future, editor-in-chief, 2002; Graduate School of Journalism, Columbia University, New York, NY, associate adjunct professor, 2002–; *Essence* magazine, contributing writer, 2002--; *Connect* magazine, editor-in-chief, 2005–.

Selected awards: University of California, Santa Barbara, W.E.B. DuBois Writing Contest, First Place Essay Winner, 1986; University of California, Santa Cruz, Friends of the UCSC Library 25th Annual Book Collection Contest, first-prize essay for *Black Women Writers: A Collection of Books*, 1991; Alicia Patterson Foundation Fellow, 2005; Henry Luce Award for Public Service Reporting; National Association of Black Journalists Award.

Addresses: *Office*—Graduate School of Journalism, Columbia University, 2950 Broadway, MC 3801, New York, NY 10027. *Web*—www.kristalbrentzook.com.

television, movies, and books for the *Village Voice* and the *LA Weekly*. She set out to turn her doctoral thesis into a work of popular nonfiction.

By the late 1980s white America had adopted cable TV and videos, and blacks were watching 44 percent more network television than the rest of the country, according to Zook's research in *Color by Fox*. The new Fox network set out to attract this audience. By 1993 Fox had the most black-produced shows in the history of television, and by 1995 black Americans accounted for 25 percent of the network's market. Zook spent a

decade interviewing television writers, executives, producers, directors, and stars. She analyzed the programs that reflected black experience and that dealt with issues of black sexuality, gender relations, social responsibility and activism, intra-racial classism and colorism, and relations between blacks and Latinos. She examined the autobiographical, improvisational, aesthetic, and dramatic attributes of programs such as *In Living Color*, *The Fresh Prince of Bel Air*, *Living Single*, the *Sinbad Show*, and *South Central*. Zook concluded: "Such shows helped us to know that our fears, desires, and memories are often collective, not individual. We may have been watching alone in our homes, but black shows of the 1990s were not unlike those conversations our grandparents used to have on front porches, in segregated cities, so far away from home." Fox eventually abandoned its black audience for more mainstream programming. *Color by Fox* was published under the auspices of the W.E.B. Du Bois Institute and received mixed reviews.

Examined the Lives of Black Women

In 1995 the Reverend Jesse L. Jackson, Sr. suggested to Zook that she interview women working in Mississippi catfish and poultry plants. Zook wrote in her preface to *Black Women's Lives*: "I went South because, as a biracial woman who was raised by two generations of African American women in an urban environment, I needed to understand the chasm between myself and those who remained in the rural fields that my grandmother had left behind as a young girl." Over the next decade Zook made nearly three dozen trips to the South, as well as to the Northeast and Northwest. *Black Women's Lives* profiled ten women, including a black Vermont organic farmer whose parents were white, a biracial California filmmaker who had been adopted by a white family, a New York cosmetics executive, and the principal of America's first sugar-free school. Zook told *Essence* in 2006: "So many of us don't fit the mainstream stereotypes of us as victims or criminals, sex objects or comedians. The women in my book are multifaceted thinkers, planners, dreamers, healers, lovers, educators and friends."

Between 2000 and 2002 Zook wrote regular features on television, music, and film for the *Washington Post*. She moved to New York City in 2002 and in 2004 she disconnected her TV. As an investigative journalist Zook focused on stories from the black community that were ignored by mainstream media. She wrote about domestic violence, including her own experiences. In an *Essence* story on missing women Zook wrote: "When Black women disappear, the media silence can be deafening. While the families of the missing struggle to bring national attention to their lost loved ones, they sift through the clues and pray for a miracle." She wrote about black women soldiers who died in the Iraq war, many of whom had joined the military to pay for their college educations. In 2006 Zook was interviewed on CNN about her investigation of the alleged rape of an exotic dancer by members of the Duke University lacrosse team, which had been sensationalized in the press. The players were eventually exonerated. Zook spent five months researching the experimental testing of HIV/AIDS drugs on 76 black foster children in New York City. By the time her special report appeared in *Essence* in 2007, the number of children known to be affected had increased to more than 500.

As of 2007 Zook was a contributing writer for *Essence* and a commentator on National Public Radio's *News and Notes*. She taught feature writing and advised graduate students at Columbia. She also led intensive writing workshops for professionals and executives. Her speaking topics included "The Essence of Truth and Justice: Empowering Women's Lives from the 1960's to the Present," "Media Monopoly: Is a Black-Owned TV Network the Impossible Dream?" and "Playing the Game: Race, Gender, and Surviving Corporate Politics." Zook was completing a book on minority ownership of the media.

Selected writings

Books

Color by Fox: The Fox Network and the Revolution in Black Television, Oxford University Press, 1999.
Black Women's Lives: Stories of Power and Pain, Nation Books, 2006.

Periodicals

"View from the War Zone," *Village Voice*, May 12, 1992.
"A Manifesto of Sorts for a Black Feminist Movement," *New York Times Magazine*, November 12, 1995, p. 686.
"Of Love and Madness: Why Women Stay When the Perfect Mate Turns Abusive," *Washington Post,* February 11, 1996, p. C5.
"Love Down Under," *Essence,* Vol. 33, No. 3, July 2002, pp. 102-106.
"Jump at de Sun," *Nation*, Vol. 276, No. 6, February 17, 2003, pp. 33-38.
Working Mother, Guest Editor, Special Issue "Best Companies for Women of Color," June 2003.
"Missing Women," *Baltimore Sun*, December 22, 2003.
"Memories in Black and Blue," *Essence*, Vol. 35, No. 7, November 2004, pp. 152, 154.
"Screened Out," *New York Times Magazine,* January 23, 2005, pp. 16-17.
"Have You Seen Her?" *Essence,* Vol. 36, No. 3, June 2005, pp. 128-132.
"They Never Made it Home: Black Women Soldiers in Iraq," *Essence,* Vol. 36, No. 1, May 2005, pp. 262-263.

(With Patrik Henry Bass) "The New York City AIDS Experiment," *Essence,* Vol. 37, No. 10, February 2007, pp. 196-201.

On-line

"Turn Off the TV," *AlterNet,* April 22, 2004, www.alternet.org/story/18487 (April 23, 2007).
"Beyond Legal Definitions, What Makes a Family?" *News & Notes,* November 20, 2006, www.npr.org/templates/story/story.php?storyId=6513392 (May 6, 2007).
"Digging at Duke," *Women's Media Center,* January 22, 2007, www.womensmediacenter.com/ex/012207.html (April 23, 2007).

Other

"Reconstructions of Nationalist Thought in Black Music and Culture," in *Rockin' the Boat: Mass Music and Mass Movements*, ed. Reebee Garafolo, South End Press, 1992.
"Ralph Farquhar's *South Central* and *Pearl's Place to Play*: Why They Failed Before Moesha Hit," in *Channeling Blackness: Studies on Television and Race in America*, ed. Darnell M. Hunt, Oxford University Press, 2005.

Sources

Books

Zook, Kristal Brent, *Color by Fox: The Fox Network and the Revolution in Black Television*, Oxford University Press, 1999.

Periodicals

Essence, March 2006, p. 78.
Washington Post, March 19, 2006, p. T7.

On-line

"Dr. Kristal Brent Zook: Curriculum Vitae," *Murdock University*, wwwmcc.murdoch.edu.au/ReadingRoom/CRCC/fellows/Zook.html (May 3, 2007).
"Faculty: Kristal Brent Zook," *The Graduate School of Journalism at Columbia University,* www.jrn.columbia.edu/faculty/zook.asp (May 3, 2007).
Kristal Brent Zook, www.kristalbrentzook.com (May 3, 2007).
"Kristal Brent Zook: Journalist/Author/Scholar," *American Program Bureau,* www.apbspeakers.com/themes/DefaultView/Site/index.aspx (May 3, 2007).

—Margaret Alic

Cumulative Nationality Index

*Volume numbers appear in **bold***

American

Aaron, Hank **5**
Abbott, Robert Sengstacke **27**
Abdul-Jabbar, Kareem **8**
Abdur-Rahim, Shareef **28**
Abele, Julian **55**
Abernathy, Ralph David **1**
Abu-Jamal, Mumia **15**
Ace, Johnny **36**
Adams Earley, Charity **13, 34**
Adams, Eula L. **39**
Adams, Floyd, Jr. **12**
Adams, Jenoyne **60**
Adams, Johnny **39**
Adams, Leslie **39**
Adams, Oleta **18**
Adams, Osceola Macarthy **31**
Adams, Sheila J. **25**
Adams, Yolanda **17**
Adams-Campbell, Lucille L. **60**
Adams-Ender, Clara **40**
Adderley, Julian "Cannonball" **30**
Adderley, Nat **29**
Adkins, Rod **41**
Adkins, Rutherford H. **21**
Agyeman, Jaramogi Abebe **10**
Ailey, Alvin **8**
Akil, Mara Brock **60**
Al-Amin, Jamil Abdullah **6**
Albright, Gerald **23**
Alcorn, George Edward, Jr. **59**
Alert, Kool DJ Red **33**
Alexander, Archie Alphonso **14**
Alexander, Clifford **26**
Alexander, Joyce London **18**
Alexander, Khandi **43**
Alexander, Margaret Walker **22**
Alexander, Sadie Tanner Mossell **22**
Alexander, Shaun **58**
Ali, Hana Yasmeen **52**
Ali, Laila **27**
Ali, Muhammad **2, 16, 52**
Allain, Stephanie **49**
Allen, Byron **3, 24**
Allen, Debbie **13, 42**
Allen, Ethel D. **13**
Allen, Marcus **20**
Allen, Robert L. **38**
Allen, Samuel W. **38**
Allen, Tina **22**
Allen-Buillard, Melba **55**
Alston, Charles **33**
Amaker, Tommy **62**

Amerie **52**
Ames, Wilmer **27**
Amos, John b8, **62**
Amos, Wally **9**
Anderson, Anthony **51**
Anderson, Carl **48**
Anderson, Charles Edward **37**
Anderson, Eddie "Rochester" **30**
Anderson, Elmer **25**
Anderson, Jamal **22**
Anderson, Marian **2, 33**
Anderson, Michael P. **40**
Anderson, Norman B. **45**
Anderson, William G(ilchrist), D.O. **57**
Andrews, Benny **22, 59**
Andrews, Bert **13**
Andrews, Raymond **4**
Angelou, Maya **1, 15**
Ansa, Tina McElroy **14**
Anthony, Carmelo **46**
Anthony, Wendell **25**
Archer, Dennis **7, 36**
Archie-Hudson, Marguerite **44**
Arkadie, Kevin **17**
Armstrong, Louis **2**
Armstrong, Robb **15**
Armstrong, Vanessa Bell **24**
Arnez J, **53**
Arnwine, Barbara **28**
Arrington, Richard **24**
Arroyo, Martina **30**
Artest, Ron **52**
Asante, Molefi Kete **3**
Ashanti **37**
Ashe, Arthur **1, 18**
Ashford, Emmett **22**
Ashford, Nickolas **21**
Ashley-Ward, Amelia **23**
Atkins, Cholly **40**
Atkins, Erica **34**
Atkins, Juan **50**
Atkins, Russell **45**
Atkins, Tina **34**
Aubert, Alvin **41**
Auguste, Donna **29**
Austin, Junius C. **44**
Austin, Lovie **40**
Austin, Patti **24**
Avant, Clarence **19**
Ayers, Roy **16**
Babatunde, Obba **35**
Bacon-Bercey, June **38**
Badu, Erykah **22**

Bahati, Wambui **60**
Bailey, Buster **38**
Bailey, Clyde **45**
Bailey, DeFord **33**
Bailey, Radcliffe **19**
Bailey, Xenobia **11**
Baines, Harold **32**
Baiocchi, Regina Harris **41**
Baisden, Michael **25**
Baker, Anita **21, 48**
Baker, Augusta **38**
Baker, Dusty **8, 43**
Baker, Ella **5**
Baker, Gwendolyn Calvert **9**
Baker, Houston A., Jr. **6**
Baker, Josephine **3**
Baker, LaVern **26**
Baker, Maxine B. **28**
Baker, Thurbert **22**
Baldwin, James **1**
Ballance, Frank W. **41**
Ballard, Allen Butler, Jr. **40**
Ballard, Hank **41**
Bambaataa, Afrika **34**
Bambara, Toni Cade **10**
Bandele, Asha **36**
Banks, Ernie **33**
Banks, Jeffrey **17**
Banks, Michelle **59**
Banks, Tyra **11, 50**
Banks, William **11**
Banner, David **55**
Baraka, Amiri **1, 38**
Barber, Ronde **41**
Barber, Tiki **57**
Barboza, Anthony **10**
Barclay, Paris **37**
Barden, Don H. **9, 20**
Barker, Danny **32**
Barkley, Charles **5**
Barlow, Roosevelt **49**
Barnes, Roosevelt "Booba" **33**
Barnes, Steven **54**
Barnett, Amy Du Bois **46**
Barnett, Etta Moten **56**
Barnett, Marguerite **46**
Barney, Lem **26**
Barnhill, David **30**
Barrax, Gerald William **45**
Barrett, Andrew C. **12**
Barrett, Jacquelyn **28**
Barrino, Fantasia **53**
Barry, Marion S(hepilov, Jr.) **7, 44**
Barthe, Richmond **15**

Basie, Count **23**
Basquiat, Jean-Michel **5**
Bass, Charlotta Spears **40**
Bassett, Angela **6, 23, 62**
Bates, Daisy **13**
Bates, Karen Grigsby **40**
Bates, Peg Leg **14**
Bath, Patricia E. **37**
Baugh, David **23**
Baylor, Don **6**
Baylor, Helen **36**
Beach, Michael **26**
Beal, Bernard B. **46**
Beals, Jennifer **12**
Beals, Melba Patillo **15**
Bearden, Romare **2, 50**
Beasley, Jamar **29**
Beasley, Phoebe **34**
Beatty, Talley **35**
Bechet, Sidney **18**
Beckford, Tyson **11**
Beckham, Barry **41**
Belafonte, Harry **4**
Bell, Derrick **6**
Bell, James "Cool Papa" **36**
Bell, James A. **50**
Bell, James Madison **40**
Bell, Michael **40**
Bell, Robert Mack **22**
Bellamy, Bill **12**
Bellamy, Terry **58**
Belle, Albert **10**
Belle, Regina **1, 51**
Belton, Sharon Sayles **9, 16**
Benét, Eric **28**
Ben-Israel, Ben Ami **11**
Benjamin, Andre **45**
Benjamin, Regina **20**
Benjamin, Tritobia Hayes **53**
Bennett, George Harold "Hal" **45**
Bennett, Gwendolyn B. **59**
Bennett, Lerone, Jr. **5**
Benson, Angela **34**
Bentley, Lamont **53**
Berry , Halle **4, 19, 57**
Berry, Bertice **8, 55**
Berry, Chuck **29**
Berry, Fred "Rerun" **48**
Berry, Mary Frances **7**
Berry, Theodore **31**
Berrysmith, Don Reginald **49**
Bethune, Mary McLeod **4**
Betsch, MaVynee **28**
Beverly, Frankie **25**

Cumulative Occupation Index

Volume numbers appear in **bold**

Art and design

Abele, Julian **55**
Adjaye, David **38**
Allen, Tina **22**
Alston, Charles **33**
Anderson, Ho Che **54**
Andrews, Benny **22**, **59**
Andrews, Bert **13**
Armstrong, Robb **15**
Bailey, Radcliffe **19**
Bailey, Xenobia **11**
Barboza, Anthony **10**
Barnes, Ernie **16**
Barthe, Richmond **15**
Basquiat, Jean-Michel **5**
Bearden, Romare **2**, **50**
Beasley, Phoebe **34**
Benjamin, Tritobia Hayes **53**
Biggers, John **20**, **33**
Biggers, Sanford **62**
Blacknurn, Robert **28**
Brandon, Barbara **3**
Brown, Donald **19**
Burke, Selma **16**
Burroughs, Margaret Taylor **9**
Camp, Kimberly **19**
Campbell, E. Simms **13**
Campbell, Mary Schmidt **43**
Catlett, Elizabeth **2**
Chase-Riboud, Barbara **20**, **46**
Collins, Paul **61**
Cortor, Eldzier **42**
Cowans, Adger W. **20**
Crite, Alan Rohan **29**
De Veaux, Alexis **44**
DeCarava, Roy **42**
Delaney, Beauford **19**
Delaney, Joseph **30**
Delsarte, Louis **34**
Donaldson, Jeff **46**
Douglas, Aaron **7**
Driskell, David C. **7**
Edwards, Melvin **22**
El Wilson, Barbara **35**
Ewing, Patrick A. **17**
Fax, Elton **48**
Feelings, Tom **11**, **47**
Fine, Sam **60**
Freeman, Leonard **27**
Fuller, Meta Vaux Warrick **27**
Gantt, Harvey **1**
Gilles, Ralph **61**
Gilliam, Sam **16**

Golden, Thelma **10**, **55**
Goodnight, Paul **32**
Green, Jonathan **54**
Guyton, Tyree **9**
Harkless, Necia Desiree **19**
Harrington, Oliver W. **9**
Hathaway, Isaac Scott **33**
Hayden, Palmer **13**
Hayes, Cecil N. **46**
Honeywood, Varnette P. **54**
Hope, John **8**
Hudson, Cheryl **15**
Hudson, Wade **15**
Hunt, Richard **6**
Hunter, Clementine **45**
Hutson, Jean Blackwell **16**
Jackson, Earl **31**
Jackson, Vera **40**
John, Daymond **23**
Johnson, Jeh Vincent **44**
Johnson, William Henry **3**
Jones, Lois Mailou **13**
King, Robert Arthur **58**
Kitt, Sandra **23**
Knox, Simmie **49**
Lawrence, Jacob **4**, **28**
Lee, Annie Francis **22**
Lee-Smith, Hughie **5**, **22**
Lewis, Edmonia **10**
Lewis, Norman **39**
Lewis, Samella **25**
Loving, Alvin, Jr., **35**, **53**
Manley, Edna **26**
Marshall, Kerry James **59**
Mayhew, Richard **39**
McCullough, Geraldine **58**
McDuffie, Dwayne **62**
McGee, Charles **10**
McGruder, Aaron **28**, **56**
Mitchell, Corinne **8**
Moody, Ronald **30**
Morrison, Keith **13**
Motley, Archibald Jr. **30**
Moutoussamy-Ashe, Jeanne **7**
Mutu, Wangechi **44**
N'Namdi, George **17**
Nugent, Richard Bruce **39**
Olden, Georg(e) **44**
Ouattara **43**
Perkins, Marion **38**
Pierre, Andre **17**
Pindell, Howardena **55**
Pinderhughes, John **47**
Pinkney, Jerry **15**

Pippin, Horace **9**
Porter, James A. **11**
Prophet, Nancy Elizabeth **42**
Puryear, Martin **42**
Reid, Senghor **55**
Ringgold, Faith **4**
Ruley, Ellis **38**
Saar, Alison **16**
Saint James, Synthia **12**
Sallee, Charles **38**
Sanders, Joseph R., Jr. **11**
Savage, Augusta **12**
Sebree, Charles **40**
Serrano, Andres **3**
Shabazz, Attallah **6**
Shonibare, Yinka **58**
Simmons, Gary **58**
Simpson, Lorna **4**, **36**
Sims, Lowery Stokes **27**
Sklarek, Norma Merrick **25**
Sleet, Moneta, Jr. **5**
Smith, Bruce W. **53**
Smith, Marvin **46**
Smith, Morgan **46**
Smith, Vincent D. **48**
Steave-Dickerson, Kia **57**
Tanksley, Ann **37**
Tanner, Henry Ossawa **1**
Thomas, Alma **14**
Thrash, Dox **35**
Tolliver, Mose **60**
Tolliver, William **9**
Tooks, Lance **62**
VanDerZee, James **6**
Wainwright, Joscelyn **46**
Walker, A'lelia **14**
Walker, Kara **16**
Washington, Alonzo **29**
Washington, James, Jr. **38**
Wells, James Lesesne **10**
White, Charles **39**
White, Dondi **34**
White, John H. **27**
Wiley, Kehinde **62**
Williams, Billy Dee **8**
Williams, O. S. **13**
Williams, Paul R. **9**
Williams, William T. **11**
Wilson, Ellis **39**
Woodruff, Hale **9**

Business

Abbot, Robert Sengstacke **27**
Abdul-Jabbar, Kareem **8**

Adams, Eula L. **39**
Adams, Jenoyne **60**
Adkins, Rod **41**
Ailey, Alvin **8**
Akil, Mara Brock **60**
Al-Amin, Jamil Abdullah **6**
Alexander, Archie Alphonso **14**
Allen, Byron **24**
Allen-Buillard, Melba **55**
Ames, Wilmer **27**
Amos, Wally **9**
Auguste, Donna **29**
Avant, Clarence **19**
Baker, Dusty **8**, **43**
Baker, Ella **5**
Baker, Gwendolyn Calvert **9**
Baker, Maxine **28**
Banks, Jeffrey **17**
Banks, William **11**
Barden, Don H. **9**, **20**
Barrett, Andrew C. **12**
Beal, Bernard B. **46**
Beamon, Bob **30**
Beasley, Phoebe **34**
Bell, James A. **50**
Bennett, Lerone, Jr. **5**
Bing, Dave **3**, **59**
Blackshear, Leonard **52**
Blackwell Sr., Robert D. **52**
Blayton, Jesse B., Sr. **55**
Bolden, Frank E. **44**
Borders, James **9**
Boston, Kelvin E. **25**
Boston, Lloyd **24**
Boyd, Gwendolyn **49**
Boyd, John W., Jr. **20**
Boyd, T. B., III **6**
Bradley, Jennette B. **40**
Brae, C. Michael **61**
Bridges, Shelia **36**
Bridgforth, Glinda **36**
Brimmer, Andrew F. **2**, **48**
Bronner, Nathaniel H., Sr. **32**
Brown, Eddie C. **35**
Brown, Les **5**
Brown, Marie Dutton **12**
Brunson, Dorothy **1**
Bryant, John **26**
Burgess, Marjorie L. **55**
Burns, Ursula **60**
Burrell, Tom **21**, **51**
Burroughs, Margaret Taylor **9**
Burrus, William Henry "Bill" **45**
Burt-Murray, Angela **59**

Shropshire, Thomas B. **49**
Siméus, Dumas M. **25**
Simmons, Kimora Lee **51**
Simmons, Russell **1, 30**
Sims, Naomi **29**
Sinbad, **1, 16**
Smith, B(arbara) **11**
Smith, Clarence O. **21**
Smith, Jane E. **24**
Smith, Joshua **10**
Smith, Willi **8**
Sneed, Paula A. **18**
Spaulding, Charles Clinton **9**
Staley, Dawn **57**
Stanford, Olivia Lee Dilworth **49**
Steinberg, Martha Jean "The Queen" **28**
Steward, David L. **36**
Stewart, Ella **39**
Stewart, Paul Wilbur **12**
Stinson, Denise L. **59**
Stringer, Vickie **58**
Sullivan, Leon H. **3, 30**
Sutton, Percy E. **42**
Taylor, Ephren W., II **61**
Taylor, Karin **34**
Taylor, Kristin Clark **8**
Taylor, Natalie **47**
Taylor, Susan L. **10**
Terrell, Dorothy A. **24**
Thomas, Franklin A. **5, 49**
Thomas, Isiah **7, 26**
Thomas-Graham, Pamela **29**
Thompson, Cynthia Bramlett **50**
Thompson, Don **56**
Thompson, John W. **26**
Tribble, Israel, Jr. **8**
Trotter, Lloyd G. **56**
Trotter, Monroe **9**
Tyson, Asha **39**
Ussery, Terdema, II **29**
Utendahl, John **23**
Van Peebles, Melvin **7**
VanDerZee, James **6**
Vaughn, Gladys Gary **47**
Vaughns, Cleopatra **46**
Walker, A'lelia **14**
Walker, Cedric "Ricky" **19**
Walker, Madame C. J. **7**
Walker, Maggie Lena **17**
Walker, T. J. **7**
Ward, Lloyd **21, 46**
Ware, Carl H. **30**
Washington, Alonzo **29**
Washington, Mary T. **57**
Washington, Regynald G. **44**
Washington, Val **12**
Wasow, Omar **15**
Watkins, Donald **35**
Watkins, Walter C. Jr. **24**
Wattleton, Faye **9**
Wein, Joyce **62**
Wek, Alek **18**
Welburn, Edward T. **50**
Wells-Barnett, Ida B. **8**
Westbrook, Kelvin **50**
Wharton, Clifton R., Jr. **7**
White, Linda M. **45**
White, Walter F. **4**
Wiley, Ralph **8**
Wilkins, Ray **47**
Williams, Armstrong **29**
Williams, O. S. **13**

Williams, Paul R. **9**
Williams, Ronald A. **57**
Williams, Terrie **35**
Williams, Walter E. **4**
Williams, Wendy **62**
Wilson, Phill **9**
Wilson, Sunnie **7, 55**
Winfrey, Oprah **2, 15, 61**
Woods, Jacqueline **52**
Woods, Sylvia **34**
Woodson, Robert L. **10**
Wright, Antoinette **60**
Wright, Charles H. **35**
Wright, Deborah C. **25**
Yoba, Malik **11**
Zollar, Alfred **40**

Dance

Acogny, Germaine **55**
Adams, Jenoyne **60**
Ailey, Alvin **8**
Alexander, Khandi **43**
Allen, Debbie **13, 42**
Atkins, Cholly **40**
Babatunde, Obba **35**
Baker, Josephine **3**
Bates, Peg Leg **14**
Beals, Jennifer **12**
Beatty, Talley **35**
Byrd, Donald **10**
Clarke, Hope **14**
Collins, Janet **33**
Davis, Chuck **33**
Davis, Sammy Jr. **18**
Dove, Ulysses **5**
Dunham, Katherine **4, 59**
Ellington, Mercedes **34**
Fagan, Garth **18**
Falana, Lola **42**
Glover, Savion **14**
Guy, Jasmine **2**
Hall, Arthur **39**
Hammer, M. C. **20**
Henson, Darrin **33**
Hines, Gregory **1, 42**
Horne, Lena **5**
Jackson, Michael **19, 53**
Jamison, Judith **7**
Johnson, Virginia **9**
Jones, Bill T. **1, 46**
Jones, Doris W. **62**
King, Alonzo **38**
McQueen, Butterfly **6, 54**
Miller, Bebe **3**
Mills, Florence **22**
Mitchell, Arthur **2, 47**
Moten, Etta **18**
Muse, Clarence Edouard **21**
Nash, Joe **55**
Nicholas, Fayard **20, 57**
Nicholas, Harold **20**
Nichols, Nichelle **11**
Powell, Maxine **8**
Premice, Josephine **41**
Primus, Pearl **6**
Ray, Gene Anthony **47**
Rhoden, Dwight **40**
Ribeiro, Alfonso **17**
Richardson, Desmond **39**
Robinson, Bill "Bojangles" **11**
Robinson, Cleo Parker **38**
Robinson, Fatima **34**
Rodgers, Rod **36**

Rolle, Esther **13, 21**
Sims, Howard "Sandman" **48**
Spears, Warren **52**
Tyson, Andre **40**
Vereen, Ben **4**
Walker, Cedric "Ricky" **19**
Walker, Dianne **57**
Washington, Fredi **10**
Williams, Dudley **60**
Williams, Vanessa L. **4, 17**
Zollar, Jawole Willa Jo **28**

Education

Achebe, Chinua **6**
Adams, Leslie **39**
Adams-Ender, Clara **40**
Adkins, Rutherford H. **21**
Aidoo, Ama Ata **38**
Ake, Claude **30**
Alexander, Margaret Walker **22**
Allen, Robert L. **38**
Allen, Samuel W. **38**
Allen-Buillard, Melba **55**
Alston, Charles **33**
Amadi, Elechi **40**
Anderson, Charles Edward **37**
Archer, Dennis **7**
Archie-Hudson, Marguerite **44**
Aristide, Jean-Bertrand **6, 45**
Asante, Molefi Kete **3**
Aubert, Alvin **41**
Awoonor, Kofi **37**
Bacon-Bercey, June **38**
Bahati, Wambui **60**
Baiocchi, Regina Harris **41**
Baker, Augusta **38**
Baker, Gwendolyn Calvert **9**
Baker, Houston A., Jr. **6**
Ballard, Allen Butler, Jr. **40**
Bambara, Toni Cade **10**
Baraka, Amiri **1, 38**
Barboza, Anthony **10**
Barnett, Marguerite **46**
Bath, Patricia E. **37**
Beckham, Barry **41**
Bell, Derrick **6**
Benjamin, Tritobia Hayes **53**
Berry, Bertice **8, 55**
Berry, Mary Frances **7**
Bethune, Mary McLeod **4**
Biggers, John **20, 33**
Black, Albert **51**
Black, Keith Lanier **18**
Blassingame, John Wesley **40**
Blockson, Charles L. **42**
Bluitt, Juliann S. **14**
Bobo, Lawrence **60**
Bogle, Donald **34**
Bolden, Tonya **32**
Bosley, Freeman, Jr. **7**
Boyd, T. B., III **6**
Bradley, David Henry, Jr. **39**
Branch, William Blackwell **39**
Brathwaite, Kamau **36**
Braun, Carol Moseley **4, 42**
Briscoe, Marlin **37**
Brooks, Avery **9**
Brown, Claude **38**
Brown, Joyce F. **25**
Brown, Sterling **10**
Brown, Uzee **42**
Brown, Wesley **23**
Brown, Willa **40**

Bruce, Blanche Kelso **33**
Brutus, Dennis **38**
Bryan, Ashley F. **41**
Burke, Selma **16**
Burke, Yvonne Braithwaite **42**
Burks, Mary Fair **40**
Burnim, Mickey L. **48**
Burroughs, Margaret Taylor **9**
Burton, LeVar **8**
Butler, Paul D. **17**
Callender, Clive O. **3**
Campbell, Bebe Moore **6, 24, 59**
Campbell, Mary Schmidt **43**
Cannon, Katie **10**
Carby, Hazel **27**
Cardozo, Francis L. **33**
Carnegie, Herbert **25**
Carruthers, George R. **40**
Carter, Joye Maureen **41**
Carter, Kenneth **53**
Carter, Warrick L. **27**
Cartey, Wilfred **47**
Carver, George Washington **4**
Cary, Lorene **3**
Cary, Mary Ann Shadd **30**
Catlett, Elizabeth **2**
Cayton, Horace **26**
Cheney-Coker, Syl **43**
Clark, Joe **1**
Clark, Kenneth B. **5, 52**
Clark, Septima **7**
Clarke, Cheryl **32**
Clarke, George **32**
Clarke, John Henrik **20**
Clayton, Constance **1**
Cleaver, Kathleen Neal **29**
Clements, George **2**
Clemmons, Reginal G. **41**
Clifton, Lucille **14**
Cobb, Jewel Plummer **42**
Cobb, W. Montague **39**
Cobb, William Jelani **59**
Cobbs, Price M. **9**
Cohen, Anthony **15**
Cole, Johnnetta B. **5, 43**
Coleman, William F., III **61**
Collins, Janet **33**
Collins, Marva **3**
Comer, James P. **6**
Cone, James H. **3**
Coney, PonJola **48**
Cook, Mercer **40**
Cook, Samuel DuBois **14**
Cook, Toni **23**
Cooper Cafritz, Peggy **43**
Cooper, Afua **53**
Cooper, Anna Julia **20**
Cooper, Edward S. **6**
Copeland, Michael **47**
Cortez, Jayne **43**
Cosby, Bill **7, 26, 59**
Cotter, Joseph Seamon, Sr. **40**
Cottrell, Comer **11**
Cox, Joseph Mason Andrew **51**
Creagh, Milton **27**
Crew, Rudolph F. **16**
Crew, Spencer R. **55**
Cross, Dolores E. **23**
Crouch, Stanley **11**
Cruse, Harold **54**
Cullen, Countee **8**
Daly, Marie Maynard **37**
Dathorne, O.R. **52**

Moore, Minyon **45**
Morial, Ernest "Dutch" **26**
Morial, Marc H. **20, 51**
Morton, Azie Taylor **48**
Moses, Robert Parris **11**
Murrell, Sylvia Marilyn **49**
Nagin, C. Ray **42, 57**
Nix, Robert N.C., Jr. **51**
Norton, Eleanor Holmes **7**
Obama, Barack **49**
O'Leary, Hazel **6**
Owens, Major **6**
Page, Alan **7**
Paige, Rod **29**
Paterson, David A. **59**
Patrick, Deval **12, 61**
Patterson, Louise **25**
Payne, Donald M. **2, 57**
Payne, William D. **60**
Perez, Anna **1**
Perkins, Edward **5**
Perkins, James, Jr. **55**
Perry, Lowell **30**
Pinchback, P. B. S. **9**
Powell, Adam Clayton, Jr. **3**
Powell, Colin **1, 28**
Powell, Debra A. **23**
Powell, Michael **32**
Raines, Franklin Delano **14**
Randolph, A. Philip **3**
Rangel, Charles **3, 52**
Raoul, Kwame **55**
Reeves, Gregory **49**
Reeves, Triette Lipsey **27**
Rice, Condoleezza **3, 28**
Rice, Norm **8**
Robinson, Randall **7, 46**
Rogers, Joe **27**
Ross, Don **27**
Rush, Bobby **26**
Rustin, Bayard **4**
Sampson, Edith S. **4**
Sanders, Malika **48**
Satcher, David **7, 57**
Sayles Belton, Sharon **9**
Schmoke, Kurt **1, 48**
Scott, David **41**
Scott, Robert C. **23**
Sears-Collins, Leah J. **5**
Shakur, Assata **6**
Shavers, Cheryl **31**
Sharpton, Al **21**
Simpson, Carole **6, 30**
Sisulu, Sheila Violet Makate **24**
Smith, Nate **49**
Smythe Haith, Mabel **61**
Slater, Rodney E. **15**
Stanton, Robert **20**
Staupers, Mabel K. **7**
Steele, Michael **38**
Stokes, Carl B. **10**
Stokes, Louis **3**
Stone, Chuck **9**
Street, John F. **24**
Sullivan, Louis **8**
Sutton, Percy E. **42**
Terry, Clark **39**
Thomas, Clarence **2, 39**
Thompson, Bennie G. **26**
Thompson, Larry D. **39**
Thompson, William C. **35**
Todman, Terence A. **55**
Towns, Edolphus **19**

Tribble, Israel, Jr. **8**
Trotter, Donne E. **28**
Tubbs Jones, Stephanie **24**
Tucker, C. Delores **12, 56**
Turnbull, Charles Wesley **62**
Turner, Henry McNeal **5**
Usry, James L. **23**
Vaughn, Gladys Gary **47**
Von Lipsey, Roderick K. **11**
Wallace, Phyllis A. **9**
Washington, Harold **6**
Washington, Val **12**
Washington, Walter **45**
Waters, Maxine **3**
Watkins, Shirley R. **17**
Watson, Diane **41**
Watt, Melvin **26**
Watts, J. C., Jr. **14, 38**
Weaver, Robert C. **8, 46**
Webb, Wellington **3**
Wharton, Clifton Reginald, Sr. **36**
Wharton, Clifton R., Jr. **7**
Wheat, Alan **14**
White, Jesse **22**
White, Michael R. **5**
Wilder, L. Douglas **3, 48**
Wilkins, Roger **2**
Williams, Anthony **21**
Williams, Eddie N. **44**
Williams, George Washington **18**
Williams, Hosea Lorenzo **15, 31**
Williams, Maggie **7**
Wilson, Sunnie **7, 55**
Wynn, Albert **25**
Young, Andrew **3, 48**

Law

Alexander, Clifford **26**
Alexander, Joyce London **18**
Alexander, Sadie Tanner Mossell **22**
Allen, Samuel W. **38**
Archer, Dennis **7, 36**
Arnwine, Barbara **28**
Bailey, Clyde **45**
Banks, William **11**
Barrett, Andrew C. **12**
Barrett, Jacqueline **28**
Baugh, David **23**
Bell, Derrick **6**
Berry, Mary Frances **7**
Berry, Theodore M. **31**
Bishop Jr., Sanford D. **24**
Bolin, Jane **22, 59**
Bolton, Terrell D. **25**
Bosley, Freeman, Jr. **7**
Boykin, Keith **14**
Bradley, Thomas **2**
Braun, Carol Moseley **4, 42**
Brooke, Edward **8**
Brown, Byrd **49**
Brown, Cora **33**
Brown, Homer S. **47**
Brown, Janice Rogers **43**
Brown, Joe **29**
Brown, Lee Patrick **1, 24**
Brown, Ron **5**
Brown, Willie L., Jr. **7**
Bryant, Wayne R. **6**
Bryant, William Benson **61**
Bully-Cummings, Ella **48**
Burke, Yvonne Braithwaite **42**
Burris, Roland W. **25**

Butler, Paul D. **17**
Bynoe, Peter C.B. **40**
Campbell, Bill **9**
Carter, Robert L. **51**
Carter, Stephen L. **4**
Chambers, Julius **3**
Cleaver, Kathleen Neal **29**
Clendenon, Donn **26, 56**
Cochran, Johnnie **11, 39, 52**
Colter, Cyrus J. **36**
Conyers, John, Jr. **4, 45**
Crockett, George, Jr. **10**
Darden, Christopher **13**
Davis, Artur **41**
Days, Drew S., III **10**
DeFrantz, Anita **37**
Diggs-Taylor, Anna **20**
Dillard, Godfrey J. **45**
Dinkins, David **4**
Dixon, Sharon Pratt **1**
Edelman, Marian Wright **5, 42**
Edley, Christopher **2, 48**
Edley, Christopher F., Jr. **48**
Ellington, E. David **11**
Ephriam, Mablean **29**
Espy, Mike **6**
Farmer-Paellmann, Deadria **43**
Fields, Cleo **13**
Finner-Williams, Paris Michele **62**
Ford, Wallace **58**
Frazier-Lyde, Jacqui **31**
Freeman, Charles **19**
Gary, Willie E. **12**
Gibson, Johnnie Mae **23**
Glover, Nathaniel, Jr. **12**
Gomez-Preston, Cheryl **9**
Graham, Lawrence Otis **12**
Gray, Fred **37**
Gray, Willie **46**
Greenhouse, Bunnatine "Bunny" **57**
Grimké, Archibald H. **9**
Guinier, Lani **7, 30**
Haley, George Williford Boyce **21**
Hall, Elliott S. **24**
Harris, Patricia Roberts **2**
Harvard, Beverly **11**
Hassell, Leroy Rountree, Sr. **41**
Hastie, William H. **8**
Hastings, Alcee L. **16**
Hatcher, Richard G. **55**
Hatchett, Glenda **32**
Hawkins, Steven **14**
Hayes, Dennis **54**
Haywood, Margaret A. **24**
Higginbotham, A. Leon, Jr. **13, 25**
Hill, Anita **5**
Hillard, Terry **25**
Hills, Oliver W. **24**
Holder, Eric H., Jr. **9**
Hollowell, Donald L. **57**
Holton, Hugh, Jr. **39**
Hooks, Benjamin L. **2**
Houston, Charles Hamilton **4**
Hubbard, Arnette Rhinehart **38**
Hunter, Billy **22**
Hurtt, Harold **46**
Isaac, Julius **34**
Jackson Lee, Sheila **20**
Jackson, Maynard **2, 41**
Johnson, Harry E. **57**
Johnson, James Weldon **5**
Johnson, Norma L. Holloway **17**
Jones, Elaine R. **7, 45**

Jordan, Vernon E. **3, 35**
Kearse, Amalya Lyle **12**
Keith, Damon J. **16**
Kennard, William Earl **18**
Kennedy, Florynce **12, 33**
Kennedy, Randall **40**
Kibaki, Mwai **60**
King, Bernice **4**
Kirk, Ron **11**
Lafontant, Jewel Stradford **3, 51**
Lewis, Delano **7**
Lewis, Reginald F. **6**
Majette, Denise **41**
Mallett, Conrad, Jr. **16**
Mandela, Nelson **1, 14**
Marsh, Henry, III **32**
Marshall, Thurgood **1, 44**
Mathis, Greg **26**
McDonald, Gabrielle Kirk **20**
McDougall, Gay J. **11, 43**
McKinnon, Isaiah **9**
McKissick, Floyd B. **3**
McPhail, Sharon **2**
Meek, Kendrick **41**
Meeks, Gregory **25**
Moose, Charles **40**
Morial, Ernest "Dutch" **26**
Motley, Constance Baker **10, 55**
Muhammad, Ava **31**
Murray, Pauli **38**
Napoleon, Benny N. **23**
Nix, Robert N.C., Jr. **51**
Noble, Ronald **46**
Norton, Eleanor Holmes **7**
Nunn, Annetta **43**
O'Leary, Hazel **6**
Obama, Barack **49**
Obama, Michelle **61**
Ogletree, Jr., Charles **12, 47**
Ogunlesi, Adebayo O. **37**
Oliver, Jerry **37**
Page, Alan **7**
Paker, Kellis E. **30**
Parks, Bernard C. **17**
Parsons, James **14**
Parsons, Richard Dean **11, 33**
Pascal-Trouillot, Ertha **3**
Patrick, Deval **12**
Payne, Ulice **42**
Payton, John **48**
Perry, Lowell **30**
Philip, Marlene Nourbese **32**
Powell, Michael **32**
Ramsey, Charles H. **21**
Raoul, Kwame **55**
Ray, Charlotte E. **60**
Redding, Louis L. **26**
Reynolds, Star Jones **10, 27, 61**
Rice, Constance LaMay **60**
Richie, Leroy C. **18**
Robinson, Malcolm S. **44**
Robinson, Randall **7, 46**
Russell-McCloud, Patricia **17**
Sampson, Edith S. **4**
Schmoke, Kurt **1, 48**
Sears-Collins, Leah J. **5**
Solomon, Jimmie Lee **38**
Sparks, Corinne Etta **53**
Steele, Michael **38**
Stokes, Carl B. **10**
Stokes, Louis **3**
Stout, Juanita Kidd **24**
Sutton, Percy E. **42**

Cumulative Subject Index

Volume numbers appear in **bold**

211

Cumulative Name Index

Volume numbers appear in **bold**

Green, Dennis 1949— **5**, **45**

Green, Grant 1935-1979 **56**

Green, Jonathan 1955— **54**

Greene, Joe 1946— **10**

Greene, Maurice 1974— **27**

Greenfield, Eloise 1929— **9**

Greenhouse, Bunnatine "Bunny" 1944— **57**

Greenlee, Sam 1930— **48**

Greenwood, Monique 1959— **38**

Gregg, Eric 1951— **16**

Gregory, Dick 1932— **1**, **54**

Gregory, Frederick 1941— **8**, **51**

Gregory, Wilton 1947— **37**

Grier, David Alan 1955— **28**

Grier, Mike 1975— **43**

Grier, Pam(ala Suzette) 1949— **9**, **31**

Grier, Roosevelt (Rosey) 1932— **13**

Griffey, George Kenneth, Jr. 1969— **12**

Griffin, Bessie Blout 1914— **43**

Griffin, LaShell 1967— **51**

Griffith, Mark Winston 1963— **8**

Griffith, Yolanda 1970— **25**

Griffith-Joyner, Florence 1959-1998 **28**

Griffiths, Marcia 1948(?)— **29**

Grimké, Archibald H(enry) 1849-1930 **9**

Grooms, Henry R(andall) 1944— **50**

Guarionex See Schomburg, Arthur Alfonso

Guillaume, Robert 1927— **3**, **48**

Guinier, (Carol) Lani 1950— **7**, **30**

Gumbel, Bryant Charles 1948— **14**

Gumbel, Greg 1946— **8**

Gunn, Moses 1929-1993 **10**

Guy, (George) Buddy 1936— **31**

Guy, Jasmine 1964(?)— **2**

Guy, Rosa 1925(?)— **5**

Guy-Sheftall, Beverly 1946— **13**

Guyton, Tyree 1955— **9**

Gwynn, Anthony Keith 1960— **18**

Habré, Hissène 1942— **6**

Habyarimana, Juvenal 1937-1994 **8**

Haddon, Dietrick 1973(?)— **55**

Hageman, Hans 19(?)(?)— **36**

Hageman, Ivan 19(?)(?)— **36**

Haile Selassie 1892-1975 **7**

Hailey, JoJo 1971— **22**

Hailey, K-Ci 1969— **22**

Hale, Clara 1902-1992 **16**

Hale, Lorraine 1926(?)— **8**

Haley, Alex (Palmer) 1921-1992 **4**

Haley, George Williford Boyce 1925— **21**

Hall, Aaron 1963— **57**

Hall, Arsenio 1955— **58**

Hall, Arthur 1943-2000 **39**

Hall, Elliott S. 1938(?)— **24**

Hall, Juanita 1901-1968 **62**

Hall, Kevan 19(??)— **61**

Hall, Lloyd A(ugustus) 1894-1971 **8**

Halliburton, Warren J. 1924— **49**

Ham, Cynthia Parker 1970(?)— **58**

Hamblin, Ken 1940— **10**

Hamer, Fannie Lou (Townsend) 1917-1977 **6**

Hamilton, Anthony 1971— **61**

Hamilton, Samuel C. 19(?)(?)— **47**

Hamilton, Virginia 1936— **10**

Hamlin, Larry Leon 1948-2007 **49**, **62**

Hammer See Hammer, M. C.

Hammer, M. C. 1963— **20**

Hammond, Fred 1960— **23**

Hammond, Lenn 1970(?)— **34**

Hampton, Fred 1948-1969 **18**

Hampton, Henry (Eugene, Jr.) 1940— **6**

Hampton, Lionel 1908(?)-2002 **17**, **41**

Hancock, Herbie Jeffrey 1940— **20**

Handy, W(illiam) C(hristopher) 1873-1937 **8**

Hani, Chris 1942-1993 **6**

Hani, Martin Thembisile See Hani, Chris

Hannah, Marc (Regis) 1956— **10**

Hansberry, Lorraine (Vivian) 1930-1965 **6**

Hansberry, William Leo 1894-1965 **11**

Hardaway, Anfernee (Deon) See Hardaway, Anfernee (Penny)

Hardaway, Anfernee (Penny) 1971— **13**

Hardaway, Penny See Hardaway, Anfernee (Penny)

Hardaway, Tim 1966— **35**

Hardin Armstrong, Lil 1898-1971 **39**

Hardin, Lillian Beatrice See Hardin Armstrong, Lil

Hardison, Bethann 19(?)(?)— **12**

Hardison, Kadeem 1966— **22**

Hardy, Nell See Carter, Nell

Hare, Nathan 1934— **44**

Harewood, David 1965— **52**

Harkless, Necia Desiree 1920— **19**

Harmon, Clarence 1940(?)— **26**

Harold, Erika 1980(?)— **54**

Harper, Ben 1969— **34**, **62**

Harper, Frances E(llen) W(atkins) 1825-1911 **11**

Harper, Frank See Harper, Hill

Harper, Hill 1973— **32**

Harper, Michael S. 1938— **34**

Harrell, Andre (O'Neal) 1962(?)— **9**, **30**

Harrington, Oliver W(endell) 1912— **9**

Harris, "Sweet" Alice See Harris, Alice

Harris, Alice 1934— **7**

Harris, Barbara 1930— **12**

Harris, Ciara Princess See Ciara

Harris, Claire 1937— **34**

Harris, Corey 1969— **39**

Harris, E. Lynn 1957— **12**, **33**

Harris, Eddy L. 1956— **18**

Harris, James, III See Jimmy Jam

Harris, Jay **19**

Harris, Leslie 1961— **6**

Harris, Marcelite Jordon 1943— **16**

Harris, Mary Styles 1949— **31**

Harris, Monica 1968— **18**

Harris, Naomie 1976— **55**

Harris, Patricia Roberts 1924-1985 **2**

Harris, Richard E. 1912(?)— **61**

Harris, Robin 1953-1990 **7**

Harrison, Alvin 1974— **28**

Harrison, Calvin 1974— **28**

Harrison, Mya See Mya

Harsh, Vivian Gordon 1890-1960 **14**

Hart, Alvin Youngblood 1963— **61**

Hart, Gregory Edward See Hart, Alvin Youngblood

Harvard, Beverly (Joyce Bailey) 1950— **11**

Harvey, Steve 1956— **18**, **58**

Harvey, William R. 1941— **42**

Haskins, Clem 1943— **23**

Haskins, James 1941-2005 **36**, **54**

Hassell, Leroy Rountree, Sr. 1955— **41**

Hastie, William H(enry) 1904-1976 **8**

Hastings, Alcee Lamar 1936— **16**

Hatcher, Richard G. 1933— **55**

Hatchett, Glenda 1951(?)— **32**

Hathaway, Donny 1945-1979 **18**

Hathaway, Isaac Scott 1874-1967 **33**

Hathaway, Lalah 1969— **57**

Haughton, Aaliyah See Aaliyah

Hawkins, "Screamin'" Jay 1929-2000 **30**

Hawkins, Adrienne Lita See Kennedy, Adrienne

Hawkins, Coleman 1904-1969 **9**

Hawkins, Erskine Ramsey 1914-1993 **14**

Hawkins, Jamesetta See James, Etta

Hawkins, La-Van 1960— **17**, **54**

Hawkins, Steven Wayne 1962— **14**

Hawkins, Tramaine Aunzola 1951— **16**

Hayden, Carla D. 1952— **47**

Hayden, Palmer 1890-1973 **13**

Hayden, Robert Earl 1913-1980 **12**

Hayes, Cecil N. 1945— **46**

Hayes, Dennis 1951— **54**

Hayes, Isaac 1942— **20**, **58**

Hayes, James C. 1946— **10**

Hayes, Roland 1887-1977 **4**

Hayes, Teddy 1951— **40**

Haynes, Cornell, Jr. See Nelly

Haynes, George Edmund 1880-1960 **8**

Haynes, Marques 1926— **22**

Haynes, Trudy 1926— **44**

Haysbert, Dennis 1955— **42**

Haywood, Gar Anthony 1954— **43**

Haywood, Jimmy 1993(?)— **58**

Haywood, Margaret A. 1912— **24**

Hazel, Darryl B. 1949— **50**

Head, Bessie 1937-1986 **28**

Healy, James Augustine 1830-1900 **30**

Heard, Gar 1948— **25**

Heard, Nathan C. 1936-2004 **45**

Hearne, John Edgar Caulwell 1926-1994 **45**

Hearns, Thomas 1958— **29**

Heavy, D 1967— **58**

Hedgeman, Anna Arnold 1899-1990 **22**

Hedgeman, Peyton Cole See Hayden, Palmer

Height, Dorothy I(rene) 1912— **2**, **23**

Hemphill, Essex 1957— **10**

Hemphill, Jessie Mae 1923-2006 **33**, **59**

Hemsley, Sherman 1938— **19**

Henderson, Cornelius Langston 1888(?)-1976 **26**

Henderson, David 1942— **53**

Henderson, Fletcher 1897-1952 **32**

Henderson, Gordon 1957— **5**

Henderson, Natalie Leota See Hinderas, Natalie

Henderson, Rickey 1958— **28**

Henderson, Stephen E. 1925-1997 **45**

Henderson, Wade 1944(?)— **14**

Hendricks, Barbara 1948— **3**

Hendrix, James Marshall See Hendrix, Jimi

Hendrix, Jimi 1942-1970 **10**

Hendrix, Johnny Allen See Hendrix, Jimi

Hendryx, Nona 1944— **56**

Hendy, Francis 195(?)— **47**

Henries, A. Doris Banks 1913-1981 **44**

Henriques, Julian 1955(?)— **37**

Henry, Aaron Edd 1922-1997 **19**

Henry, Clarence "Frogman" 1937— **46**

Henry, Lenny 1958— **9**, **52**

Henson, Darrin 1970(?)— **33**

Henson, Matthew (Alexander) 1866-1955 **2**

Henson, Taraji 1971— **58**

Hercules, Frank 1911-1996 **44**

Herenton, Willie W. 1940— **24**

Herman, Alexis Margaret 1947— **15**

Hernandez, Aileen Clarke 1926— **13**

Hernton, Calvin C. 1932-2001 **51**

Hickman, Fred(erick Douglass) 1951— **11**

Higginbotham, A(loyisus) Leon, Jr. 1928-1998 **13**, **25**

Higginbotham, Jack See Higginbotham, Jay C.

Higginbotham, Jay C. 1906-1973 **37**

Hightower, Dennis F(owler) 1941— **13**

Hill, Anita (Faye) 1956— **5**

Hill, Beatrice See Moore, Melba

Hill, Bonnie Guiton 1941— **20**

Hill, Calvin 1947— **19**

Hill, Donna 1955— **32**

Hill, Dulé 1975(?)— **29**

Hill, Errol 1921— **40**

Hill, Grant (Henry) 1972— **13**

Hill, Janet 1947— **19**

Hill, Jesse, Jr. 1927— **13**

Hill, Lauryn 1975— **20**, **53**

Hill, Leslie Pinckney 1880-1960 **44**

Hill, Oliver W. 1907— **24**

Hill, Tamia See Tamia

Hillard, Terry 1954— **25**

Hilliard, David 1942— **7**

Hilliard, Earl F. 1942— **24**

Hilliard, Wendy 196(?)— **53**

Himes, Chester 1909-1984 **8**

Hinderas, Natalie 1927-1987 **5**

Hine, Darlene Clark 1947— **24**

Hines, Earl "Fatha" 1905-1983 **39**

Hines, Garrett 1969— **35**

Hines, Gregory (Oliver) 1946-2003 **1**, **42**

Hinton, Milt 1910-2000 **30**

Hinton, William Augustus 1883-1959 **8**